SELECTIONS

FROM THE

UNPUBLISHED WRITINGS

OF

JONATHAN EDWARDS,

OF AMERICA.

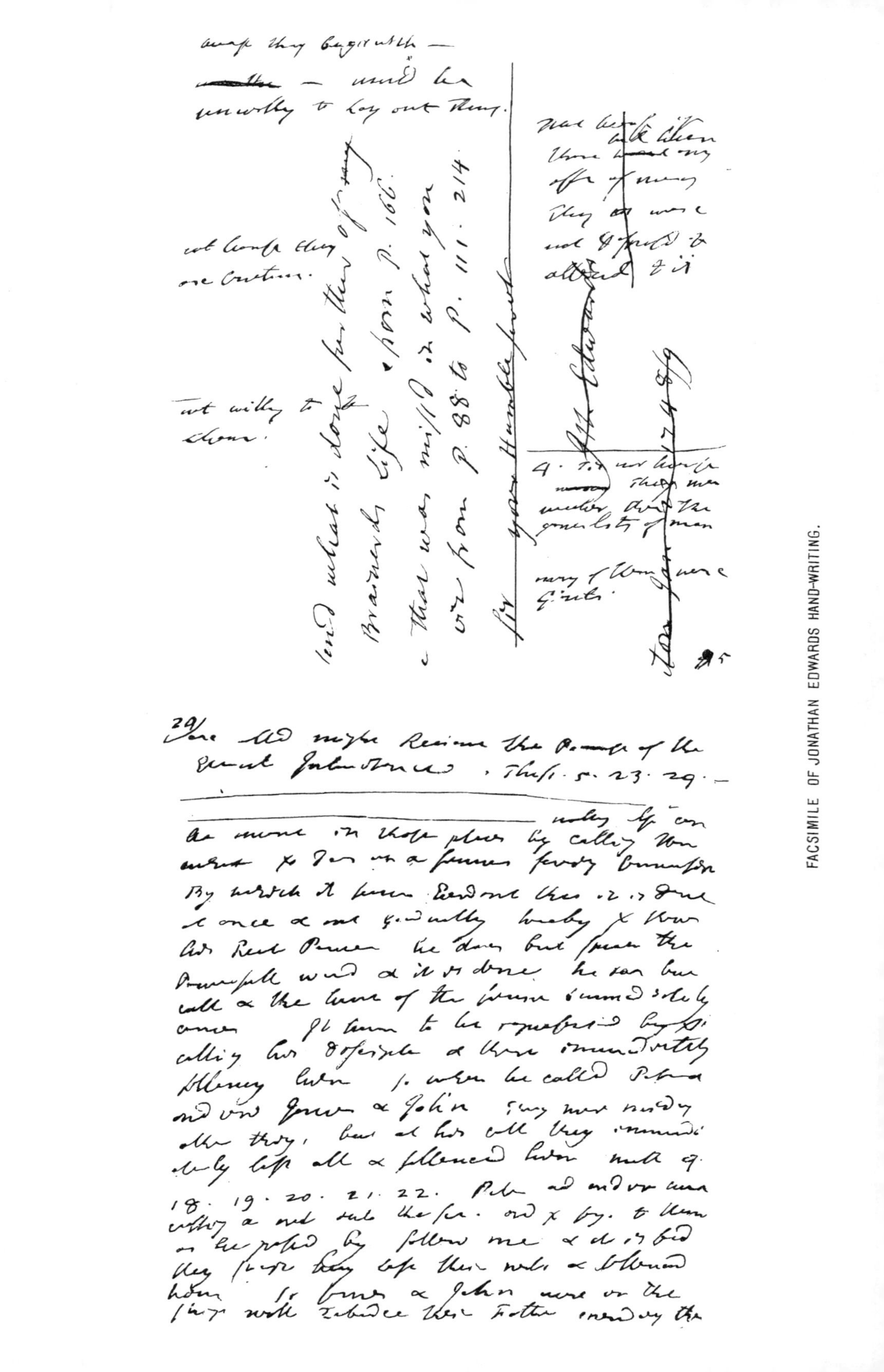

FACSIMILE OF JONATHAN EDWARDS HAND-WRITING.

SELECTIONS

FROM THE

UNPUBLISHED WRITINGS

OF

JONATHAN EDWARDS

OF AMERICA.

EDITED FROM THE ORIGINAL MSS., WITH FACSIMILIES
AND AN INTRODUCTION

BY THE

REV. ALEXANDER B. GROSART,
KINROSS.

"I consider JONATHAN EDWARDS the greatest of the sons of men. He ranks with the brightest luminaries of the Christian Church, not excluding any country, or any age, since the apostolic."

ROBERT HALL

"This remarkable man, *the* metaphysician of America....His power of subtile argument, PERHAPS UNMATCHED, CERTAINLY UNSURPASSED AMONG MEN, was joined, as in some of the ancient Mystics, with a character which raised his piety to fervour."

SIR JAMES MACKINTOSH

"Edwards comes nearer Bishop Butler as a philosophical divine than any other theologian with whom we are acquainted."

ROBERT MOREHEAD

Soli Deo Gloria Publications
...for instruction in righteousness...

Soli Deo Gloria Publications
213 W. Vincent Street, Ligonier, PA 15658
(412) 238-7741

*

Selections from the Unpublished Writings of Jonathan Edwards
was first printed for private circulation in 1865
by Rev. Alexander B. Grosart.

This Soli Deo Gloria Reprint is 1992.

*

ISBN 10877611-43-3

Introduction to the Twentieth Century Edition of "Selections from the Unpublished Writings of Jonathan Edwards"

Soli Deo Gloria has given us this first re-publishing of the Grosart work since its original private printing for 300 subscribers in 1865 (delayed by the "deplorable" Civil War). This is a useful Edwards event for several reasons.

First, the sermons here were never published elsewhere, to my knowledge.

Second, Grosart claims "scrupulous accuracy" in his transcription, though one sermon I checked against the manuscript was quite imperfect. However, the essential Edwards message remains lucid.

Third, the sermon on 2 Timothy 3:16 is Edwards's fullest development of the doctrine of biblical inspiration.

Fourth, The Treatise on Grace was one of Edwards's greatest disserations, not published again until Paul Helm's valuable edition in 1971.

Fifth, some of the "Annotations on Passages of the Bible" have not yet been published elsewhere. Also, "Directions for Judging of Persons' Experiences" apparently is not even listed in Thomas H. Johnson's The Printed Writings of Jonathan Edwards, 1703-1758.

Grosart found the Reverend Tryon Edwards, great-grandson of Jonathan, at his Connecticut pastorate, where he had the general collection. With Tryon Edwards, Grosart read many of the MSS before taking ("pirating," according to Stephen Stein and others) many with him to Scotland. I have seen many sermon manuscripts in Beinecke Library at Yale with the A.B.G., or Alex. Grosart, marked in red.

Grosart's hope of producing a more adequate biography with Tryon Edwards never materialized. It is feared that some of the MSS subsequently never materialized either. However, the Scottish clergyman did follow Selections with "The Handwriting of Famous Divines: Jonathan Edwards, M.A." Sunday at Home 31 (May): 458-60. This reprints Edwards's letter of 13 July 1751 to William Hogg, Edinburgh, about his settlement in Stockbridge; reproduces the closing lines in Edwards's handwriting; and suggests, contrary to received opinion, that Edwards was compassionate as evident in the many tear-stained manuscript pages of Sinners in the Hands of an Angry God. (M.X. Lesser, Jonathan Edwards, A Reference Guide Boston, G.H. Hall & Co., 1981) p.97

John H. Gerstner, Ph.D.
Ligonier, PA
November, 1992

CONTENTS.

* It has not been deemed necessary to insert here a list of the texts, (upwards of three hundred, besides others incidentally noticed), seeing they are given in the regular order of the Books as arranged in our English Bible.—G.

FACSIMILES.

JONATHAN EDWARDS

Born at Windsor, Connecticut	5th Oct. 1703
His father was the Rev. Timothy Edwards, pastor of a church in Windsor for sixty years.	
Became a Student of Yale College, Newhaven, in	1716
Graduated B.A.	1719-20
"Licensed" as a Minister of the Gospel	1722
"Preached" for eight months to a congregation of English Presbyterians, in the years	1722–23
Returned to Windsor and passed M.A. at "Yale"	1723–24
"Tutor" at Yale	1724 *seq.*
"Accepted" a "call" to be "Colleague" with his maternal Grandfather, at Northampton, Mass.	1726
Ordained	1727
Married Miss Sarah Pierpont	1727
Left Northampton	1750–51
Removed to Stockbridge, Mass., where he preached to the Indians and a few white settlers	1751–52
His treatise on "The Will" published in	1754
Chosen to be President of the College of New Jersey, Princeton .	1757
Died 22d March	1758

TO

JOHN VEITCH ESQ., M.A.,

PROFESSOR OF LOGIC AND RHETORIC IN THE UNIVERSITY OF GLASGOW,

I Dedicate

THESE "REMAINS" OF A GREAT THINKER,

IN

MEMORIAL OF COLLEGE-DAYS,

WHILE FELLOW-STUDENTS

UNDER

HAMILTON AND WILSON;

WITH HIGH ADMIRATION AND REGARD,

ALEXANDER B. GROSART.

INTRODUCTION.

TEN years ago I crossed the Atlantic in order to consult and arrange with the representatives of JONATHAN EDWARDS, about a complete and really worthy edition of the Works, published and unpublished, of that "master in Israel." Commissioned by Publishers of position and character thereto, and the way having been prepared by correspondence, I had immediate access given me to all the MANUSCRIPTS of Edwards, . . . these having been committed to the keeping of the Rev. Tryon Edwards, D.D., of New London, Connecticut, "as sole permanent trustee, by all the then surviving grandchildren of their author." * Very pleasant, if onerous, was the labour of examining the numerous MSS.; which were found to embrace,—besides papers of rare biographical interest and value,—the originals of some of the works already published, and a mass of his ordinary "sermons," in part fully written out, in larger part half-written out, and in largest part in simple "notes,"—these three classes being of very various worth. The treasure of the whole proved to be a Treatise on Grace, carefully finished and prepared for the press: and second to it, if second, an interleaved Bible, containing numerous ANNOTATIONS. Circumstances, which it is not at all needful to state here, have hitherto prevented the carrying out of the scheme of a complete collective edition of the Works: but a forlorn hope is indulged, that if the deplorable Civil war were ended, it may yet be achieved under the joint-editorship of the above Rev. Dr Tryon Edwards and myself.

Meantime, in response to very frequent and urgent requests addressed to me, I have personally transcribed from the original MSS. now in my possession, the contents of the present volume.

* Introduction to Edwards's "Charity and its Fruits; or, Christian Love as manifested in the Heart and Life." Edited from the Original MSS. by Tryon Edwards, D.D. (London: Nisbet & Co. 1852. 8vo.), page iv.: an inestimable book.

With a collective edition of the Works in possible prospect, I did not deem myself at liberty to *publish* anything; but there seems no valid objection to the *printing* of a limited impression for subscribers only, willing and wishful to share the cost with the Editor.

I may briefly notice the several portions of our Selections.

I. Treatise on Grace.—This Manuscript was found by itself, carefully placed within folds of thick paper, and tied up with a silk ribbon. It proved to be arranged into chapters and sections, all paged; and, in short, precisely as now printed. Our facsimile prefixed to the title-page, shews the size and appearance of the original. Many of the pages have interlineations and erasures; but there can be no doubt that the Manuscript was intended for publication.

It is possible that I may have the usual bias of a discoverer and editor. But I shall be surprised if this Treatise do not at once take rank with its kindred one, on "the Religious Affections." There is in it, I think, the massive argumentation of his great work, on "The Will;" but there is, in addition, a fineness of spiritual insight, a holy fervour not untinged with the pathetic "frenzy" of the English Mystics, as of Peter Sterry and Archbishop Leighton, and—especially toward the close—a rapturous exultation in the "excellency and loveliness" of God, a *glow* in iteration, of the wonder and beauty and blessedness of Divine Love, and a splendour of assertion of the claims, so to speak, of God the Holy Spirit, which it would be difficult to over-estimate. . . . .

II. Annotations on the Bible.—I give an account of the copy of Holy Scripture whence these Annotations are drawn, in the Note prefixed to them. It is perhaps necessary to explain *that not one of these has been hitherto printed.* In the "Works" as supplemented by Mr Robert Ogle of Edinburgh,* there is a series of "Notes on the Bible," and in the "Works" as now in circulation in America,† a few pages (seven in all) are occupied with "Observations upon Particular

* This supplement is titled volume IX. and volume X. of the Works, intending thereby to range with Williams's edition in 8 vols. royal 8vo, and the American below. The former contains, I. Notes on the Bible, (pp. 397;) and, II. Types of the Messiah. The latter, I. Miscellaneous Observations; II. Seventeen Occasional Sermons. Those who have Williams's edition ought to possess themselves of these; and those also who have the American edition, inasmuch as none of their contents are in the one, and only a comparatively small part in the other. Messrs Ogle & Murray, South Bridge, Edinburgh, are the present publishers, and few copies remain.

† 4 vols. 8vo, vol. iii. pp. 547-553. See footnote at end of this Introduction.

Passages of Scripture," the former omitting the latter, and the latter, strange to say, omitting the former, as well as other equally important portions of Edwards's writings. But the present *is a wholly independent series,*—the old Bible having been in the possession of one of the grandchildren until the general committing of all in 1849–50 to Dr Tryon Edwards, as stated *ante.* In the "Notes on the Bible" mentioned above, there are various references to "the Blank Bible," which were not understood, but now are, in the light of our recovery of the present Annotations.

Students of Edwards have always prized "above rubies" the "Notes" and "Observations" already extant; and I run no great hazard in anticipating that those now for the first time printed, will be equally valued. They seem to us to be of a more richly *experimental* character than the others, while there is the same acumen, quickness in discernment of Scriptural harmonies and parallelisms, soundness of interpretation of difficulties, happy accommodation, sweetness and tenderness of enforcement, overshadowed at times with solemn appeal, and rare ingenuity of "improvement,"—as the Puritans were wont to call it.

III. Directions for Judging of Persons' Experiences.—I have come upon this searching and very precious MS. since the issuing of my Proposals. It evidently formed the author's guide in his test-conversations with enquirers during the great Awakenings or Revivals. This—as well as eight instead of *two* sermons—is substituted for specimens of the original MS. of the treatise on "The Will," as explained onwards.

IV. Sermons.—As stated, the great mass of the Edwards's MSS. consists of his "Sermons." From among these a noble volume might be gathered, that is, of fully written out and magnificent Discourses: and another of equal weight and value, consisting of select passages from those less perfect, and, *as a whole,* of ordinary type, together with what clerics know as "skeletons" or "sketches,"—many of them, as No. 2 of our selection will shew, mammoth-boned. I have given *eight* Sermons: Nos. 3 and 4, 5 and 6, and 7 and 8, consisting of two Sermons in each case from one text—in place of *two* Sketch-sermons only, as originally designed and announced—to illustrate the usual style of preparation by Jonathan Edwards for the pulpit. No. 1 is the more frequent example of his preparations; No 2 is fuller, and is peculiarly interesting, as being one of those delivered to the Indians of Stockbridge; Nos. 3 and 4 are still fuller; Nos. 5 and 6 yet more so; and Nos. 7 and 8 elaborate, but, as will be seen, not filled up, so far as the wording goes. I have selected the last, as being on a difficult passage,—which is at once assumed to mean that which strikes our common sense as its only meaning,—and because it furnishes us with a well-nigh *awsome* specimen of the purged and Dantesque style of Edwards's grandest preaching, as well as, in its final "Applications" and "Directions," of his unexpected, and pungent, and penetrating rebukes of prevalent sin. It should make a fine picture to call up the scene of the great Preacher delivering the sermon on "The Word of God" to the swarthy Indians, in what was then the outskirts of civilisation, though, as we can testify, a finer landscape now is nowhere to be seen; nor found, a more winsome or kindly Community.

The common notion is that Edwards was what is called a "*Reader*" of his Sermons. Never was anything more untrue. Having gone over every page, line, and word that the great Preacher has left behind him, as preserved by Dr Tryon Edwards, I beg to state that the exception is to find a fully written-out Sermon. On great occasions, and during "The Revivals," he evidently prepared with fulness and verbal accuracy: and the tradition is that the most extraordinary of all his sermons,—perhaps the most extraordinary that ever has fallen from uninspired lips, and not less so in its momentous results,—"Sinners in the Hands of an Angry God," was read very closely, amid such a hush of awe and silent dropping of tears as we conceive of at the base of Sinai's flaming peaks, and as still thrill in the recollection of descendants of the hearers in New England. But his MSS. shew, beyond all gainsaying, that his rule—in the proportion of 95 to 100—was to jot down the leading thoughts and illustrations, and trust to the suggestions of the moment for the recall of previous study, and meditation, and prayer, and for the language.

Let not, then, the great name of JONATHAN EDWARDS be adduced in support of the practice of invariably "reading" Sermons; a practice that, *except in rare instances,* quenches all real eloquence, breaks the spell of influence, unlooses the links of the electric chain that ought to bind a speaker and his audience and pass and repass thrills of feeling, and, above all, leads to frauds of the most damaging and perilous sort.

Our facsimile will shew the thing better than any words. Such "Notes," be it kept in mind, compose the great mass of Edwards's ordinary and habitual preparations.

V. Letters.—I have not printed any of Edwards's "Letters," reserving those obtained, and others expected, for his "Life," one day to be written; and than which few comparable have been lived. I possess already priceless and hitherto unknown materials for a worthy Biography.

Finally: I had intended adding specimens, with facsimiles, of the original Manuscripts of the treatise on "The Will;" but a critical examination of the MSS. has revealed such valuable *unpublished materials,* such remarkable uncoverings of the processes of that master-book, such suggestive studies, and such jottings-down, at the moment, of profound thinking and speculation, under the heading of "The Mind," as should far exceed our limits. It is possible that I may prepare an edition of the Treatise, embracing these Studies and Preparations. If so, the friends into whose hands I now place this present volume may expect to hear of it.

It only remains to add, that the several MSS. of our Selections are given with *scrupulous accuracy.* Sometimes a word has been dropped, and I have inserted it; but invariably within brackets [ ]. I have adhered to the contractions of the age,—*e.g.*, "'tis" for "it is," "don't" for "do not," "'em" for "them," &c.; because we have herein a characteristic which is noticeable in the history of language and literature. Sometimes I would fain have corrected, what is now regarded as an ungrammatical construction, a clumsy phrase; but that had been to import into the eighteenth, rules of the nineteenth century. Another has said, "Edwards's style, like Butler's, is very much that of a man thinking aloud; yet, in both these authors, the train of thinking in their own minds is more clearly exhibited to us than, perhaps, by any other author, whilst they shew us, with great truth and distinctness, what their notions are, and how they came by them, with very little concern about the form of expression in which they are conveyed."*

This Volume is printed uniform in size with, by far the best edition extant of, the "Works,"—viz., that by Williams, and the supplementary volumes by Ogle. Its broad margins will also admit of its cutting down to range with the American edition,† which, spite of its singularly careless omissions and now worn stereotypes, has

* Encyc. Brit., as before.

† New York, 4 volumes 8vo., with double indices, 8th edition, 1851: now the property, it is believed, of the Messrs Carter, Broadway, who have done more for the higher theological literature of America, than, perhaps, any other American publishers. As a Scotchman, it may be allowed me to congratulate my "brither Scots," on the honourable position they have honourably won for themselves.

advantages over the others in its full Indices, and is, indeed, the only one, (save the somewhat inconvenient two huge volumes bearing the imprint of Bohn,) *in print.* "Charity and its Fruits," noticed *ante,* is unfortunately a small 8vo.

ALEXANDER B. GROSART.

1ST MANSE,
KINROSS, *December 26th,* 1864.

TREATISE ON GRACE.

NOTE.

See Introduction I., page 12.—G.

TREATISE ON GRACE.

CHAPTER I.

[SHEWING] THAT COMMON AND SAVING GRACE DIFFER, NOT ONLY IN DEGREE, BUT IN NATURE AND KIND.

SUCH phrases as common grace, and special or saving grace, may be understood as signifying either diverse kinds of influence of God's Spirit on the hearts of men, or diverse fruits and effects of that influence. The Spirit of God is supposed sometimes to have some influence upon the minds of men that are not true Christians, and [it is supposed] that those dispositions, frames, and exercises of their minds that are of a good tendency, but are common to them with the saints, are in some respect owing to some influence or assistance of God's Spirit. But as there are some things in the hearts of true Christians that are peculiar to them, and that are more excellent than any thing that is to be found in others, so it is supposed that there is an operation of the Spirit of God different, and that the value which distinguishes them is owing to a higher influence and assistance than the virtues of others. So that sometimes the phrase, *common grace*, is used to signify that kind of action or influence of the Spirit of God, to which are owing those religious or moral attainments that are common to both saints and sinners, and so signifies as much as common assistance; and sometimes those moral or religious attainments themselves that are the fruits of this assistance, are intended. So likewise the phrase, *special* or *saving* grace, is sometimes used to signify that peculiar kind or degree of operation or influence of God's Spirit, whence saving actions and attainments do arise in the godly, or, which is the same thing, special and saving assistance; or else to signify that distinguishing saving virtue itself, which is the fruit of this assistance. These phrases are more frequently understood in the latter sense, viz., not for common and special assistance, but for common and special, or saving virtue, which is the fruit of that assistance, and so I would be understood by these phrases in this discourse.

And that special or saving grace in this sense is not only different from common grace in degree, but entirely diverse in nature and kind, and that natural men not only have not a sufficient degree of virtue to be saints, but that they have no degree of that grace that is in godly men, is what I have now to shew.

1. *This is evident by what Christ says in* John iii. 6, where Christ, speaking of Regeneration, says—" That which is born of the flesh is flesh, and that which is born of the Spirit is spirit." Now, whatever Christ intends by the terms flesh and spirit in the words, yet this much is manifested and undeniable, that Christ here intends to shew Nicodemus the necessity of a new birth, or another birth than his natural birth, and that, from this argument, that a man that has been the subject only of the first birth, has nothing of that in his heart which he must have in order to enter into the kingdom. He has nothing at all of that which Christ calls spirit, whatever that be. All that a man [has] that has been the subject only of a natural birth don't go beyond that which Christ calls flesh, for however it may be refined and exalted, yet it cannot be raised above flesh. 'Tis plain, that by flesh and spirit, Christ here intends two things entirely different in nature, which cannot be one from the other. A man cannot have anything of a nature superior to flesh that is not born again, and therefore we must be " born again." That by flesh and spirit are intended certain moral principles, natures, or qualities, entirely different and opposite in their nature one to another, is manifest from other texts, as particularly: Gal. v. 17—" For the flesh lusteth against the spirit, and the spirit against the flesh : and they are contrary the one to the other ; so that ye cannot do the things which ye would ;" Ver. 19, " Now the works of the flesh are manifest, which are these : Adultery, fornication," &c. Ver. 22—" But the fruit of the Spirit is love, joy, peace," &c. ; and by Gal. vi. 8—" For he that soweth to the flesh shall of the flesh reap corruption : but he that soweth to the Spirit shall of the Spirit reap life everlasting." Rom. viii. 6–9— " For to be carnally minded is death, but to be spiritually minded is life and peace," &c. 1 Cor. iii. 1—" And I, brethren, could not speak unto you as unto spiritual, but as unto carnal, even as unto babes in Christ." So that it is manifest by this, that men that have been the subjects only of the first birth, have no degree of that moral principle or quality that those that are new born have, whereby they have a title to the kingdom of heaven. This principle or quality comes out then no otherwise than by birth, and the birth that it must come by is not, cannot be, the first birth, but it must be a new birth. If men that have no title to the kingdom of heaven, could have something of the Spirit, as well as flesh, then Christ's argument would be false. It is plain, by Christ's reasoning, that those that are not in a state of salvation, cannot have these two opposite principles in their hearts together, some flesh and some spirit, lusting one against the other as the godly have, but that they have flesh only.

2. *That the only principle in those that are savingly converted, whence gracious acts flow, which in the language of Scripture is called the Spirit, and set in opposition to the flesh, is that which others not*

only have not a sufficient degree of, but have nothing at all of, is further manifest, *because the Scripture asserts both negatively, that those that have not the Spirit are not Christ's.* Rom. viii. 9—"But ye are not in the flesh but in the Spirit, if so be that the Spirit of God dwell in you. Now if any man have not the Spirit of Christ, he is none of His;" *and also* [positively] *that those that have the Spirit are His.* 1 John iii. 24—"Hereby we know that he abideth in us by the Spirit which he hath given us." And our having the Spirit of God dwelling in our hearts is mentioned as a certain sign that persons are entitled to heaven, and is called the earnest of the future inheritance, (2 Cor. i. 22, and v. 5, Eph. i. 14;) which it would not be if others that had no title to the inheritance might have some of it dwelling in them.

Yea, that those that are not true saints have nothing of the Spirit, no part nor portion of it, is still more evident, because not only a having any particular motion of the Spirit, but a being *of the Spirit* is given as a sure sign of being in Christ. 1 John iv. 13—"Hereby know we that we dwell in Him, and He in us, because He hath given us *of His Spirit.*" If those that are not true saints have any degree of that spiritual principle, then though they have not so much, yet they have *of it,* and so that would be no sign that a person is in Christ. If those that have not a saving interest in Christ have nothing of the Spirit, then they have nothing; no degree of those graces that are the fruits of the Spirit, mentioned in Gal. v. 22—"But the fruit of the Spirit is love, joy, peace, longsuffering, gentleness, goodness, faith, meekness, temperance." Those fruits are here mentioned with that very design, that we may know whether we have the Spirit or no.

3. *Those that are not true saints, and in a state of salvation, not only have not so much of that holy nature and Divine principle that is in the hearts of the saints, but they do not partake of it,* because a being "*partakers of the Divine nature*" is spoken of as the peculiar privilege of true saints, (2 Pet. i. 4.) It is evident that it is the true saints that the Apostle is there speaking of. The words in this verse with the foregoing are these: "According as his Divine power hath given to us all things that pertain to life and godliness, through the knowledge of Him that hath called us to glory and virtue; whereby are given to us exceeding great and precious promises; that by these ye might be partakers of the Divine nature; having escaped the corruption that is in the world through lust." The "Divine nature" and "lust" are evidently here spoken of as two opposite principles in man. Those that are in the world, and that are the men of the world, have only the latter principle; but to be partakers of the Divine nature is spoken of as peculiar to them that are distinguished and separated from the world, by the free and sovereign grace of God giving them all things that pertain to life and godliness, giving the knowledge of Him and calling them to glory and virtue, and giving them the exceeding great and precious promises of the gospel, and that have escaped the corruption of the world of wicked men. And a being partakers of the Divine nature is spoken of, not only

as peculiar to the saints, but as one of the highest privileges of the saints.

4. *That those that have not a saving interest in Christ have no degree of that relish and sense of spiritual things or things of the Spirit, of their Divine truth and excellency, which a true saint has, is evident by* 1 Cor. ii. 14—"The natural man receiveth not the things of the Spirit of God, for they are foolishness unto him, neither can he know them, because they are spiritually discerned." A natural man is here set in opposition to a spiritual one, or one that has the Spirit, as appears by the foregoing and following verses. Such we have shewn already the Scripture declares all true saints to be, and no other. Therefore by natural men are meant those that have not the Spirit of Christ and are none of His, and are the subjects of no other than the natural birth. But here we are plainly taught that a natural man is perfectly destitute of any sense, perception, or discerning of those things of the Spirit. [We are taught that] by the words "he neither does nor can know them, or discern them;" so far from this they are "foolishness unto him;" he is a perfect stranger, so that he does not know what the talk of such things means; they are words without a meaning to him; he knows nothing of the matter any more than a blind man of colours.

Hence it will follow, that the sense of things of religion that a natural man has, is not only not to the same degree, but nothing of the same nature with that which a true saint has. And besides, if a natural person has the fruit of the Spirit, which is of the same kind with what a spiritual person has, then he experiences within himself the things of the Spirit of God; and how then can he be said to be such a stranger to them, and have no perception or discerning of them?

The reason why natural men have no knowledge of spiritual things is, because they have nothing of the Spirit of God dwelling in them. This is evident by the context: for there we are told that it is by the Spirit that these things are taught, (verses 10-12;) and godly persons in the next verse are called spiritual, because they have the Spirit dwelling in them. Hereby the sense again is confirmed, for natural men are in no degree spiritual; they have only nature and no Spirit. If they had anything of the Spirit, though not in so great a degree as the godly, yet they would be taught spiritual things, or things of the Spirit, in proportion to the measure of the Spirit that they had. The Spirit that searcheth all things would teach them in some measure. There would not be so great a difference that the one could perceive nothing of them, and that they should be foolishness to them, while to the other they appear divinely and remarkably wise and excellent, as they are spoken of in the context, (verses 6-9,) and as such the apostle spoke here of discerning them.

The reason why natural men have no knowledge or perception of spiritual things is, because they have none of the anointing spoken of, (1 John ii. 27:) "The anointing which ye have received of Him, abideth in you, and you need not that any man teach you." This anointing is evidently spoken of here, as a thing peculiar to true saints. Ungodly men never had any degree of that holy oil poured upon them, and therefore have no discerning of spiritual things. Therefore none of that sense that natural men have of things of religion, is of the same nature with what the godly have. But to these they are totally blind. Therefore in conversion the eyes of the blind are opened. The world is wholly unacquainted with the Spirit of God, as appears by John xiv. 17, where we read about "the Spirit of truth whom the world cannot receive, because it knoweth Him not."

5. *Those that go for those in religion that are not true saints and in a state of salvation have no charity, as is plainly implied in the beginning of the* XIII.th *chapter of the* 1*st Epistle to the Corinthians.* Therefore they have no degree of that kind of grace, disposition, or affection, that is so called. So Christ elsewhere reproves the Pharisees, those high pretenders to religion among the Jews, that they had not the love of God in them, (John v. 42.)

6. *That those that are not true saints have no degree of that grace that the saints have is evident, because they have no communion or fellowship with Christ.* If those that are not true saints partake of any of that Spirit, those holy inclinations and affections, and gracious acts of soul that the godly have from the indwelling of the Spirit of Christ, then they would have communion with Christ. The communion of saints with Christ does certainly very much consist in that receiving of His fulness and partaking of His grace spoken of, John i. 16—"Of his fulness have all we received, and grace for grace;" and in partaking of that Spirit which God gives not by measure unto Him. Partaking of Christ's holiness and grace, His nature, inclinations, tendencies, love, and desires, comforts and delights, must be to have communion with Christ. Yea, a believer's communion *with* the Father and the Son does mainly consist in his partaking of the Holy Ghost, as appears by 2 Cor. xiii. 14—"The grace of the Lord Jesus Christ, and the love of God, and the *communion* of the Holy Ghost."

But that unbelievers have no fellowship or communion with Christ appears, (1.) because they are not united to Christ. They are not in Christ. For the Scripture is very plain and evident in this, that those that are in Christ are actually in a state of salvation, and are justified, sanctified, accepted of Christ, and shall be saved. Phil. iii. 8, 9—"Yea doubtless, and I count all things but loss for the excellency of the knowledge of Christ Jesus my Lord: for whom I have suffered the loss of all things, and do count them but dung, that I may win Christ, and be found *in Him.*" 2 Cor. v. 17—"If any man be *in Christ,* he is a new creature: old things are passed away; behold, all things are become new." 1 John ii. 5—"But whoso keepeth His word, in him verily is the love of God perfected: hereby know we that we are *in Him;*" and iii. 24—"He that keepeth His commandments dwelleth in Him, and He in him: and hereby we know that He abideth in us, by the Spirit which He hath given us." But those that are not in Christ, and are not united to Him, can have no degree of communion with Him. For there is no communion without union. The members can have no communion with the head or participation of its life and health unless they are united to it. The branch must be united with the vine, otherwise there can be no communication from the vine to it, nor any partaking of any degree of its sap, or life, or influence. So without the union of the wife to the husband, she can have no communion in his goods. (2.) The Scripture does more directly teach that it is only true saints that have communion with Christ, as particularly this is most evidently spoken of as what belongs to the saints, and to them only, in 1 John i. 3, together with verses 6, 7—"That which we have seen and heard declare we unto you, that ye also may have fellowship with us: and truly our fellowship is with the Father, and with his Son Jesus Christ." Ver. 6—"If we say that we have fellowship with him, and walk in darkness, we lie, and do not the truth: but if we walk in the light, as He is in the light, we have fellowship one with another, and the blood of Jesus Christ His Son cleanseth us from all sin." Also in 1 Cor. i. 9—"God is faithful, by whom ye were called unto the fellowship of His Son Christ Jesus our Lord."

7. *The Scripture speaks of the actual being of a truly holy and gracious principle in the heart, as inconsistent with a man's being a sinner or a wicked man.* 1 John iii. 9—"Whosoever is born of God doth not commit sin; for his seed remaineth in him: and he cannot sin, because he is born of God." Here it is needless to dispute what is intended by this seed, whether it be a principle of true virtue and a holy nature in the soul, or whether it be the word of God as the cause of that virtue. For let us understand it in either sense, it comes to much the same thing in the present argument; for if by the seed is meant the word of God, yet when it is spoken of as abiding in him that is born again, it must be intended, with respect to its effect, as a holy principle in his heart: for the word of God does not abide in one that is born again more than another, any other way than in its effect. The word of God abides in the heart of a regenerate person as a holy seed, a Divine principle there, though it may be but as a seed, a small thing. The seed is a very small part of the plant, and is its first principle. It may be in the heart as a grain of mustard-seed, may be hid, and seem to be in a great measure buried in the earth. But yet it is inconsistent with wickedness. The smallest degrees and first principles of a Divine and holy nature and disposition are inconsistent with a state of sin; whence it is said "he cannot sin." There is no need here of a critical inquiry into the import of that expression; for doubtless so much at least is implied through this, "his seed being in him," as is inconsistent with his being a sinner or a wicked man. So that this heavenly plant of true holiness cannot be in the heart of a sinner, no, not so much as in its first principle.

8. *This is confirmed by the things that conversion is represented by in the Scriptures, particularly its being represented as a work of creation.* When God creates He does not merely establish and perfect the things which were made before, but makes wholly and

immediately something entirely new, either out of nothing, or out of that which was perfectly void of any such nature, as when He made man of the dust of the earth. "The things that are seen are not made of things that do appear." Saving grace in man is said to be the new man or a new creature, and corrupt nature the old man. If that nature that is in the heart of a godly man be not different in its nature and kind from all that went before, then the man might possibly have had the same things a year before, and from time to time from the beginning of his life, but only not quite to the same degree. And how then is grace in him, the new man or the new creature?

Again, conversion is often compared to a resurrection. Wicked men are said to be dead, but when they are converted they are represented as being by God's mighty and effectual power raised from the dead. Now there is no medium between being dead and alive. He that is dead has no degree of life; he that has the least degree of life in him is alive. When a man is raised from the dead, life is not only in a greater degree, but it is all new.

The same is manifest by conversion being represented as a new birth or as regeneration. Generation is not only perfecting what is old, but 'tis a begetting from the new. The nature and life that is then received has then its beginning: it receives its first principles.

Again, conversion in Scripture is represented as an opening of the eyes of the blind. In such a work those have light given them that were totally destitute of it before. So in conversion, stones are said to be raised up children to Abraham: while stones they are altogether destitute of all those qualities that afterwards render them the living children of Abraham, and not only had them not in so great a degree. Agreeably to this, conversion is said to be a taking away a heart of stone and a giving a heart of flesh. The man while unconverted has a heart of stone which has no degree of that life and sense that the heart of flesh has, because it yet remains a stone, than which nothing is further from life and sense.

Inference 1.—From what has been said, I would observe *that it must needs be that conversion is wrought at once.* That knowledge, that reformation and conviction that is preparatory to conversion may be gradual, and the work of grace after conversion may be gradually carried on, yet that work of grace upon the soul whereby a person is brought out of a state of total corruption and depravity into a state of grace, to an interest in Christ, and to be actually a child of God, is in a moment.

It must needs be the consequence; for if that grace or virtue that a person has when he is brought into a state of grace be entirely different in nature and kind from all that went before, then it will follow that the last instant before a person is actually a child of God and in a state of grace, a person has not the least degree of any real goodness, and of that true virtue that is in a child of God.

Those things by which conversion is represented in Scripture hold forth the same thing. In creation something is brought out of nothing in an instant. God speaks and it is done, He commands and it stands fast. When the dead are raised, it is done in a moment. Thus when Christ called Lazarus out of his grave, it was not a gradual work. He said, "Lazarus, come forth," and there went life with the call. He heard His voice and lived. So Christ, John v. 25—"Verily, verily, I say unto you, The hour is coming, and now is, when the dead shall hear the voice of the Son of God: and they that hear shall live,"—which words must be understood of the work of conversion. In creation, being is called out of nothing and instantly obeys the call, and in the resurrection the dead are called into life: as soon as the call is given the dead obey.

By reason of this instantaneousness of the work of conversion, one of the names under which conversion is frequently spoken of in Scripture, is *calling:* Rom. viii. 28–30—"And we know that all things work together for good to them that love God, to them who are the called according to His purpose. For whom He did foreknow, He also did predestinate to be conformed to the image of His Son, that He might be the firstborn among many brethren. Moreover whom He did predestinate, them He also called: and whom He called, them He also justified: and whom He justified, them He also glorified." Acts ii. 37–39—"Now when they heard this, they were pricked in their heart, and said unto Peter and to the rest of the apostles, Men and brethren what shall we do? Then Peter said unto them, Repent, and be baptized every one of you in the name of Jesus Christ for the remission of sins, and ye shall receive the gift of the Holy Ghost. For the promise is unto you, and to your children, and to all that are afar off, even as many as the Lord our God shall call." Heb. ix. 15, (last clause)—"That they which are called might receive the promise of the eternal inheritance." 1 Thess. v. 23, 24—"And the very God of peace sanctify you wholly. . . . Faithful is he that calleth you, who also will do it." Nothing else can be meant in those places by calling than what Christ does in a sinner's saving conversion. By which it seems evident that it is done at once and not gradually; whereby Christ, through His great power, does but speak the powerful word and it is done, He does but call and the heart of the sinner immediately comes. It seems to be symbolised by Christ's calling His disciples, and their immediately following Him. So when he called Peter, Andrew, James, and John, they were minding other things; but at His call they immediately left all and followed Him. Matt. iv. 18–22—Peter and Andrew were casting a net into the sea, and Christ says to them as He passed by, Follow me; and it is said, they straightway left their nets and followed Him. So James and John were in the ship with Zebedee their father mending their nets, and He called them, and immediately they left the ship and their father and followed Him. So when Matthew was called: Matt. ix. 9—"And as Jesus passed forth from thence, He saw a man, named Matthew, sitting at the receipt of custom: and He saith unto him, Follow me. And he arose and followed Him." Now whether they were then converted or not, yet doubtless Christ in thus calling His first disciples to a visible following of Him, represents to us the manner in which He would call men to be truly His disciples and spiritually to follow Him in all ages. There is something immediately and instantaneously put into their hearts at that call that they had nothing of before, that effectually disposes them to follow.

It is very manifest that almost all the miracles of Christ that He wrought when on earth were types of His great work of converting sinners, and the manner of His working those miracles holds forth the instantaneousness of the work of conversion. Thus when He healed the leper, which represented His healing us of our spiritual leprosy, He put forth His hand and touched him, and said, "I will; be thou clean." And immediately his leprosy was cleansed. Matt. viii. 3; Mark i. 42; Luke v. 13. And so, in opening the eyes of the blind, which represents His opening the eyes of our blind souls, (Matt. xx. 30, &c.,) He touched their eyes, and immediately their eyes received sight, and they followed Him. So Mark x. 52; Luke xviii. 43. So when He healed the sick, which represents His healing our spiritual diseases, or conversion, it was done at once. Thus when He healed Simon's wife's mother, (Mark i. 31,) He took her by the hand and lifted her up; and immediately the fever left her, and she ministered unto them. So when the woman which had the issue of blood touched the hem of Christ's garment, immediately the issue of blood stanched, (Luke viii. 44.) So the woman that was bowed together with the spirit of infirmity, when Christ laid His hands upon her, immediately she was made straight, and glorified God, (Luke xiii. 12, 13;) which represents that action on the soul whereby He gives an upright heart, and sets the soul at liberty from its bondage to glorify Him. So the man at the pool of Bethesda, when Christ bade him rise, take up his bed and walk, (he) was immediately made whole, (John v. 8, 9) After the same manner Christ cast out devils, which represents His dispossessing the devil of our souls in conversion; and so He settled the winds and waves, representing His subduing, in conversion, the heart of the wicked, which is like the troubled sea, when it cannot rest; and so He raised the dead, which represented His raising dead souls.

The same is confirmed by those things which conversion is compared to in Scripture. It is often compared to a resurrection. Natural men (as was said before) are said to be dead, and to be raised when they are converted by God's mighty effectual power from the dead. Now, there is no medium between being dead and alive; he that is dead has no degree of life in him, he that has the least degree of life in him is alive. When a man is raised from the dead, life is not only in a greater degree in him than it was before, but it is all new. The work of conversion seems to be compared to a raising the dead to life, in this very thing, even its instantaneousness, or its being done, as it were, at a word's speaking. As in John v. 25, (before quoted)—"Verily, verily, I say unto you, the hour is coming and now is when the dead shall hear the voice of the Son of God, and they that hear shall live." He speaks here of a work of conversion, as appears by the preceding verse; and by the words themselves, which speak of the time of this raising the dead, not only as to come hereafter, but as what was already come. This shews conversion to be an immediate instantaneous work, like to the change made on Lazarus when Christ called him from the grave: there went life with the call, and Lazarus was immediately alive. Immediately before the call sinners are dead or wholly destitute of life, as appears by the expression, "*The dead* shall hear the voice," and immediately after the call they are alive; yea, there goes life with the word, as is evident, not only because it is said they shall live, but also because it is said, they shall hear His voice. The first moment they have any life is the moment when Christ calls, and as soon as they are called, which further appears by what was observed before, even that a being called and converted are spoken of in Scripture as the same thing.

The same is confirmed (as observed before) from conversion being compared to a work of creation, which is a work wherein something is made either out of nothing, or out of that having no degree of the same kind of qualities and principles, as when God made man of the dust of the earth. Thus it is said, "If any man be in Christ he is a new creature;" which obviously implies that he is an exceeding diverse kind of creature from what he was before he was in Christ, that the principle or qualities that he has by which he is a Christian, are entirely new, and what there was nothing of, before he was in Christ.

Inference 2. Hence we may learn that *it is impossible for men to convert themselves* by their own strength and industry, with only a concurring assistance helping in the exercise of their natural abilities and principles of the soul, and securing their improvement. For what is gained after this manner is a gradual acquisition, and not something instantaneously begotten, and of an entirely different nature, and wholly of a separate kind, from all that was in the nature of the person the moment before. All that men can do by their own strength and industry is only gradually to increase and improve and new-model and direct qualities, principles, and perfections of nature that they have already. And that is evident, because a man in the exercise and improvement of the strength and principles of his own nature has nothing but the qualities, powers, and perfections that are already in his nature to work with, and nothing but them to work upon; and therefore 'tis impossible that by this only, anything further should be brought to pass, than only a new modification of what is already in the nature of the soul. That which is only by an improvement of natural qualities, principles, and perfections—let these things be improved never so much and never so industriously, and never so long, they'll still be no more than an improvement of those natural qualities, principles, and perfections; and therefore not anything of an essentially distinct and superior nature and kind.

'Tis impossible (as Dr Clarke observes) "that any effect should have any perfection that was not in the cause: for if it had, then that perfection would be caused by nothing."* 'Tis therefore utterly impossible that men's natural perfections and qualities in that exercise, and however assisted in that exercise, should produce in the soul a principle or perfection of a nature entirely different from all of them, or any manner of improvement or modification of them.

The qualities and principles of natural bodies, such as figure or motion, can never produce anything beyond themselves. If infinite comprehensions and divisions be eternally made, the things must still be eternally the same, and all their possible effects can never be anything but repetitions of the same. Nothing can be produced by only those qualities of figure and motion, beyond figure and motion: and so nothing can be produced in the soul by only its internal principles, beyond these principles or qualities, or new improvements and modifications of them. And if we suppose a concurring assistance to enable to a more full and perfect exercise of those natural principles and qualities, unless the assistance or influence actually produces something beyond the exercise of internal principle: still, it is the same thing. Nothing will be produced but only an improvement and new modification of those principles that are exercised. Therefore it follows that saving grace in the heart, can't be produced in man by mere exercise of what perfections he has in him already, though never so much assisted by moral suasion, and never so much assisted in the exercise of his natural principles, unless there be something more than all this, viz., an immediate infusion or operation of the Divine Being upon the soul. Grace must be the immediate work of God, and properly a production of His Almighty power on the soul.

* The well-known *a priori* argument of this eminent thinker, if somewhat uncertain divine, entitled " A Demonstration of the Being and Attributes of God."—G.

CHAPTER II.

SHEWING WHEREIN ALL SAVING GRACE DOES SUMMARILY CONSIST.

THE next thing that arises for consideration is, What is the nature of this Divine principle in the soul that is so entirely diverse from all that is naturally in the soul? Here I would observe,—

1. *That that saving grace that is in the hearts of the saints, that within them [which is] above nature, and entirely distinguishes 'em from all unconverted men, is radically but one*—i.e., *however various its exercises are, yet it is but one in its root; 'tis one individual principle in the heart.*

'Tis common for us to speak of various graces of the Spirit of God as though they were so many different principles of holiness, and to call them by distinct names as such,—repentance, humility, resignation, thankfulness, &c. But we err if we imagine that these in their first source and root in the heart are properly distinct principles. They all come from the same fountain, and are, indeed, the various exertions and conditions of the same thing; only different denominations according to the various occasions, objects, and manners, attendants and circumstances of its exercise. There is some one holy principle in the heart that is the essence and sum of all grace, the root and source of all holy acts of every kind, and the fountain of every good stream, into which all Christian virtues may ultimately be resolved, and in which all duty and [all] holiness is fulfilled.

Thus the Scripture represents it. Grace in the soul is one fountain of water of life, (John iv. 14,) and not various distinct fountains. So God, in the work of Regeneration, implants one heavenly seed in the soul, and not various different seeds. 1 John iii. 9—"Whosoever is born of God doth not commit sin; for His *seed* remaineth in him." . . . The Day [that] has arisen on the soul is but one. The oil in the vessel is simple and pure, conferred by one holy anointing. All is "wrought" by one individual work of the Spirit of God. And thus it is there is a consentanation* of graces. Not only is one grace in some way allied to another, and so tends to help and promote one another, but one is really implied in the other. The nature of one involves the nature of another. And the great reason of it is, that all graces have one common essence, the original principle of all, and is but one. Strip the various parts of the Christian soul of their circumstances, concomitants, appendages, means, and

* Query, = harmony, *i.e.*, from consentaneous ?—G.

occasions, and consider that which is, as it were, their *soul* and essence, and all appears to be the same. [I observe]

2. That principle in the soul of the saints, which is the grand Christian virtue, and which is the soul and essence and summary comprehension of all grace, *is a principle of Divine Love.* This is evident,

(1.) *Because we are abundantly taught in the Scripture that Divine Love is the sum of all duty;* and that all that God requires of us is fulfilled in it,—*i.e.*, That Love is the sum of all duty of the heart, and its exercises and fruits the sum of all [the] duty of life. But if the duty of the heart, or all due dispositions of hearts, are all summed up in love, then undoubtedly all grace may be summed up in LOVE.

The Scripture teaches us that all our duty is summed up in love; or, which is the same thing, that 'tis the sum of all that is required in the Law; and that, whether we take the Law as signifying the Ten Commandments, or the whole written Word of God. So, when by the Law is meant the Ten Commandments: Rom. xiii. 8—"Owe no man anything, but to love one another: for he that loveth another hath fulfilled the law;" and, therefore, several of these commandments are there rehearsed. And again, in ver. 10, "Love is the fulfilling of the Law." And unless love was the sum of what the Law required, the Law could not be fulfilled in Love. A law is not fulfilled but by obedience to the sum of what it contains. So the same Apostle again: 1 Tim. i. 5—"Now the end of the commandment is charity" [love.]

If we take the Law in a yet more extensive sense for the whole written Word of God, the Scripture still teaches us that Love is the sum of what is required in it. [Thus] Matt. xxii. 40. There Christ teaches us that on these two precepts of loving God and our neighbour hang all the Law and the Prophets,—that is, all the written Word of God. So that what was called the Law and the Prophets was the whole written Word of God that was then extant. The Scripture teaches this of each table of the Law in particular.

Thus, the Lawyer that we read of in the X.th chapter of Luke, vv. 25–28, mentions the love of God and our neighbour as the sum of the two Tables of the Law; and Christ approves of what he says. When he stood up and tempted Christ with this question, "Master, what shall I do to inherit eternal life?" Christ asks him what was required of him "in the Law?" He makes answer, "Thou shalt love the Lord thy God with all thy heart, and with all thy soul, and with all thy strength, and with all thy mind, and thy neighbour as thyself;" and Christ replies, "Thou hast answered right; this do, and thou shalt live;" as much as to say, "Do this, then thou hast fulfilled the whole Law."

So in Matthew xxii., vv. 36–38, that commandment, "Thou shalt love the Lord thy God with all thy heart, and with all thy soul, and with all thy mind," is given by Christ himself as the sum of the first Table of the Law, in answer to the question of the Lawyer, who asked Him, "Which is the great commandment of the Law?" And in the next verse, loving our neighbours as ourselves is mentioned as the sum of the second Table, as it is also in Romans xiii. 9, where most of the precepts of the second Table are rehearsed over in particular: "For this, Thou shalt not commit adultery, Thou shalt not kill, Thou shalt not steal, Thou shalt not bear false witness, Thou shalt not covet; and if there be any other commandment, it is briefly compreprehended in this saying, namely, Thou shalt love thy neighbour as thyself."

The Apostle James seems to teach the same thing. James ii. 8—"If ye fulfil the royal law according to the scripture, Thou shalt love thy neighbour as thyself, ye do well."

Thus frequent, express, and particular is the Scripture in teaching us that all duty is comprehended in Love. The Scripture teaches us, in like manner, of nothing else. This is quite another thing than if Religion in general had only sometimes gone under the name of the Love of God, as it sometimes goes by the name of the fearing of God, and sometimes the knowledge of God, and sometimes feeling of God.

This argument does fully and irrefragably prove that all grace, and every Christian disposition and habit of mind and heart, especially as to that which is primarily holy and Divine in it, does summarily consist in Divine Love, and may be resolved into it: however, with respect to its kinds and manner of exercise and its appendages, it may be diversified. For certainly there is no duty of heart, or due disposition of mind, but what is included in the "Law and the Prophets," and is required by some precept of that Law and rule which He has given mankind to walk by. But yet the Scripture affords us other evidences of the truth of this.

(2.) *The Apostle speaks of Divine Love as that which is the essence of all Christianity in the XIII.th chapter of* [*the*] 1*st* [*Epistle* to the] *Corinthians.* There the Apostle evidently means a comparison between the gifts of the Spirit and the grace of the Spirit. In the foregoing chapter the Apostle had been speaking of the gifts of the Spirit throughout, such as the gift of wisdom, the gift of knowledge, the gift of faith, the gift of healing or working miracles, prophecy, discerning spirits, speaking with tongues, &c.; and in the last verse in the chapter he exhorts the Corinthians to "covet earnestly the best gifts;" but adds, "and yet I shew you a more excellent way," and so proceeds to discourse of the saving grace of the Spirit under the name of *ἀγάπη*, love, and to compare this saving grace in the heart with those gifts. Now, 'tis manifest that the comparison is between the gifts of the Spirit that were common to both saints and sinners, and that saving grace that distinguishes true saints; and, therefore, charity or love is here understood by Divines as intending the same thing as sincere grace of heart.

By love or charity here there is no reason to understand the Apostle [as speaking] only of love to men, but that principle of Divine Love that is in the heart of the saints in the full extent, which primarily has God for its object. For there is no reason to think that the Apostle doesn't mean the same thing by charity here as he does in the VIII.th chapter of the same Epistle, where he is comparing the same two things together, knowledge and charity, as he does here. But there he explains himself to mean by charity the love of God: [verses 1–3]—"Now, as touching things offered unto idols, we know that we all have knowledge. Knowledge puffeth up, but charity edifieth. And if any man think that he knoweth anything, he knoweth nothing yet as he ought to know. But if any man love God, the same is known of Him," &c.*

'Tis manifest that Love or charity is here (chap. xiii.) spoken of as the very essence of all Christianity, and is the very thing wherein a gracious sincerity consists. For the Apostle speaks of it as the most excellent, the most necessary, and essential thing of all, without which all that makes the greatest, and fairest, and most glittering show in Religion is nothing—without which, "if we speak with the tongues of men and angels, we are become as sounding brass and tinkling cymbals"—and without which, though we have "the gift of prophecy, and understand all mysteries and all knowledge, and have all faith, so that we could remove mountains, and should bestow all our goods to feed the poor, and even give our bodies to be burned, we are nothing." Therefore, how can we understand the Apostle any otherwise than that this is the very thing whereof the essence of all consists; and that he means the same by charity as a gracious charity, as indeed it is generally understood. If a man does all these things here spoken, makes such glorious prophecies, has such knowledge, such faith, and speaks so excellently, and performs such excellent external acts, and does such great things in religion as giving all his goods to the poor and giving his body to be burned, what is wanting but one thing? The very quintessence of all Religion, the very thing wherein lies summarily the sincerity, spirituality, and divinity of Religion. And that, the Apostle teaches us, is LOVE.

And further, 'tis manifestly the Apostle's drift to shew how this excellent principle does radically comprehend all that is good. For he goes on to shew how all essences of good and excellent dispositions and exercises, both towards God and towards man, are virtually contained and will flow from this one principle: "Love suffereth long, and is kind, envieth not, . . . endureth all things," &c. The words of this last verse especially respects duties to God, as the former did duties to men, as I would shew more particularly afterwards.†

* The paragraph commencing, "In love or charity," down to this, is an after-insertion.—G.

† In the MS. on this page there is placed a passage within brackets, which it is deemed better to remove to a footnote, as interrupting the general argument and line of illustration :—

"Here it may be noted, by the way, that by charity 'believing all things, hoping all things,' the Apostle has undoubtedly respect to the same faith and hope that in other parts of the chapter are mentioned together and compared with charity, [as I think might be sufficiently made manifest, if it were proper here to spend time upon it.] And not believing and hoping, in the case of our neighbour, which the Apostle had spoken of before, in the last words of verse 5th, and had plainly summed up all parts of charity towards our neighbour in the 6th verse. And then in this verse the Apostle proceeds to mention other exercises or fruits of charity quite of another kind—viz., patience under suffering, faith and hope, and perseverance." The clause placed within [ ] is deleted in the MS.—G.

Thus the Apostle don't only represent love or charity as the most excellent thing in Christianity, and as the quintessence, life and soul of all Religion, but as that which virtually comprehends all holy virtues and exercises. And because Love is the quintessence and soul of all grace, wherein the divinity and holiness of all that belongs to charity does properly and essentially consist; therefore, when Christians come to be in their most perfect state, and the Divine nature in them shall be in its greatest exaltation and purity, and be free from all mixtures, stripped of these appurtenances and that clothing that it has in the present state; and [when] it shall lose many other of its denominations, especially from the peculiar manner and exercises accommodated to the imperfect circumstances of the present state, they will be what will remain. All other names will be swallowed up in the name of charity or love, as the Apostle, agreeably to his chapter on this, (1 Cor. chap. xiii.,) observes in verses 8-10—"Charity never faileth. . . . But when that *which is perfect is come*, then that which is in part shall be done away." And, therefore, when the Apostle, in the last verse, speaks of charity as the greatest grace, we may well understand him in the same sense as when Christ speaks of the command to love God, &c., as the greatest commandment—viz., that among the graces, that is the source and sum of all graces, as that commanded is spoken of as the sum of all commands, and requiring that duty which is the ground of all other duties.

It must be because Charity is the quintessence and soul of all duty and all good in the heart that the Apostle says that it is "the end of the commandment," for doubtless the main end of the commandment is to promote that which is most essential in Religion and constituent of holiness.

3. *Reason bears witness to the same thing.*

(1.) *Reason testifies that Divine Love is so essential in Religion that all Religion is but hypocrisy and a "vain show" without it.* What is Religion but the exercise and expressions of regard to the Divine Being? But certainly if there be no love to Him, there is no sincere regard to Him; and all pretences and show of respect to Him, whether it be in word or deed, must be hypocrisy, and of no value in the eyes of Him who sees the heart. How manifest is it that without love there can be no true honour, no sincere praise! And how can obedience be hearty, if it be not a testimony of respect to God? The fear of God without love is no other than the fear of devils; and all that outward respect and obedience, all that resignation, that repentance and sorrow for sin, that form in religion, that outward devotion that is performed merely from such a fear without love, is all of it a practical lie, as in Psalm lxvi. 3—". . . How terrible art Thou in Thy works! through the greatness of Thy power shall Thine enemies submit themselves unto Thee." In the original it is "shall Thine enemies lie unto Thee"—*i.e.*, shall yield a feigned or lying obedience and respect to Thee, when still they remain enemies in their hearts. There is never a devil in hell but what would perform all that many a man [has] performed in religion, that had no love to God; and a great deal more if they were in like circumstances and the like hope of gain by it, and be as much of a devil in his heart as he is now. The Devil once seemed to be religious from fear of torment: Luke viii. 28—"When he saw Jesus, he cried out, and fell down before Him, and with a loud voice said, What have I to do with Thee, Jesus, Thou Son of God Most High? I beseech Thee, torment me not." Here is external worship. The Devil is religious; he prays—he prays in a humble posture; he falls down before Christ, he lies prostrate; he prays earnestly, he cries with a loud voice; he uses humble expressions—"I beseech Thee, torment me not;" he uses respectful, honourable, adoring expressions—"Jesus, Thou Son of God Most High." Nothing was wanting but LOVE.

And with respect to duties towards men, no good offices would be accepted by men one from another, if they saw the heart, and knew they did not proceed from any respect in the heart. If a child carry it very respectfully to his father, either from a strong fear, or from hope of having the larger inheritance when his father is dead, or from the like consideration, and not at all from any respect to his father in his heart; if the child's heart were open to the view of his father, and he plainly knew that there was no real regard to him, Would the child's outward honour and obedience be acceptable to the parent? So if a wife should carry it very well to her husband, and not at all from any love to him, but from other considerations plainly seen, and certainly known by the husband, Would he at all delight in her outward respect any more than if a wooden image were contrived to make respectful motions in his presence?

If duties towards men are [to be] accepted of God as a part of Religion and the service of the Divine Being, they must be performed not only with a hearty love to men, but that love must flow from regard to Him.

(2.) Reason shews *that all good dispositions and duties are wholly comprehended in, and will flow from, Divine Love.* Love to God and men implies all proper respect or regard to God and men; and all proper acts and expressions of regard to both will flow from it, and therefore all duty to both. To regard God and men in our heart as we ought, and to have that nature of heart towards them that we ought, is the same thing. And, therefore, a proper regard or love comprehends all virtue of heart; and he that shews all proper regard to God and men in his practice, performs all that in practice towards them which is his duty. The Apostle says, Romans. xiii. 10—"Love works no ill to his neighbour." 'Tis evident by his reasoning in that place, that he means more than is expressed—that love works no ill but all good, all our duty to our neighbour: which Reason plainly shews. And as the Apostle teaches that love to our neighbour works no ill but all good towards our neighbour; so, by a parity of reason, love to God works no ill, but all our duty towards God.

A Christian love to God, and Christian love to men, are not properly two distinct principles in the heart. These varieties are radically the same; the same principle flowing forth towards different objects, according to the order of their existence. God is the First Cause of all things, and the Fountain and Source of all good; and men are derived from Him, having something of His image, and are the objects of His mercy. So the first and supreme object of Divine Love is God; and men are loved either as the children of God or His creatures, and those that are in His image, and the objects of His mercy, or in some respects related to God, or partakers of His loveliness, or at least capable of happiness.

That love to God, and a Christian love to men, are thus but one in their root and foundation-principle in the heart, is confirmed by several passages in the First Epistle of John: chap. iii. verses 16, 17—"Hereby perceive we the love of God, because He laid down His life for us: and we ought to lay down our lives for the brethren. But whoso hath this world's goods, . . . how dwelleth the love of God in him?" Chap. iv. 20, 21—"If a man say, I love God and hateth his brother, he is a liar: for he that loveth not his brother whom he hath seen, how can he love God whom he hath not seen? And this commandment have we from him, That he who loveth God love his brother also." Chap. v. 1, 2—"Whosoever believeth that Jesus is the Christ is born of God: and every one that loveth Him that begat, loveth him also that is begotten of Him. By this we know that we love the children of God, when we love God, and keep His commandments."

Therefore to explain the nature of Divine Love, what is principally requisite is to explain the nature of love to God. For this may especially be called Divine Love; and herein all Christian love or charity does radically consist, for this is the fountain of all.

As to a definition of Divine Love, things of this nature are not properly capable of a definition. They are better felt than defined. Love is a term as clear in its signification, and that does as naturally suggest to the mind the thing signified by it, as any other term or terms that we can find out or substitute in its room. But yet there may be a great deal of benefit in descriptions that may be given of this heavenly principle though they all are imperfect. They may serve to limit the signification of the term and distinguish this principle from other things, and to exclude counterfeits, and also more clearly to explain some things that do appertain to its nature.

Divine Love, as it has God for its object, may be thus described. 'Tis the soul's relish of the supreme excellency of the Divine nature, inclining the heart to God as the chief good.

The first thing in Divine Love, and that from which everything that appertains to it arises, is a relish of the excellency of the Divine nature; which the soul of man by nature has nothing of.

The first effect that is produced in the soul, whereby it is carried above what it has or can have by nature, is to cause it to relish or taste the sweetness of the Divine relation. That is the first and most fundamental thing in Divine Love, and that from which everything else that belongs to Divine Love naturally and necessarily proceeds. When once the soul is brought to relish the excellency of the

Divine nature, then it will naturally, and of course, incline to God every way. It will incline to be with Him and to enjoy Him. It will have benevolence to God. It will be glad that He is happy. It will incline that He should be glorified, and that His will should be done in all things. So that the first effect of the power of God in the heart in REGENERATION, is to give the heart a Divine taste or sense; to cause it to have a relish of the loveliness and sweetness of the supreme excellency of the Divine nature; and indeed this is all the immediate effect of the Divine Power that there is, this is all the Spirit of God needs to do, in order to a production of all good effects in the soul. If God, by an immediate act of His, gives the soul a relish of the excellency of His own nature, other things will follow of themselves without any further act of the Divine power than only what is necessary to uphold the nature of the faculties of the soul. He that is once brought to see, or rather to taste, the superlative loveliness of the Divine Being, will need no more to make him long after the enjoyment of God, to make him rejoice in the happiness of God, and to desire that this supremely excellent Being may be pleased and glorified.* And if this be true, then the main ground of true love to God is the excellency of His own nature, and not any benefit we have received, or hope to receive, by His goodness to us. Not but that there is such a thing as a gracious gratitude to God for mercies bestowed upon us; and the acts and fruits of His goodness to us may [be,] and very often are, occasions and incitements of the exercise of true love to God, as I must shew more particularly hereafter. But love or affection to God, that has no other good than only some benefit received or hoped for from God, is not true love. [If it be] without any sense of a delight in the absolute excellency of the Divine nature, [it] has nothing Divine in it. Such gratitude towards God requires no more to be in the soul than that human nature that all men are born with, or at least that human nature well cultivated and improved, or indeed not further vitiated and depraved than it naturally is. It is possible that natural men, without the addition of any further principle than they have by nature, may be affected with gratitude by some remarkable kindness of God to them, as that they

* In the MS. the following is placed within brackets at this place, and so again it interrupts the argument and illustration. It is transferred to this footnote:—

"Love is commonly distinguished into a love of complacence and love of benevolence. Of these two a love of complacence is first, and is the foundation of the other, —*i.e.*, if by a love of complacence be meant a relishing a sweetness in the qualifications of the beloved, and a being pleased and delighted in his excellency. This, in the order of nature, is before benevolence, because it is the foundation and reason of it. A person must first relish that wherein the amiableness of nature consists, before he can wish well to him on the account of that loveliness, or as being worthy to receive good. Indeed, sometimes love of complacence is explained something differently, even for that joy that the soul has in the presence and possession of the beloved, which is different from the soul's relish of the beauty of the beloved, and is a fruit of it, as benevolence is. The soul may relish the sweetness and the beauty of a beloved object, whether that object be present or absent, whether in possession or not in possession; and this relish is the foundation of love of benevolence, or desire of the good of the beloved. And it is the foundation of love of affection to the beloved object when absent; and it is the foundation of one's rejoicing in the object when present; and so it is the foundation of everything else that belongs to Divine Love."—G.

should be so affected with some great act of kindness of a neighbour. A principle of self-love is all that is necessary to both. But Divine Love is a principle distinct from self-love, and from all that arises from it. Indeed, after a man is come to relish the sweetness of the supreme good there is in the nature of God, self-love may have a hand in an appetite after the enjoyment of that good. For self-love will necessarily make a man desire to enjoy that which is sweet to him. But God's perfections must first savour appetite and [be] sweet to men, or they must first have a taste to relish sweetness in the perfection of God, before self-love can have any influence upon them to cause an appetite after the enjoyment of that sweetness. And therefore that divine taste or relish of the soul, wherein Divine Love doth most fundamentally consist, is prior to all influence that self-love can have to incline us to God; and so must be a principle quite distinct from it, and independent of it.

CHAPTER III.

SHEWING HOW A PRINCIPLE OF GRACE IS FROM THE SPIRIT OF GOD.

I. *That this holy and Divine principle, which we have shewn does radically and summarily consist in Divine Love, comes into existence in the soul by the power of God in the influences of the Holy Spirit, the Third Person in the blessed Trinity, is abundantly manifest from the Scriptures.*

Regeneration is by the Spirit: John iii. 5, 6—"Verily, verily, I say unto thee, Except a man be born of water, and of the Spirit, he cannot enter into the kingdom of God. That which is born of the flesh is flesh; and that which is born of the Spirit is spirit." And verse 8—"The wind bloweth where it listeth, and thou hearest the sound thereof, but canst not tell whence it cometh, and whither it goeth: so is every one that is born of the Spirit."

The renewing of the soul is by the Holy Ghost: Titus iii. 5—"Not by works of righteousness which we have done, but according to His mercy He saved us, by the washing of regeneration, and renewing of the Holy Ghost." A new heart is given by God's putting His Spirit within us: Ezekiel xxxvi. 26, 27—"A new heart also will I give you, and a new spirit will I put within you; and I will take away the stony heart out of your flesh, and I will give you an heart of flesh. And I will put my Spirit within you, and cause you to walk in my statutes, and ye shall keep my judgments and do them." Quickening of the dead soul is by the Spirit: John vi. 63—"It is the Spirit that quickeneth." Sanctification is by the Spirit of God: 2 Thess. ii. 13—"God hath from the beginning chosen you to salvation through sanctification of the Spirit, and belief of the truth." Romans xv. 16—"That the offering up of the Gentiles might be acceptable, being sanctified by the Holy Ghost." 1 Cor. vi. 11—"Such were some of you: but ye are washed, but ye are sanctified, but ye are justified in the name of the Lord Jesus, and by the Spirit of our God." 1 Peter i. 2—"Elect according to the foreknowledge of God the Father, through sanctification of the Spirit, unto obedience and sprinkling of the blood of Jesus Christ." All grace in the heart is the fruit of the Spirit: Gal. v. 22, 23—"But the fruit of the Spirit is love, joy, peace, long-suffering, gentleness, goodness, faith, meekness, temperance." Eph. v 9—"The fruit of the Spirit is in all goodness, and righteousness, and truth." Hence the Spirit of God is called the Spirit of grace, (Heb. x. 29.)

This doctrine of a gracious nature being by the immediate influence of the Spirit of God, is not only taught in the Scriptures, but is irrefragable to Reason. Indeed there seems to be a strong disposition in men to disbelieve and oppose the doctrine of true disposition, to disbelieve and oppose the doctrine of immediate influence of the Spirit of God in the hearts of men, or to diminish and make it as small and remote a matter as possible, and put it as far out of sight as may be. Whereas it seems to me, true virtue and holiness would naturally excite a prejudice (if I may so say) in favour of such a doctrine; and that the soul, when in the most excellent frame, and the most lively exercise of virtue,—love to God and delight in Him,—would naturally and unavoidably think of God as kindly communicating Himself to him, and holding communion with him, as though he did as it were see God smiling on him, giving to him and conversing with him; and that if he did not so think of God, but, on the contrary, should conceive that there was no immediate communication between God and him, it would tend greatly to quell his holy motions of soul, and be an exceeding damage to his pleasure.

No good reason can be given why men should have such an inward disposition to deny any immediate communication between God and the creature, or to make as little of it as possible. 'Tis a strange disposition that men have to thrust God out of the world, or to put Him as far out of sight as they can, and to have in no respect immediately and sensibly to do with Him. Therefore so many schemes have been drawn to exclude, or extenuate, or remove at a great distance, any influence of the Divine Being in the hearts of men, such as the scheme of the Pelagians, the Socinians, &c. And therefore these doctrines are so much ridiculed that ascribe much to the immediate influence of the Spirit, and called enthusiasm, fanaticism, whimsy, and distraction; but no mortal can tell for what.

If we make no difficulty of allowing that God did immediately make the whole Universe at first, and caused it to exist out of nothing, and that every individual thing owes its being to an immediate, voluntary, arbitrary* act of Almighty power, why should we make a difficulty of supposing that He has still something immediately to do with the things that He has made, and that there is an arbitrary* influence still that God has in the Creation that He has made?

And if it be reasonable to suppose it with respect to any part of the Creation, it is especially so with respect to reasonable creatures, who are the highest part of the Creation, next to God, and who are most immediately made for God, and have Him for their next Head, and are created for the business wherein they are mostly concerned. And above all, in that wherein the highest excellency of this highest rank of beings consist, and that wherein he is most conformed to God, is nearest to Him, and has God for his most immediate object.

It seems to me most rational to suppose that as we ascend in the order of being we shall at last come immediately to God, the First Cause. In whatever respect we ascend, we ascend in the order of time and succession.

II. *The Scripture speaks of this holy and Divine principle in the heart as not only from the Spirit, but as being spiritual.* Thus

* and * That is=self choice, uncontrolled.—G.

saving knowledge is called spiritual understanding: Col. i. 9—"We desire that ye might be filled with the knowledge of His will in all wisdom and spiritual understanding." So the influences, graces, and comforts of God's Spirit are called spiritual blessings: Eph. i. 3—"Blessed be the God and Father of our Lord Jesus Christ, who hath blessed us with all spiritual blessings in heavenly places in Christ." So the imparting of any gracious benefit is called the imparting of a spiritual gift: Rom. i. 11—"For I long to see you, that I may impart unto you some spiritual gift." And the fruits of the Spirit which are offered to God are called spiritual sacrifices: 1 Peter ii. 5—"A spiritual priesthood to offer up spiritual sacrifices, acceptable to God by Jesus Christ." And a spiritual person signifies the same in Scripture as a gracious person, and sometimes one that is much under the influence of grace: 1 Cor. ii. 15—"He that is spiritual judgeth all things, yet he himself is judged of no man;" and iii. 1—"And I, brethren, could not speak unto you as unto spiritual but as unto carnal." Gal. vi. 1—"If a man be overtaken in a fault, ye which are spiritual restore such an one in the spirit of meekness." And to be graciously minded is called in Scripture a being spiritually minded: Rom. viii. 6—"To be spiritually minded is life and peace."

Concerning this, two things are to be noted.

1. *That this Divine principle in the heart is not called spiritual, because it has its seat in the soul or spiritual part of man, and not in his body.* It is called spiritual, not because of its relation to the spirit of man, in which it is, but because of its relation to the Spirit of God, from which it is. That things are not called spiritual because they appertain not to the body but the spirit of man is evident, because gracious or holy understanding is called spiritual understanding in the forementioned passage, (Col. i. 9.) Now, by spiritual understanding cannot be meant that understanding which has its seat in the soul, to distinguish it from other understanding that has its seat in the body, for all understanding has its seat in the soul; and that things are called spiritual because of their relation to the Spirit of God is most plain, by the latter part of the 2d chapter of 1st Corinthians. There we have both those expressions, one immediately after another, evidently meaning the same thing: verses 13, 14—"Which things also we speak, not in the words which man's wisdom teacheth, but which the Holy Ghost teacheth; comparing spiritual things with spiritual. But the natural man receiveth not the things of the Spirit of God." And that by the spiritual man is meant one that has the Spirit is also as plainly evident by the context: verses 10-12—"God hath revealed *them* unto us by His Spirit: for the Spirit searcheth all things, yea, the deep things of God. For what man knoweth the things of a man," &c. Also ver. 15—"He that is spiritual judgeth all things," by which is evidently meant the same as he that hath the Spirit that "searcheth all things," as we find in the foregoing verses. So persons are said to be spiritually minded, not because they mind things that relate to the soul or spirit of man, but because they mind things that relate to the

Spirit of God: Romans viii. 5, 6—"For they that are after the flesh do mind the things of the flesh; but they that are after the Spirit the things of the Spirit. For to be carnally minded is death; but to be spiritually minded is life and peace."

2. *It must be observed that where this holy Divine principle of saving grace wrought in the mind is in Scripture called spiritual, what is intended by the expression is not merely nor chiefly that it is from the Spirit of God, but that it is of the nature of the Spirit of God.* There are many things in the minds of some natural men that are from the influence of the Spirit, but yet are by no means spiritual things in the scriptural sense of the word. The Spirit of God convinces natural men of sin, (John xvi. 8.) Natural men may have common grace, common illuminations, and common affections, that are from the Spirit of God, as appears by Hebrews vi. 4. Natural men have sometimes the influences of the Spirit of God in His common operations and gifts, and therefore God's Spirit is said to be striving with them, and they are said to resist the Spirit, (Acts vii. 51;) to grieve and vex God's Holy Spirit, (Eph. iv. 30; Isaiah lxiii. 10;) and God is said to depart from them even as the Spirit of the Lord departed from Saul: 1 Sam. xvi. 14—"But the Spirit of the Lord departed from Saul, and an evil spirit from the Lord troubled him."

But yet natural men are not in any degree spiritual. The great difference between natural men and godly men seems to be set forth by this, that the one is natural and carnal, and the other spiritual; and natural men are so totally destitute of that which is Spirit, that they know nothing about it, and the reason given for it is because they are not spiritual, (1 Cor. ii. 13-15.) Indeed sometimes those miraculous gifts of the Spirit that were common are called spiritual because they are from the Spirit of God; but for the most part the term seems to be appropriated to its gracious influences and fruits on the soul, which are no otherwise spiritual than the common influences of the Spirit that natural men have, in any other respect than this, that this saving grace in the soul, is not only from the Spirit, but it also partakes of the nature of that Spirit that it is from, which the common grace of the Spirit does not. Thus things in Scripture language are said to be earthly, as they partake of an earthly nature, partake of the nature of the earth; so things are said to be heavenly, as they in their nature agree with those things that are in heaven; and so saving grace in the heart is said to be spiritual, and therein distinguished from all other influences of the Spirit, that it is of the nature of the Spirit of God. It partakes of the nature of that Spirit, while no common gift of the Spirit doth so.

But here an enquiry may be raised, viz.:—

Enq. *How does saving grace partake of the nature of that Spirit that it is from, so as to be called on that account spiritual, thus essentially distinguishing it from all other effects of the Spirit?* for every effect has in some respect or another the nature of its cause, and the common convictions and illuminations that natural men have are in some respects [of] the nature of the Spirit of God; for there is light and understanding and conviction of truth in these common illuminations, and so they are of the nature of the Spirit of God—that is, a discerning spirit and a spirit of truth. But yet saving grace, by its being called spiritual, as though it were thereby distinguished from all other gifts of the Spirit, seems to partake of the nature of the Spirit of God in some very peculiar manner.

Clearly to satisfy this enquiry, we must do these two things:—1. We must bear in mind what has already been said of the nature of saving grace, and what I have already shewn to be that wherein its nature and essence lies, and wherein all saving grace is radically and summarily comprised—viz., a principle of Divine Love. 2. We must consider what the Scripture reveals to be in a peculiar manner the nature of the Holy Spirit of God, and in an enquiry of this nature I would go no further than I think the Scripture plainly goes before me. The Word of God certainly should be our rule in matters so much above reason and our own notions.

And here I would say—

(1.) That I think *the Scripture does sufficiently reveal the Holy Spirit as a proper Divine Person;* and thus we ought to look upon Him as a distinct personal agent. He is often spoken of as a person, revealed under personal characters and in personal acts, and it speaks of His being acted on as a person, and the Scripture plainly ascribes every thing to Him that properly denotes a distinct person; and though the word person be rarely used in the Scriptures, yet I believe that we have no word in the English language that does so naturally represent what the Scripture reveals of the distinction of the Eternal Three,—Father, Son, and Holy Ghost,—as to say they are one God but three persons.

(2.) *Though all the Divine perfections are to be attributed to each person of the Trinity, yet the Holy Ghost is in a peculiar manner called by the name of Love*—Ἀγάπη, the same word that is translated charity in the XIII.th chapter of 1st Corinthians. The Godhead or the Divine essence is once and again said to be Love: 1 John iv. 8—"He that loveth not, knoweth not God; for God is love." So again, ver. 16—"God is love; and he that dwelleth in love, dwelleth in God, and God in him." But the Divine essence is thus called in a peculiar manner as breathed forth and subsisting in the Holy Spirit; as may be seen in the context of these texts, as in the 12th and 13th verses of the same chapter—"No man hath seen God at any time. If we love one another, God dwelleth in us, and His love is perfected in us. Hereby know we that we dwell in Him, and He in us, because He hath given us of His Spirit." It is the same argument in both these verses: in the 12th verse the apostle argues that if we have love dwelling in us, we have God dwelling in us; and in the 13th verse he clears the face of the argument by this, that this love which is dwelling in us is God's Spirit. And this shews that the foregoing argument is good, and that if love dwells in us, we know God dwells in us indeed, for the Apostle supposes it as a thing granted and allowed that God's Spirit is God. The Scripture elsewhere does abundantly teach us that the way in which God dwells in the saints is by His Spirit, by their being the temples of the Holy Ghost. Here this Apostle teaches us the same thing. He says, "We know that He dwelleth in us, that He hath given us His Spirit;" and this is manifestly to explain what is said in the foregoing verse—viz., that God dwells in us, inasmuch as His love dwells in us; which love he had told us before—ver. 8—is God himself. And afterwards, in the 16th verse, he expresses it more fully, that this is the way that God dwells in the saint—viz., because this love dwells in them, which is God.

Again the same is signified in the same manner in the last verses of the foregoing chapter. In the foregoing verses, speaking of love as a true sign of sincerity and our acceptance with God, beginning with the 18th verse, he sums up the argument thus in the last verse: "And hereby we know that He abideth in us, by the Spirit which He hath given us.

We have also something very much like this in the apostle Paul's writings.

Gal. v. 13-16—"Use not liberty for an occasion to the flesh, but by love serve one another. For all the law is fulfilled in one word, even in this, Thou shalt love thy neighbour as thyself. But if ye bite and devour one another, take heed that ye be not consumed one of another. This I say then, Walk in the Spirit, and ye shall not fulfil the lust of the flesh." Here it seems most evident that what the apostle exhorts and urges in the 13th, 14th, and 15th verses,—viz., that they should walk in love, that they might not give occasion to the gratifying of the flesh,—he does expressly explain in the 16th verse by this, that they should walk in the Spirit, that they might not fulfil the lust of the flesh; which the great Mr Howe takes notice of in his "Sermons on the Prosperous State of the Christian Interest before the End of Time," p. 185, published by Mr Evans. His words are, "Walking in the Spirit is directed with a special eye and reference unto the exercise of this love; as you may see in Galatians v., the 14th, 15th, and 16th verses compared together. All the law is fulfilled in one word, (he means the whole law of the second table,) even in this, Thou shalt love thy neighbour as thyself. But if ye bite and devour one another, (the opposite to this love, or that which follows on the want of it, or from the opposite principle,) take heed that ye be not consumed one of another. This I say then, (observe the inference,) Walk in the Spirit, and ye shall not fulfil the lust of the flesh. To walk in the Spirit is to walk in the exercise of this love."

So that as the Son of God is spoken of as the wisdom, understanding, and *Λογος* of God, (Proverbs viii.; Luke xi. 49; John i., at the beginning,) and is, as Divines express things, the personal Wisdom of God; so the Spirit of God is spoken of as the Love of God, and may with equal foundation and propriety be called the personal Love of God. We read in the beloved disciple's writings of these two—*Λογος* and *Ἀγάπη*, both of which are said to be God, (John i. 1; 1 John iv. 8-16.) One is the Son of God, and the other the Holy Spirit. There are two things that God is said to be in this First Epistle of

John—light and love: chap. i. 5—"God is light." This is the Son of God, who is said to be the wisdom and reason of God, and the brightness of His glory; and in the 4th chapter of the same epistle he says, "God is love," and this he applies to the Holy Spirit.

Hence the Scripture symbol of the Holy Ghost is a dove, which is the emblem of love, and so was continually accounted (as is well known) in the heathen world, and is so made use of by their poets and mythologists, which probably arose partly from the nature and manner of the bird, and probably in part from the tradition of the story of Noah's dove, that came with a message of peace and love after such terrible manifestations of God's wrath in the time of the deluge. This bird is also made use of as an emblem of love in the Holy Scriptures; as it was on that message of peace and love that God sent it to Noah, when it came with an olive-leaf in its mouth, and often in Solomon's Song: Cant. i. 15—"Thou hast doves' eyes:" Cant. v. 12—"His eyes are as the eyes of doves:" Cant. v. 2—"Open to me, my love, my dove," and in other places in that song.

This bird, God is pleased to choose as the special symbol of His Holy Spirit in the greatest office or work of the Spirit that ever it has or will exert—viz., in anointing Christ, the great Head of the whole Church of saints, from which Head this holy oil descends to all the members, and the skirts of His garments, as the sweet and precious ointment that was poured on Aaron's head, that great type of Christ. As God the Father then poured forth His Holy Spirit of love upon the Son without measure, so that which was then seen with the eye—viz., a dove descending and lighting upon Christ—signified the same thing as what was at the same time proclaimed to the Son—viz., This is my beloved Son, in whom I am well pleased. This is the Son on whom I pour forth all my love, towards whom my essence entirely flows out in love. See Matt. iii. 16, 17; Mark i. 10, 11; Luke iii. 22; John i. 32, 33.

This was the anointing of the Head of the Church and our great High Priest, and therefore the holy anointing oil of old with which Aaron and other typical high priests were anointed was the most eminent type of the Holy Spirit of any in the Old Testament. This holy oil, by reason of its soft-flowing and diffusive nature, and its unparalleled sweetness and fragrancy, did most fitly represent Divine Love, or that Spirit that is the Deity, breathed forth or flowing out and softly falling in infinite love and delight. It is mentioned as a fit representation of holy love, which is said to be like the precious ointment on the head, that ran down upon the beard, even Aaron's beard, that went down to the skirts of his garments. It was from the fruit of the olive-tree, which it is known has been made use of as a symbol of love or peace, which was probably taken from the olive-branch brought by the dove to Noah in token of the Divine favour; so that the olive-branch and the dove that brought it, both signified the same thing—viz., love, which is specially typified by the precious oil from the olive-tree.

God's love is primarily to Himself, and His infinite delight is in Himself, in the Father and the Son loving and delighting in each other. We often read of the Father loving the Son, and being well pleased in the Son, and of the Son loving the Father. In the infinite love and delight that is between these two persons consists the infinite happiness of God: Prov. viii. 30.—"Then I was by him, as one brought up with him: and I was daily his delight, rejoicing always before him;" and therefore seeing the Scripture signifies that the Spirit of God is the Love of God, therefore it follows that Holy Spirit proceeds from or is breathed forth from, the Father and the Son in some way or other infinitely above all our conceptions, as the Divine essence entirely flows out and is breathed forth in infinitely pure love and sweet delight from the Father and the Son; and this is that pure river of water of life that proceeds out of the throne of the Father and the Son, as we read at the beginning of the XXII.[d] chapter of the Revelation; for Christ himself tells us that by the water of life, or living water, is meant the Holy Ghost, (John vii. 38, 39.) This river of water of life in the Revelation is evidently the same with the living waters of the sanctuary in Ezekiel, (Ezek. xlvii. 1, &c.;) and this river is doubtless the river of God's pleasure, or of God's own infinite delight spoken of in Ps. xxxvi. 7–9—"How excellent is thy loving-kindness, O God! therefore the children of men put their trust under the shadow of thy wings. They shall be abundantly satisfied with the fatness of thy house; and thou shalt make them drink of the river of thy pleasures. For with thee is the fountain of life." The river of God's pleasures here spoken of is the same with the fountain of life spoken of in the next words. Here, as was observed before, the water of life by Christ's own interpretation is the Holy Spirit. This river of God's pleasures is also the same with the fatness of God's house, the holy oil of the sanctuary spoken of in the next preceding words, and is the same with God's love, or God's excellent loving-kindness, spoken of in the next preceding verse.

I have before observed that the Scripture abundantly reveals that the way in which Christ dwells in the saint is by His Spirit's dwelling in them, and here I would observe that Christ in His prayer, in the XVII.[th] chapter of John, seems to speak of the way in which He dwells in them as by the indwelling of the love wherewith the Father has loved Him: John xvii. 26—"And I have declared unto them thy name, and will declare it; that the love wherewith thou hast loved me may be in them, and I in them." The beloved disciple that wrote this Gospel having taken [such] particular notice of this, that he afterwards in his first epistle once and again speaks of Love's dwelling in the saints, and the Spirit's dwelling in them being the same thing.

Again, the Scripture seems in many places to speak of love in Christians as if it were the same with the Spirit of God in them, or at least as the prime and most natural breathing and acting of the Spirit in the soul. So Rom. v. 5—"Because the love of God is shed abroad in our hearts by the Holy Ghost, which is given unto us:" Col. i. 8—"Who also declared unto us your love in the Spirit:" 2 Cor. vi. 6—"By kindness, by the Holy Ghost, by love unfeigned:" Phil. ii. 1—"If there be therefore any consolation in Christ, if any comfort of love, if any fellowship of the Spirit, if any bowels and mercies, fulfil ye my joy, that ye be like-minded, having the same love, being of one accord, of one mind."

The Scripture therefore leads us to this conclusion, though it be infinitely above us to conceive how it should be, that yet as the Son of God is the personal word, idea, or wisdom of God, begotten by God, being an infinitely perfect, substantial image or idea of Himself, (as might be very plainly proved from the Holy Scripture, if here were proper occasion for it ;) so the Holy Spirit does in some ineffable and inconceivable manner proceed, and is breathed forth both from the Father and the Son, by the Divine essence being wholly poured and flowing out in that infinitely intense, holy, and pure love and delight that continually and unchangeably breathes forth from the Father and the Son, primarily towards each other, and secondarily towards the creature, and so flowing forth in a different subsistence or person in a manner to us utterly inexplicable and inconceivable, and that this is that person that is poured forth into the hearts of angels and saints.

Hence 'tis to be accounted for, that though we often read in Scripture of the Father loving the Son, and the Son loving the Father, yet we never once read either of the Father or the Son loving the Holy Spirit, and the Spirit loving either of Them. It is because the Holy Spirit is the Divine love itself, the love of the Father and the Son. Hence also it is to be accounted for, that we very often read of the love both of the Father and the Son to men, and particularly their love to the saints; but we never read of the Holy Ghost loving them, for the Holy Ghost is that love of God and Christ that is breathed forth primarily towards each other, and flows out secondarily towards the creature. This also will well account for it, that the apostle Paul so often wishes grace, mercy, and peace from God the Father, and from the Lord Jesus Christ, in the beginning of his epistles, without even mentioning the Holy Ghost, because the Holy Ghost is Himself the love and grace of God the Father and the Lord Jesus Christ. He is the Deity wholly breathed forth in infinite, substantial, intelligent, love : from the Father and Son first towards each other, and secondarily freely flowing out to the creature, and so standing forth a distinct personal subsistence.

Both the holiness and happiness of the Godhead consists in this love. As we have already proved, all creature holiness consists essentially and summarily in love to God and love to other creatures; so does the holiness of God consist in His love, especially in the perfect and intimate union and love there is between the Father and the Son. But the Spirit that proceeds from the Father and the Son is the bond of this union, as it is of all holy union between the Father and the Son, and between God and the creature, and between the creatures among themselves. All seems to be signified in Christ's prayer in the XVII.th chapter of John, from the 21st verse. Therefore this Spirit of love is the "bond of perfectness" (Col. iii. 14) throughout the whole blessed society or family in heaven and earth, consisting of the Father, the Head of the family, and the Son, and all His saints that are the disciples, seed, and spouse of the Son. The happiness of God doth also consist in this love; for doubtless the happiness of God consists in the infinite love He has to, and delight He has in Himself; or in other words, in the infinite delight there is between the Father and the Son, spoken of in Prov. viii. 30. This delight that the Father and the Son have in each other is not to be distinguished from Their love of complacence one in another, wherein love does most essentially consist, as was observed before. The happiness of the Deity, as all other true happiness, consists in love and society.

Hence it is that the Spirit of God, the third person in the Trinity, is so often called the Holy Spirit, as though "Holy" were an epithet some way or other peculiarly belonging to Him, which can be no other way than that the holiness of God does consist in Him. He is not only infinitely holy as the Father and the Son are, but He is the holiness of God itself in the abstract. The holiness of the Father and the Son does consist in breathing forth this Spirit. Therefore He is not only called the Holy Spirit, but the Spirit of holiness: Rom. i. 4—"According to the Spirit of holiness."

Hence also the river of "living waters," or waters of life, which Christ explains in the VII.th [chapter] of John, of the Holy Spirit, is in the forementioned Psalm [xxxvi. 8] called the "river of God's pleasures;" and hence also that holy oil with which Christ was anointed, which I have shewn was the Holy Ghost, is called the "oil of gladness:" Heb. i. 9—"Therefore God, even thy God, hath anointed thee with the oil of gladness above thy fellows." Hence we learn that God's fulness does consist in the Holy Spirit. By fulness, as the term is used in Scripture, as may easily be seen by looking over the texts that mention it, is intended the good that any one possesses. Now the good that God possesses does most immediately consist in His joy and complacence that He has in Himself. It does objectively, indeed, consist in the Father and the Son; but it doth most immediately consist in the complacence in these elements. Nevertheless the fulness of God consists in the holiness and happiness of the Deity. Hence persons, by being made partakers of the Holy Spirit, or having it dwelling in them, are said to be "partakers of the fulness of God" or Christ. Christ's fulness, as Mediator, consists in His having the Spirit given Him "not by measure," (John iii. 34.) And so it is that He is said to have "the fulness of the Godhead," [which] is said "to dwell in Him bodily," (Col. ii. 9.) And as we, by receiving the Holy Spirit from Christ, and being made partakers of His Spirit, are said "to receive of His fulness, and grace for grace." And because this Spirit, which is the fulness of God, consists in the love of God and Christ; therefore we, by knowing the love of Christ, are said "to be filled with all the fulness of God," (Eph. iii. 19.) For the way that we know the love of Christ, is by having that love dwelling in us, as 1 John iv. 13; because the fulness of God consists in the Holy Spirit. Hence our communion with God the Father and God the Son consists in our possessing of the Holy Ghost, which is Their Spirit. For to have communion or fellowship with either, is to partake with Them of Their good in

Their fulness in union and society with Them. Hence it is that we read of the saints having fellowship and communion with the Father and with the Son; but never of their having fellowship with the Holy Ghost, because the Holy Ghost is that common good or fulness which they partake of, in which their fellowship consists. We read of the communion of the Holy Ghost; but not of communion with Him, which are two very different things.

Persons are said to have communion with each other when they partake with each other in some common good; but any one is said to have communion of anything, with respect to that thing they partake of, in common with others. Hence, in the apostolical benediction, he wishes the "grace of the Lord Jesus Christ, and the love of God the Father, and the communion or partaking of the Holy Ghost." The blessing wished is but one—viz., the Holy Spirit. To partake of the Holy Ghost is to have that love of the Father and the grace of the Son.

From what has been said, it follows that the Holy Spirit is the *summum* of all good. 'Tis the fulness of God. The holiness and happiness of the Godhead consists in it; and in communion or partaking of it consists all the true loveliness and happiness of the creature. All the grace and comfort that persons here have, and all their holiness and happiness hereafter, consists in the love of the Spirit, spoken of Rom. xv. 30; and joy in the Holy Ghost, spoken of Rom. xiv. 17; Acts ix. 31, xiii. 52. And, therefore, that which in Matt. vii. 11—"If ye then, being evil, know how to give good gifts unto your children, how much more shall your Father which is in heaven, give good things to them that ask Him?"—is in Luke xi. 13, expressed thus:—"If ye then, being evil, know how to give good gifts unto your children; how much more shall your heavenly Father give the Holy Spirit to them that ask Him?" Doubtless there is an agreement in what is expressed by each Evangelist: and giving the Holy Spirit to them that ask, is the same as giving good things to them that ask; for the Holy Spirit is the sum of all good.

Hence we may better understand the economy of the Persons of the Trinity as it appears in the part that each one has in the affair of Redemption, and shews the equality of each Person concerned in that affair, and the equality of honour and praise due to each of Them. For that work, glory belongs to the Father and the Son, that They so greatly loved the world. To the Father, that He so loved the world, that He gave His only-begotten Son, who was all His delight, who is His infinite objective Happiness. To the Son, that He so loved the world, that He gave Himself. But there is equal glory due to the Holy Ghost on this account, because He is the Love of the Father and the Son, that flows out primarily towards God, and secondarily towards the elect that Christ came to save. So that, however wonderful the love of the Father and the Son appear to be, so much the more glory belongs to the Holy Spirit, in whom subsists that wonderful and excellent love.

It shews the infinite excellency of the Father thus:—That the Son so delighted in Him, and prized His honour and glory, that when He had a mind to save sinners, He came infinitely low, rather than men's salvation should be the injury of that honour and glory. It shewed the infinite excellency and worth of the Son, that the Father so delighted in Him, that for His sake He was ready to quit His own; yea, and receive into favour those that had deserved infinitely ill at His hands. Both shews the infinite excellency of the Holy Spirit, because He is that delight of the Father and the Son in each other, which is manifested to be so great and infinite by these things.

What has been said shews that our dependence is equally on each Person in this affair. The Father approves and provides the Redeemer, and Himself accepts the price of the good purchased, and bestows that good. The Son is the Redeemer, and the price that is offered for the purchased good. And the Holy Ghost is the good purchased; [for] the Sacred Scriptures seem to intimate that the Holy Spirit is the sum of all that Christ purchased for man, (Gal. iii. 13, 14.)

What Christ purchased for us is, that we might have communion with God in His good, which consists in partaking or having communion of the Holy Ghost, as I have shewn. All the blessedness of the redeemed consists in partaking of the fulness of Christ, their Head and Redeemer, which, I have observed, consists in partaking of the Spirit that is given Him not by measure. This is the vital sap which the creatures derive from the true vine. This is the holy oil poured on the Head, that goes down to the members. Christ purchased for us that we should enjoy the Love: but the love of God flows out in the proceeding of the Spirit; and He purchased for them that the love and joy of God should dwell in them, which is by the indwelling of the Holy Spirit.

The sum of all spiritual good which the saints have in this world, is that spring of living water within them which we read of, (John iv. 10;) and those rivers of living waters flowing from within them which we read of, (John vii. 38, 39,) which we are there told is the Holy Spirit. And the sum of all happiness in the other world, is that river of living water which flows from the throne of God and the Lamb, which is the river of God's pleasures, and is the Holy Spirit; which is often compared in Sacred Scripture to water, to the rain and dew, and rivers and floods of waters, (Isa. xliv. 3, xxxii. 15, xli. 17, 18, compared with John iv. 14, xxxv. 6, 7, xliii. 19, 20.)

The Holy Spirit is the purchased possession and inheritance of the saints, as appears, because that little of it which the saints have in this world is said to be the earnest of that purchased inheritance, (Eph. i. 13, 14; 2 Cor. i. 22., v. 5.) 'Tis an earnest of that which we are to have a fulness of hereafter. The Holy Ghost is the great subject of all gospel promises, and therefore is called the Spirit of promise, (Eph. i. 13.) He is called the promise of the Father, (Luke xxiv. 49.)

The Holy Ghost being a comprehension of all good things promised in the gospel, we may easily see the force of the Apostle's inquiry: Gal. iii. 2—"This only would I know, Received ye the Spirit by the works of the Law, or by the hearing of faith?" So that in the offer of Redemption 'tis of God of whom our good is purchased, and 'tis God that purchases it, and 'tis God also that is the thing purchased. Thus all our good things are of God, and through God, and in God, as Rom. xi. 36—"For of Him, and through Him, and to Him, and in Him, [as εἰς is rendered in 1 Cor. viii. 6,] are all things: to whom be glory for ever." All our good is of God the Father, and through God the Son, and all is in the Holy Ghost, as He is Himself all our good. And so God is Himself the portion and purchased inheritance of His people. Thus God is the Alpha and Omega in this affair of Redemption.

If we suppose no more than used to be supposed about the Holy Ghost, the honour of the Holy Ghost in the work of Redemption is not equal in any sense to the Father and the Son's; nor is there an equal part of the glory of this work belonging to Him. Merely to apply to us, or immediately to give or hand to us blessing purchased, after it is purchased, is subordinate to the other two Persons,—is but a little thing to the purchaser of it by the paying an infinite price by Christ, by Christ's offering up Himself a sacrifice to procure it; and 'tis but a little thing to God the Father's giving His infinitely dear Son to be a sacrifice for us to procure this good. But according to what has now been supposed, there is an equality. To be the wonderful love of God, is as much as for the Father and the Son to exercise wonderful love; and to be the thing purchased, is as much as to be the price that purchases it. The price, and the thing bought with that price, answer each other in value; and to be the excellent benefit offered, is as much as to offer such an excellent benefit. For the glory that belongs to Him that bestows the gospel, arises from the excellency and value of the gift, and therefore the glory is equal to that excellency of the benefit. And so that Person that is that excellent benefit, has equal glory with Him that bestows such an excellent benefit.

But now to return: from what has been now observed from the Holy Scriptures of the nature of the Holy Spirit, may be clearly understood why grace in the hearts of the saints is called spiritual, in distinction from other things that are the effects of the Spirit in the hearts of men. For by this it appears that the Divine principle in the saints is of the nature of the Spirit; for as the nature of the Spirit of God is Divine Love, so Divine Love is the nature and essence of that holy principle in the hearts of the saints.

The Spirit of God may operate and produce effects upon the minds of natural men that have no grace, as He does when He assists natural conscience and convictions of sin and danger. The Spirit of God may produce effects upon inanimate things, as of old He moved on the face of the waters. But He communicates holiness in His own proper nature only, in those holy effects in the hearts of the saints. And, therefore, those holy effects only are called spiritual; and the saints only are called spiritual persons in Sacred Scripture.

Men's natural faculties and principles may be assisted by the operation of the Spirit of God on their minds, to enable them to exert those acts which, to a greater or lesser degree, they exert naturally. But the Spirit don't at all communicate Himself in it in His own nature, which is Divine Love, any more than when He moved upon the face of the waters.

Hence also we may more easily receive and understand a doctrine that seems to be taught us in the Sacred Scripture concerning grace in the heart—viz., that it is no other than the Spirit of God itself dwelling and acting in the heart of a saint,—which the consideration of these things will make manifest:—

(1.) That the Sacred Scriptures don't only call grace spiritual, but "spirit."

(2.) That when the Sacred Scriptures call grace spirit, the Spirit of God is intended; and that grace is called "Spirit" no otherwise than as the name of the Holy Ghost, the Third Person in the Trinity is ascribed to it.

1. This holy principle is often called by the name of "spirit" in Sacred Scripture. So in John iii. 6—"That which is born of the Spirit is spirit." Here by flesh and spirit, we have already shewn, are intended those two opposite principles in the heart, corruption and grace. So by flesh and spirit the same things are manifestly intended in Gal. v. 17—"For the flesh lusteth against the spirit, and the spirit against the flesh: and these are contrary the one to the other; so that ye cannot do the things that ye would." This that is here given as the reason why Christians cannot do the things that they would, is manifestly the same that is given for the same thing in the latter part of the VIIth chapter of the Romans. The reason there given why they cannot do the things that they would is, that the law of the members war with [and] against the law of the mind; and, therefore, by the law of the members and the law of the mind are meant the same as the flesh and spirit in Galatians. Yea, they are called by the same name of the flesh and spirit there, in that context, in the continuation of the same discourse in the beginning of the next chapter:—"Therefore there is no condemnation to them that are in Christ Jesus, that walk not after the flesh, but after the Spirit." Here the Apostle evidently refers to the same two opposite principles warring one against another, that he had been speaking of in the close of the preceding chapter, which he here calls flesh and spirit as he does in his Epistle to the Galatians.

This is yet more abundantly clear by the next words, which are, "For the law of the spirit of life in Christ Jesus hath made me free from the law of sin and death." Here these two things that in the preceding verse are called "flesh and spirit," are in this verse called "the law of the spirit of life" and "the law of sin and death," evidently speaking still of the same law of our mind and the law of sin spoken of in the last verse of the preceding chapter. The Apostle goes on in the VIIIth chapter to call aversation* and grace by

* *Sic.* Query . . . . opposition? or = turning from?—G.

the names of flesh and spirit, (verses 4–9, and again verses 12, 13.) These two principles are called by the same names in Matt. xxvi. 41—"The spirit indeed is willing, but the flesh is weak." There can be no doubt but that the same thing is intended here by the flesh and spirit as (compare what is said of the flesh and spirit here and in these places) in the VIIth and VIIIth chapters of Romans, and Gal. v. Again, these two principles are called by the same words in Gal. vi. 8. If this be compared with the 18th verse of the foregoing chapter, and with Romans viii. 6 and 13, none can doubt but the same is meant in each place.

2. If the Sacred Scriptures be duly observed, where grace is called by the name of "spirit," it will appear that 'tis so called by an ascription of the Holy Ghost, even the Third Person in the Trinity, to that Divine principle in the heart of the saints, as though that principle in them were no other than the Spirit of God itself, united to the soul, and living and acting in it, and exerting itself in the use and improvement of its faculties.

Thus it is in the VIIIth chapter of Romans, as does manifestly appear by verses 9–16—"But you are not in the flesh, but in the spirit, if so be the Spirit of God dwell in you," &c. "Now, if any man have not the Spirit of Christ, he is none of His," &c.

Here the Apostle does fully explain himself what he means when he so often calls that holy principle that is in the hearts of the saints by the name "spirit." This he means, the Spirit of God itself dwelling and acting in them. In the 9th verse he calls it the Spirit of God, and the Spirit of Christ in the 10th verse. He calls it Christ in them in the 11th verse. He calls it the Spirit of Him that raised up Jesus from the dead dwelling in them; and in the 14th verse he calls it the Spirit of God. In the 16th verse he calls it the Spirit itself. So it is called the Spirit of God in 1 Cor. ii. 11, 12. So that that holy, Divine principle, which we have observed does radically and essentially consist in Divine Love, is no other than a communication and participation of that same infinite Divine Love, which is GOD, and in which the Godhead is eternally breathed forth; and subsists in the Third Person in the blessed Trinity. So that true saving grace is no other than that very love of God—that is, God, in One of the Persons of the Trinity, uniting Himself to the soul of a creature, as a vital principle, dwelling there and exerting Himself by the faculties of the soul of man, in His own proper nature, after the manner of a principle of nature.

And we may look back and more fully understand what the apostle John means when he says once and again, "God is Love," and "He that dwelleth in Love dwelleth in God, and God in him," and "If we love one another, God dwelleth in us," and "His Love is perfected in us," [and] "Hereby we know that we dwell in Him and He in us, because He has given us of His Spirit."

By this, also, we may understand what the apostle Peter means in his 2d Epistle i. 4, that the saints are made "partakers of the Divine nature." They are not only partakers of a nature that may, in some sense, be called Divine, because 'tis conformed to the nature of God; but the very Deity does, in some sense, dwell in them. That holy and Divine love dwells in their hearts, and is so united to human faculties, that 'tis itself become a principle of new nature. That love, which is the very native tongue and spirit of God, so dwells in their souls that it exerts itself in its own nature in the exercise of those faculties, after the manner of a natural or vital principle in them.

This shews us how the saints are said to be the "temples of the Holy Ghost" as they are.*

By this, also, we may understand how the saints are said to be made "partakers of God's holiness," not only as they partake of holiness that God gives, but partake of that holiness by which He himself is holy. For it has been already observed, the holiness of God consists in that Divine Love in which the essence of God really flows out.

This also shews us how to understand our Lord when He speaks of His joy being fulfilled in the saints: John xvii. 13—"And now I come unto thee; and these things I speak in the world, that they might have My joy fulfilled in themselves." It is by the indwelling of that Divine Spirit, which we have shewn to be God the Father's and the Son's infinite Love and Joy in each other. In the 13th verse He says He has spoken His word to His disciples, "that His joy might be fulfilled;" and in verse 26th He says, "And I have declared unto them Thy name, and will declare it; that the love wherewith Thou hast loved Me may be in them, and I in them."

And herein lies the mystery of the vital union that is between Christ and the soul of a believer, which orthodox Divines speak so much of, Christ's love—that is, His Spirit is actually united to the faculties of their souls. So it properly lives, acts, and exerts its nature in the exercise of their faculties. By this Love being in them, He is in them, (John xvii. 26;) and so it is said, 1 Cor. vi. 17—"But he that is joined to the Lord is one spirit."

And thus it is that the saints are said to live, "yet not they, but Christ lives in them," (Gal. ii. 20.) The very promise of spiritual life in their souls is no other than the Spirit of Christ himself. So that they live by His life, as much as the members of the body live by the life of the Lord, and as much as the branches live by the life of the root and stock. "Because I live, ye shall live also," (John xiv. 19.) "We are dead: but our life is hid with Christ in God," (Col. iii. 3.) "When Christ, who is our life, shall appear," (Col. iii. 4.)

There is a union with Christ, by the indwelling of the Love of Christ, two ways. First, as 'tis from Christ, and is the very Spirit and life and fulness of Christ; and second, as it acts to Christ. For the very nature of it is love and union of heart to Him.

Because the Spirit of God dwells as a vital principle or a principle of new life in the soul, therefore 'tis called the "Spirit of life," (Rom. viii. 2;) and the Spirit that "quickens." (John vi. 63.)

* 1 Cor. iii. 16, 17, vi. 19; 2 Cor. vi. 16.—G.

The Spirit of God is a vital principle in the soul, as the breath of life is in the body: Ezek. xxxvii. 5—"Thus saith the Lord God unto these bones, I will cause breath to enter into you, and ye shall live;" and so verses 9, 10. . . . .

That principle of grace that is in the hearts of the saints is as much a proper communication or participation of the Spirit of God, the Third Person in the Trinity, as that breath that entered into these bodies is represented to be a participation of the wind that blew upon them. The prophet says, "Come from the four winds, O breath, and breathe upon these slain that they may live," is now the very same wind and the same breath; but only was wanted to these bodies to be a vital principle in them, which otherwise would be dead. And therefore Christ himself represents the communication of His Spirit to His disciples by His breathing upon them, and communicating to them His breath, (John xx. 22.)

We often, in our common language about things of this nature, speak of a principle of grace. I suppose there is no other principle of grace in the soul than the very Holy Ghost dwelling in the soul and acting there as a vital principle. To speak of a habit of grace as a natural disposition to act grace, as begotten in the soul by the first communication of Divine light, and as the natural and necessary consequence of the first light, it seems in some respects to carry a wrong idea with it. Indeed the first exercise of grace in the first light has a tendency to future acts, as from an abiding principle, by grace and by the covenant of God; but not by any natural force. The giving one gracious discovery or act of grace, or a thousand, has no proper natural tendency to cause an abiding habit of grace for the future; nor any otherwise than by Divine constitution and covenant. But all succeeding acts of grace must be as immediately, and, to all intents and purposes, as much from the immediate acting of the Spirit of God on the soul, as the first; and if God should take away His Spirit out of the soul, all habits and acts of grace would of themselves cease as immediately as light ceases in a room when a candle is carried out. And no man has a habit of grace dwelling in him any otherwise than as he has the Holy Spirit dwelling in him in his temple, and acting in union with his natural faculties, after the manner of a vital principle. So that when they act grace, 'tis, in the language of the Apostle, "not they, but Christ living in them." Indeed the Spirit of God, united to human faculties, acts very much after the manner of a natural principle or habit. So that one act makes way for another, and so it now settles the soul in a disposition to holy acts; but that it does, so as by grace and covenant, and not from any natural necessity.

Hence the Spirit of God seems in Sacred Scripture to be spoken of as a quality of the persons in whom it resided. So that they are called spiritual persons; as when we say a virtuous man, we speak of virtue as the quality of the man. 'Tis the Spirit itself that is the only principle of true virtue in the heart. So that to be truly virtuous is the same as to be spiritual.

And thus it is not only with respect to the virtue that is in the hearts of the saints on earth, but also the perfect virtue and holiness of the saints in heaven. It consists altogether in the indwelling and acting of the Spirit of God in their habits. And so it was with man before the Fall; and so it is with the elect, sinless angels. We have shewn that the holiness and happiness of God consist in the Holy Spirit; and so the holiness and happiness of every holy or truly virtuous creature of God, in heaven or earth, consist in the communion of the same Spirit.

ANNOTATIONS ON PASSAGES OF HOLY SCRIPTURE;

FROM

PRESIDENT EDWARDS'S INTERLEAVED BIBLE.

NOTE.

THE following is the title-page of the Bible from whence these "Notes" are drawn: —"Verbum Dei. THE HOLY BIBLE, Containing the Old Testament and the New; Newly translated out of the originall Tongue; and with the former translations diligently compared and revised: London: Printed by the Companie of Stationers. 1652. Cor mundum circa in me Deus, Psalm 51." 4to. On a flyleaf there is the signature of a former possessor of the Bible, thus: "Benjamin Pierpont, His Book AD: 1728." This was probably a son of the Rev. James Pierpont of New Haven, New England, whose third wife, Mary, grand-daughter of the famous THOMAS HOOKER, was mother of the wife of Jonathan Edwards. Of "Benjamin" himself nothing seems to be known. Immediately underneath the other is, "Jonathan Edwards his Book 1748." Mr Pierpont records, on the reverse of the title-page, that the interleaving paper consisted of "432 leaves," and the volume itself of "396 leaves." He has also interspersed a few commonplace observations. Edwards's heading for his "Notes" is, "Miscellaneous Observations on the Holy Scriptures."—G.

OLD TESTAMENT.

GENESIS.

1. Gen. ii. 3—"And God blessed the seventh day, and sanctified it," &c.] It is rendered very probable by Bedford in his "Scripture Chronology,"* that this first Sabbath being the first day of Adam's life, and so the first day from whence he began to reckon time, was the first day of his week; and so, that the first day of the week was the day that God sanctified to be kept by all nations and ages, excepting the change that was made of the day of the Sabbath for the Israelitish nation after the coming out of Egypt, till the resurrection of Christ; and also that the "deep sleep" that was fallen on Adam in which God took from him one of his ribs and made Eve of it, was on the night before. If so, then as Christ rose from the dead on the first day of the week, so Adam on the same day rose from his first sleep. As Christ on that day rose from that death that He died, by which He purchased and obtained the Church, being by that means created anew; so Adam rose from that "deep sleep" that he slept, which made way for her formation, and by which he obtained her. As when Adam arose from his deep sleep, God brought the woman to him, whose being, his deep sleep had made way for, and gave her to him; so when Christ rose from the dead, God brought the Church to Him: it was gathered and brought home to Christ in an extraordinary manner, soon after His resurrection. As Adam rose and received his wife, "bone of his bone, and flesh of his flesh," and taken out of himself, from near his heart; so Christ received His Church that is "of his flesh and of his bones," (Eph. v. 30,) and as the product of His most dear dying love. As this day was a day wherein God was refreshed, and rejoiced in beholding His works, and a day of rejoicing to Adam in that he then received his wife, and a day of rejoicing to Eve, being then first received into union with her companion; so the day of Christ's resurrection was a day of rejoicing to God the Father, to Christ, and also to the Church, which was then begotten again to a living hope by the resurrection.

2. Gen. ii. 17—"In the day," &c.] It does not seem to me

* 1730 folio.—G.

necessary that we should understand this, that death should be executed upon him in that day when he ate. But that it may be understood in the same manner as Solomon's words to Shimei, (1 Kings ii. 37.) Death was executed upon Shimei many days after he had done that thing. The thing that God would signify to Adam by this expression seems to me to be, that if he but once presumed to taste that fruit, he should die. You shall not be waited upon to see whether you will do it again, but as soon as ever you have eaten, that very day shall death be made sure to you, you shall be bound to die, given over to death without any more waiting upon you; as that was what Solomon would signify to Shimei; that if he but once went over the brook Kedron, he should die; (see note on 1 Kings ii. 37,) and so these words signify that perfect obedience was the condition of God's covenant that was made with Adam, as they signify that for one act of disobedience he should die. See Ezek. xxxiii. 12—[" Thou shalt die."] (See POOL, Synop. *in loc.*) *

3. Gen iii. 15—" I will put enmity between thee and the woman, and between thy seed and her seed: it shall bruise thy head, and thou shalt bruise his heel."] Here the pronoun "he," the verb "bruise," and the affix "his" are all of the singular number, as Bedford observes in p. 166 of his "Scripture Chronology,"† which shews that by "seed" is meant a particular person, and not her posterity in general; which observation is agreeable to that which the apostle Paul makes, (Gal. iii. 16,) referring to what is said in Gen. xxii. 17, 18, where the singular pronoun or affix "his," and the singular verb "possess," is in like manner used when speaking of that "seed of Abraham," who should "possess the gate of his enemies," and "in whom all the families of the earth should be blessed." Bedford in his "Scripture Chronology" says the Jewish Paraphrasts express this text thus: "There shall be a remedy to mankind: but there shall be no remedy to thee the serpent. But there shall be a remedy to them in the latter age of the world, even in the days of King Messiah, who shall remember what thou didst in the beginning of the world;" and says, that Maimonides, a learned Jew, justly admires [= wonders] that the seed of the woman should be only mentioned, and not of Adam, without whom she could have no seed, and which must therefore be his seed; and that it should be said of "*her* seed," not of "his," that it bruised the serpent's head. "This," saith he, "is one of the passages in Scripture which is most wonderful, and not to be understood according to the letter, but contains great wisdom in it." In the old Creation, the woman was taken out of the man; in the new Creation, the man is taken out of the woman. God in the new creation honours the inferior; as man, the inferior nature, is honoured above the angels.

4. Gen. iii. 21—"Coats of *skins*."] Our first parents, who were become naked, were clothed at the expense of life. Beasts were slain,

* The well-known "Synopsis Criticorum," filling five large folios. Best edition is, Utrecht, 1684.—G.

† As before under Gen. ii. 3.—G.

and resigned up their lives to afford them clothing to cover their nakedness. The skin signifies the life, as in Job ii. 4—"Skin for skin"—*i.e.*, life for life. These beasts typified Jesus Christ. Probably they were beasts slain in sacrifice; but if not, if they were slain by God on purpose to clothe Adam and Eve, the type is no less lively. See Exod. xxxvi. 14.

5. Gen. iv. 23, 24—"And Lamech said unto his wives, Adah and Zillah, here my voice; ye wives of Lamech, . . I have slain a man," &c.] The probable design of the Holy Spirit in relating this, is to shew the great increase of the depravity and corruption of the world of Cain's posterity, and those that adhered to them at that day, in the generation next to the Flood. This is shewn in the particular instance of Lamech, the chief man of Cain's posterity in his day. Lamech had been guilty of murder, he had slain some man that he had had a quarrel with, and he justifies himself in it, and endeavours to satisfy his wives that he shall escape with impunity, from the instance of Cain, whose life God had protected, and even took especial care that no man should kill him; and had declared if any man killed him, vengeance should be taken on him sevenfold, though the man he slew was his brother and a righteous man, and had done him no injury. But this man he had slain in, or for his wounding, (as the words are interpreted by some learned men, (see Pool, Synop. *in loc.*) See instance Joshua xxiv. 32, בְּמֵאָה קְשִׂיטָה for an hundred pieces of silver,)—*i.e.*, the man he had slain had injured and wounded him; and therefore if Cain should be avenged sevenfold, doubtless he seventy and sevenfold. By this speech to his wives he shews his impenitence, presumption, and great insensibility. When Cain had slain his brother, his conscience greatly troubled him; but Lamech, with great obduracy, shakes off all remorse, and as it were bids defiance to all fear and trouble about the matter. That he should set the price of his life so high; that he should imagine that the vengeance due to the man that should take it away ought to be so vastly beyond that which was threatened for the killing of Cain, must be owing to a prodigious pride of heart, esteeming himself a man of such great value, and accounting it so heinous a thing for any to hurt or wound him; and then it shews a vile abuse of God's goodness, long-suffering, and forbearance, in the instance of Cain, which ought to have led men to repentance. But instead of this, that instance of God's forbearance probably was so abused as to be one great occasion of that violence that the earth was filled with in Lamech's days. The sins for which the old world was destroyed were chiefly sensuality, pride, violence, presumption, a stupid, seared conscience, and abusing God's patience, of each of which Lamech (the head of that wicked world) is here set forth [as] an example, in his polygamy and his murder, (which probably was some way occasioned by his polygamy,) and in this speech to his wives about what he had done. It need not be wondered at that Lamech should express his mind to his wives any more than that Ahab and Haman should express the wicked workings of their hearts to their wives, [1 Kings

xxi. 5, 6; Eph. v. 10–14;] and it is the less to be wondered at in Lamech's case, for it is natural to suppose that his wives, knowing what he had done, were full of fear lest the friends of the persons murdered would avenge themselves on him and his family, and that they themselves should lose their lives by the means; which would be more natural still if the quarrel he had had with the young man that was slain, was about his wives, as is probable. This may well account for the earnestness of Lamech's speech to his wives, as we may well suppose it would require some pains to remove their fears in such a case.

6. Gen. iv. 25—"Hath appointed *me*," &c.] Eve does not say, God hath appointed *us* another seed, but hath appointed *me*. She speaks of Abel and Seth, the righteous children of Adam and Eve, as *her* seed; and so the Church, or generation of the righteous which was to proceed from Seth, she calls *her* seed, doubtless with respect to the promise, (chap. iii. 15.)

7. Gen. iv. 26—"And to Seth, to him also," &c.] The right translation probably is, "Then began men to call by the name of the Lord," or "in the name of the Lord,"—*i.e.*, then they began to call themselves and their children by or in His name, signifying that then the people of God,—of whom Seth was the principal man, and, as it were, their head leader and chief priest, being with his posterity appointed another seed (seed or generation of God) instead of Abel,—I say, then the people of God, openly to distinguish themselves from the wicked apostate world of the posterity of Cain and those that joined with them, began to appear in a visibly distinct society, being called the children of God, when the others were called the children of men. The children and posterity were looked upon as being in the name of the father and upholding his name. See Numb. xxvii. 4; Deut. ix. 14, xxv. 7; 1 Sam. xxiv. 21; 2 Sam. xiv. 7, xviii. 18; Ruth iv. 5; Job xviii. 17; Isa. xiv. 22; Gen. xlviii. 16, compared with Numb. vi. 27. On the birth of Enos, it probably first began to be a custom for parents openly to dedicate their children to God and call them by His name, and, as it were, insert them into His name by bringing them to the place of public worship, the transaction being performed by the parents' solemn declaration and covenant, attended with prayer and sacrifice. See Pool, Synop. *in loc.*

8. Gen. v. 20—"Shall comfort us."] How Noah would comfort the Church of God, we may be led to understand by the manner in which the like expression is used in Ezek. xiv. 22.

9. Gen. v. 24—"Enoch walked," &c.] That Enoch and Elias were translated, shews that it is not because the redemption of Christ was not sufficient, that the saints are not wholly freed from death, so as never to taste it. God saw fit that there should be these instances of it, probably partly for this end, to manifest this. If all mankind had died without one exception, it would have been ready to lead us to think it absolutely necessary that the justice or truth of God required, and that these didn't allow of one being redeemed from it; and that the redemption of Christ in that point failed of sufficiency.

What is absolutely universal, we are ready to look upon as absolutely necessary; and the translation of these saints is the more credible, because at the end of the world all the saints that are found living when Christ comes, shall be translated without dying. If all shall be translated, why not one or two before?

10. Gen. vii. 2, 3—"Of clean beasts and clean fowls by sevens."] Three couples for breed[ing,] and the seventh for sacrifice, (chap. viii. 20,) as in the distribution of the days of the week. See HENRY *in loc.*

11. Gen. ix. 12-14.] Such a promise of God that He would no more destroy the earth by a flood of waters, and such a token of this covenant, was very necessary for the comfort of Noah and his sons, after they had been so terrified by such an awful dispensation of God. For probably before the Flood they had never seen any such thick clouds and such showers of rain as are common since. The air and fluids of the earth being then so much purer, as not to be disposed thus to such thick and dark condensing of vapours. God's way of watering the ground seems to be that mentioned in Gen. ii. 6, of causing a mist to go up and descend in gentle dews. The rainbow here seems to be a new thing, which it would not have been if there had been such clouds and showers before the Flood as since. Noah and his sons, therefore, would have been likely to have been put into a terrible consternation from time to time, when they saw the heavens all covered with thick and dark clouds, and the water descending in great showers of rain, for fear the world was going to be drowned again with a flood; but God having told Noah, as in these verses, their seeing the rainbow, as was common after showers, especially great showers, would be a great comfort to them. That beautiful pleasant appearance, the rainbow, was a token of the covenant. So God's covenant with His people is represented by the staff called beauty in Zech. xi. 10.

12. Gen. xii. 14—"For ever."] Such a phrase sometimes signifies no longer than "till the year of jubilee;" so Exod. xxi. 6. But if this phrase is limited by the year of jubilee, which came at the end of every fifty years, no wonder that it should be spoken of as what should be continued for ever, which was to last to the end of the ages of that dispensation, till the coming of Christ, and the introduction of the glorious gospel-day, the great thing typified by the jubilee. There were some ordinances which were only for one particular time; so were several in the XIIth chapter of Exodus, such as eating the paschal lamb with their staff in their hand, &c., and their sprinkling the blood on the door-posts. Many ordinances were only occasional precepts to be observed on the occasion of God's appearance at Mount Sinai, and the occasion of building the tabernacle, the occasion of setting apart the tribe of Levi and the family of Aaron, consecrating the tabernacle, altar, &c. The occasion of the destruction of Korah and his company; the occasion of their being plagued with fiery serpents; the occasion of their passing through Jordan; the occasion of the siege of Jericho, &c. Some ordinances were in

force only during their continuing in the wilderness, as the ordinances concerning their encampments and marches, their gathering and disposing of the manna, their bringing all the beasts they killed to eat to the door of the tabernacle, &c. It is in contradistinction to these that the ordinances that were to be continued throughout the ages of their dispensation and of the Jewish state in Canaan, are called perpetual or everlasting statutes ; and in this view, and as compared with those transitory and temporary statutes, they might well be so called.

13. Gen. xiv. 5, 6.] Thus God is pleased to honour His servant Abraham. First, He orders that in Providence, that shews the great strength of the enemy, by giving the victory over so many people and those that were so mighty. They subdue the race of the giants that were in these lands ; and then He gives them an easy prey to Abraham and his family, His little flock, and shews that the weakness of God is stronger than the greatest strength of men, when hand joins in hand and mighty princes are combined together. Abraham takes them in their greatest glory, and just after they had taken their richest prize, that which they took from that wealthy country of the plain of Sodom. In their highest pride and exaltation and triumph, they are suddenly brought down as Nebuchadnezzar and Belshazzar were. Thus God often deals with man. There seems to be a special hand of God with them to enable them to conquer those giants from the favour He bore to His servants Abraham and Lot, and to evacuate those countries of them that He designed to give to their posterity for a possession. See Deut. ii. 18, 19, &c. They gave not God the glory of this great victory, but took it to themselves, as Nebuchadnezzar did the building of Babylon ; therefore God destroyed them. That race of giants that were in and about Canaan, was probably the only race of giants upon earth. God had long war with them, and they were all destroyed ; for the sake of His people, the race was entirely extirpated. They seemed to have been raised up for that end, that they might be types of the devils, and that their being destroyed before His people, might be a type of the victory Christ obtains over the devils for the sake of His people. See Josh. x.

14. Gen. xv. 1.] In what God says to Abraham, He has respect to what is related in the foregoing chapter. There, it is related how wonderfully God had protected him from his enemies, and given him the victory over them ; and therefore God on this occasion bids Abraham not to " fear," and tells him that He is his shield. In the preceding chapter it is also related how that Abraham had refused the reward that the King of Sodom had offered him ; and therefore God here tells him that He is his exceeding great reward, which He was sufficient for, being the possessor of heaven and earth, as Abraham on that occasion observed, in verses 19th and 22d of foregoing chapter.

15. Gen. xvii. 12—" And he that is eight days old," &c.] One reason why they were not to be circumcised till they were eight days old, was because the child was legally impure till then. It was born

impure, being defiled with blood, and it was seven days before it was clean; both the mother and child were unclean seven days on that account, they being both defiled with that blood, as Levit. xii. 2, 3.

16. Gen. xvii. 14—"That soul shall be cut off from his people."] This and other parallel texts in the Law of Moses are not necessarily to be understood of death. It is very agreeable to the use of such expressions elsewhere, that he that is excommunicated, deprived, either by the judgment of ecclesiastical judges or by the immediate judgment of God, of all union or communion with the congregation or Church of God's people, should be said to be cut off from His people and cut off from the congregation of the Lord. Joshua says to the Gibeonites, Joshua ix. 23. . . . In the original it is "There shall not be cut off from you a bondsman." (The word "cut off" in the original being the same as in the other case)—*i.e.*, no one of you shall be separated from the rest of your company, so as not to partake with him or have communion with him in servitude. So God says, Num. iv. 18—*i.e.*, let them not be separated from them and from a participation in their privileges. Here, again, the word in the original is the same: as it also is Zech. iv. 2, where it is implied that not only those that are dead, but those who are separated from the inhabitants and benefits of the city by captivity, are cut off from the city. So divorcement in Scripture is "cutting off," the word being from the same root in the original, (Deut. xxiv. 1, 3; Isa. l. 1.) However, God's depriving His people of church privileges, or of the privileges of His visible people, is compared to this very thing.

17. Gen. xviii. 18, 19.] By these verses it is manifest—

(1.) That absolute promises already made may yet, in a sort, depend on future conditions; for the promise here mentioned had been made already absolutely over and over. But yet Abraham's future commanding his children and his household after him, is mentioned as the condition of it; and then after that [there] remains another condition—viz., that they keep the way of the Lord to do justice and judgment.

(2.) That the promise is absolutely made before the performance of all the conditions, because the performance of the future conditions is so certainly connected with what was already found in Abraham, that it was certainly consequent, and taken as already fulfilled. This may illustrate the dependence of a sinner's salvation on his future universal obedience and perseverance, though it be already absolutely promised.

(3.) Hereby it is manifest that, ordinarily, a thorough care and endeavour in the education of children will be successful.

(4.) That when God admits children into covenant with their parents, and so admits them to be the subjects of the visible seal of the Covenant, it is, as it were, on a dependence on the future religion and piety of the children, as so ordinarily consequent on it that it may be looked upon as virtually included in it.

18. Gen. xix. 1—"And Lot sat in the gate of Sodom."] Where he probably sat exhorting and reproving the people; for the gate of

the city seems of old to be the place of resort on all public occasions, not only the place the judges sat to judge the people, but where their teachers sat to instruct and reprove them, (Isa. xxix. 21 ; Amos v. 10.) The judges might properly do this, but others might also do it who did not take upon themselves the office of judges. If Lot was now reproving the people, and striving to persuade them to repent and reform, he thus [shewed that he] had "no fellowship with the unfruitful works of darkness," but rather reproved them; and God rewarded his withstanding and resisting the stream of the general wickedness of that people, by sending angels on a most kind and merciful errand to him, while in the exercise of his fortitude and opposition; and it is observable that just before the destruction of the people, God used extraordinary means to reclaim them by Lot's reproofs, (who was a preacher of righteousness as well as Noah, 2 Pet. ii. 5–9,) and their destruction came upon them just on the manifestation of the highest and most desperate degree of obstinacy in them, in their despising his reproofs, and most horrid wickedness towards Lot and the angels immediately after. Lot having lately been reproving the people in the gate, the place of judgment, made them the more ready to say, as they do in ver. 9—"This fellow came in to sojourn, and he will needs be a judge."

19. Gen. xxii. 8—"God will provide Himself a lamb."] Fulfilled in Christ. We may observe here an instance of the harmony between the Old and New Testaments, in that it is according to the Old Testament, as well as in that it is not unreasonable, that God Himself should provide the sacrifice by which sins against Himself should be atoned for, and His own anger appeased. Abraham did not only tell his son that God would provide Himself, but He actually did provide a ram for Abraham, to offer up as a burnt-offering. Again, we may observe here that which may confirm us, that the prophecies of the prophets often, according to the mind of the Holy Ghost, had respect to those things which the prophets themselves had no thought of. For Abraham, when he said "God will provide Himself a lamb," had no thought of any other than that Isaac was to be the lamb that was to be offered and that God had provided for Himself. See John xi. 51.

20. Gen. xxiv. 12.] Abraham's servant obtained a wife for his master's son, not merely by delivering his message, but by prayer joined with it. So the ministers of Christ win souls, not only by preaching, but by earnest prayer to God for their conversion.

21. Gen. xxvi. 5.] If God had such respect to Abraham's righteousness and obedience, and particularly to his offering up his son in obedience to God, as to give the earthly Canaan to his seed, much more will God have such a respect to the righteousness of Christ, and His offering up Himself in obedience to God, as for the sake of this to give His seed the heavenly Canaan.

22. Gen. xxvii. 4.] It was probably the manner, in those days, for parents, when they grew old and expected to die in a little time, to make a feast and to eat and drink with their children, when they gave

them their blessing and their dying charges, and so did, as it were, make their Will. Their dying testament, or blessing, was something like a Covenant; but it was the manner of those, when they made a Covenant with any, to make a feast and eat and drink together, (chap. xxvi. 30, xxxi. 46.) When they gave their children the blessing, they then, as it were, took their leave of them. And when near friends took their leave one of another, they were wont to eat and drink together. So Rebekah's friends took their leave of her, (Gen. xxxiv. 54.) So did the Levite's father-in-law take leave of him and his daughter, the Levite's wife, in Judges xix. So God, when He makes His testament or covenant with us, doth it, as it were, at a feast. Of old, when the people entered into solemn covenant with God, they were wont to make a feast and feasted before the Lord; and almost all solemnities were attended with feasting. The Patriarchs thus blessing their children before their death, exhibits to us a proof of the covenant of grace, which is, as it were, Christ's Last Will and Testament to His people.

23. Gen. xxviii. 11, 12.] There seems to be a double representation in this story. It seems to be a type that has respect to two things.

(1.) By Jacob sleeping and having heaven opened to him, and God appearing in heaven as his covenant-God, and the angels of God ascending and descending on him, seems to be represented Christ, which is confirmed by what Christ says, (John i. 51,) in which Christ plainly alludes to what is said here in ver. 12; and Jacob's sleep here, seems to represent the death of Christ. As Jacob in his sleep has the gate of heaven opened and a ladder set on the earth, on the land of Canaan, whose top reached to heaven, and the angels of God ascending and descending on it, and God appearing in heaven revealing Himself as the covenant-God of him and his seed, and promising that his seed shall be as the dust of the earth, and that in him and his seed all the families of the earth should be blessed. So Christ, by His death, procured that the gate of heaven should be opened towards the earth, and that there should be a union between heaven and earth, and that there should be a way from heaven to the earth procured, as it were, a ladder, by which there might be an ascent from this sinful miserable world to heaven. Christ procured this way to heaven for His covenant people, for His spiritual posterity, and therefore the foot of the ladder is set on the land of Canaan, the land of His people, on Jacob's land, or the land of Jacob's posterity; and Christ, by His death, procured that the angels of God might ascend and descend to and from the land of Canaan, in and through His mediation, or on His ladder, to be ministering spirits to the inhabitants of Canaan, (Heb. i. 14.) So through the death of Christ, God appears as the covenant-God of Him and His seed, promising to give heaven to Him and His seed, as in ver. 14 He promises to give Canaan to Jacob and his seed, and also, as bound in Covenant, to multiply His seed as the dust of the earth, as here to Jacob, (Isa. liii. 10;) and promising to give Him the Gentiles in all parts of the world, or from the four winds of heaven, to be His seed, (which was accomplished soon after the death of Christ,) as here He promises to Jacob that he should spread abroad to the west, and to the east, and to the north, and to the south, and as promising that "in him all the families of the earth should be blessed." Note that Christ is evidently called by the name of Israel, one of the names of Jacob, in Isa. xlix. 3, which renders it more probable that Jacob is here a type of Christ.

(2.) Jacob here represents a believer, or rather believers collectively, as the Church is spiritual Israel, of whom Jacob, or Israel, is the father; and the stone that he slept or rested upon represents Christ, who is from time to time compared to a stone; and that Christ is represented by this stone seems more evident, because he anointed it, (ver. 18.) Thereby He is represented—that is, Christ, or the anointed, and is called so, not only as He is anointed of God, but also as anointed by His people, (see Dan. ix. 25; Mark xiv. 3;) and another thing that confirms that this stone is a type of Christ, is what Jacob says of it in ver. 22, for Christ is the house of God, "in Whom dwells all the fulness of the Godhead bodily." It was He that was signified by the Tabernacle and Temple, as is evident by what Christ says of His own body, for, says He, "destroy," &c.; and the Lamb is said to be the temple of the New Jerusalem, (Rev. xxi. 22.) And it is still further evident by the use that he put it to, for he set it up for a pillar—*i.e.*, for an altar, (see Exod. xxiv. 4.) For the oil that Jacob poured on it was to consecrate it as an altar, and was also as an offering to God on the altar, as the precious ointment that Mary poured on the head of Christ was an offering to Christ and to God through Him. And this will be more evident if we compare what is said here with chap. xxxv. 14, where we have an account that Jacob in the same place set up a pillar of stone (and probably it was the same stone) and poured a drink-offering thereon, and poured oil thereon. What we are told of, chap. xxxv. 7—"And he built there an altar, and called it El-beth-el: because there God appeared unto him, when he fled from the face of his brother." This altar probably (as I have observed) is the same spoken of in ver. 14, on which he poured a drink-offering and oil—viz., the stone which he set up for a pillar, which was probably the same stone that is spoken of in this place, or that that stone at least was a principal stone in the altar. But this he calls El-beth-el,—*i.e.*, the God of Bethel,—because it represented the God of Bethel, or Jesus Christ, who is that God. Jacob promises, at the end of this chapter, that when God should return him again into his own land in peace, that this stone which he had set up for a pillar should be God's house—*i.e.*, this very place shall be that which I will make the place of worship, (and therefore he set up the stone that he slept on for a pillar or monument whereby to remember the place;) and this very stone shall be the altar on which I will worship and offer offerings to God: as we are told of David, when he had built an altar in the threshing-floor of Ornan the Jebusite, in the place where the angel appeared to him; (1 Chron. xxii. 1,) which accordingly was the place where the Temple was built. And therefore, when Jacob was returned to Canaan and seemed to be negligent of his promise, God put him in mind of it, and commanded him to go and dwell there and make that the place of his worship, (Gen. xxxv. 1;) and therefore, doubtless, the stone that he set up when he came there, that we have account of, (verses 14, 15,) was in the very same place, and, we have all reason to think, the same stone. There God talked with him again then, and we have an account (ver. 13) that God went up from him in the place He talked with him, which denoted that place where God appeared. There was the gate or entrance into heaven, as he says this place is, and so doubtless was the same spot. Besides that, we find Jacob calls it by the same name, ver. 15. . . . Hence we may learn that their altars of old were types of Christ, especially in His Divine nature. They represented Him who is the "rock" of Israel, (see Judges xiii. 19.) And therefore it was the manner of the heathen to set up pillars or small altars instead of images, as Bedford in his "Scripture Chronology," and other historians have observed: which was strictly forbidden to the children of Israel, (Levit. xxvi. 1, and so Deut. xvi. 22;) and the children of Israel were required to destroy the pillars of the people of the land, (Deut. vii. 5, and xii. 3;) and hence the children of Israel were strictly forbidden to have any other altar but one,—no other but the altar of the Lord, because God was one, and Christ was one, and because altars represented Christ. This is not the only place where the name of God is given to an altar. We have the like in Exod. xvii. 15. Jacob's sleeping or resting on this stone, (for this stone, we are told, was his pillow,) typifies God's people believing in or resting on Christ. Christ invites the weary to come to Him, and promises that in Him they shall have rest. Jacob, while resting on this stone, has heaven's gate opened to him, and a ladder reaching from him to God in heaven; so it is by faith in Christ that God's people have heaven's gate opened to them, and have a way prepared for them to ascend and come to God in heaven. Jacob, while resting on this stone, has God appearing to him as his covenant-God; so it is through faith in Christ that God becomes their covenant-God, and whereby they become interested in the promises of that covenant of grace, and it is by faith that they become related to heaven and have the privilege of the ministration of angels. Jacob's sleep here represents both death and rest. If we look on Jacob here as a type of Christ, his sleep is a type of death. If as a type of the Church, or of the Israel of God, then it represents spiritual rest. But let us take the type which way we will, we may observe that the great privilege and blessing is obtained, of having heaven's gate opened and a way to heaven from the earth, and the ministration of angels is enjoyed in Bethel, in the house of God,—*i.e.*, in God's Church, —and in the improvement of the ordinances of His house.

24. Gen. xxix. 27—"Fulfil her week."] By this it is evident that then, in those days, their time was divided out into weeks, or parcels of seven days, as it is now, by which may rationally be argued that the Sabbath was then observed among them, that it was an institution

for the times before Moses, and that the remembrance of the institution was kept up in the world throughout the ages that preceded the Mosaic Dispensation. For the weekly division of time had its rise from the appointment of one day in seven to be observed as a Sabbath, and it was the observing the Sabbath that upheld this division.

25. Gen. xxx. 1.] It is an observation in the fulfilling of Scripture, that when God's people have an immediate desire and pressing after an outward thing, they have their design sometimes answered, but therewith a sharp reproof from God; and usually find small satisfaction in their enjoying that about which they were so unsober in their pursuit. "Give children," &c., said Rachel: she got children, and she died in bringing one of them forth.

26. Gen. xxxi. 24—"Good or bad."] *i.e.*, Say nothing at all to him to compel him, to oblige him to return again, or to bring him again under thy service, or to oblige him to resign to thee any of his wives, or cattle, or substance. Say nothing that has such a tendency, or with any such view, whether it seem right and just to you or wrong, good or evil. I leave not you to judge of the rightness of what you shall say with this view, but charge thee to say nothing at all in the least to infringe on his liberty or his possessions. Laban came out after Jacob with such intentions, and he was now meditating what he would say to this purpose. His head was exceeding full of matter, but God charges him to suppress all, and not say one word tending to the design on which he was pursuing Jacob, however right and reasonable it might appear to him. God knew the heart of Laban, and He speaks to his heart. He knew how ready he would be to plead that the design he was upon was just, and that what he had meditated to say to Jacob was good and just. But God prevents him, by charging him to say nothing to the purpose he was pursuing, let it be good or bad.

27. Gen xxxii. 31.] Jacob goes away with a blessing, but yet halting on his thigh. God commonly, when He bestows some extraordinary spiritual blessing and peculiar favour, also at the same time brings some temporal affliction or difficulty, as Paul when admitted to the third heavens had a thorn in the flesh at the same time, lest he should be exalted above measure. Jacob's halting on his thigh represents the saints getting along with difficulty and trouble, disappointment of their temporal aims, and their failing in the steps they take, as what nature aims at and desires. Jacob's lameness after he had the blessing, made him lean more on his staff, so the saints' afflictions they meet with in the world, make them live more by faith, (see ver. 10, and Num. xxi. 18.) Jacob himself when he had the blessing had with it that kind of lameness of which his halting on his thigh was a type, and so he had ever since he first stole the blessing from Esau. He presently upon it suffered banishment, went away poor and solitary, with nothing but his staff, to Padanaram. There he met with crosses and disappointments: he was cheated with Leah instead of Rachel, for whom he served seven

years, and was forced to serve another seven years. Rachel, his most beloved wife, was a great while barren, and after he had suffered twenty years' exile from his father's house, and hard service and a great deal of trouble from his father-in-law, he was forced to steal away, and his journey was attended with great difficulty and peril: he was in great danger first from Laban, and then from Esau, and was forced to purchase safety from him with the loss of great part of his substance. He made him a present of five hundred and eighty of his cattle, and was forced greatly to bow and cringe besides; and then his daughter Dinah was defiled, which doubtless was a very sorrowful thing to him; and then he had more sorrow by the cruelty and treachery of Simeon and Levi's two sons, which made him to stink in the nostrils of the inhabitants of the country, so that he was in fear of his life from them; and then Rachel, his most beloved wife, died in bringing forth her second child; and then Reuben, his first-born son, was guilty of incest with one of his own concubines, which must needs be a great grief to him; and then he had most bitter affliction in the loss of his beloved son Joseph; and then, doubtless, had a great deal of sorrow from the great sins and calamities there were in Judah and his family; and then there was a sore famine, and Jacob and his family were put to a great deal of trouble to get provision to support themselves, and he had much exercise, perplexity, and distress in the affair managed between Joseph and his brethren; and then he and all his family [had] as it were a second banishment from the land of Canaan, the land promised to him in Egypt, an idolatrous country, and never returned any more alive. That Jacob, who was so often blessed of God, and to whom God so frequently ministered such abundant favours to, should yet meet with so much trouble and sorrow in this life is a great evidence of a future state. The same may be observed concerning David. Halting is put elsewhere for affliction or adversity: Ps. xxv. 15—"But in mine adversity they rejoiced;" in the original, "in my halting," (Micah iv. 6, 7; Zeph. iii. 19.)

28. Gen. xxxvii. 24.] The pit was empty, there was no water in it. Joseph's brethren intended to famish him, or kill him with hunger and thirst, and it was so ordered afterwards that they would have died with famine had not they come and bowed down to Joseph to the earth for relief.

29. Gen. xxxvii. 31–33.] Joseph's brethren deceive Jacob their father by the blood of a kid instead of his son Joseph's, his best beloved son; as he, being Esau's brother, had deceived Isaac his father with the flesh and skin of a kid, instead of his son Esau's skin and his venison, who was Isaac's best beloved son. Thus is Jacob punished by God's providence, (see xxix. 25.)

30. Gen. xli. 40, &c.] This signifies the Father's investing of Christ the Mediator with the government of the Church and the world. Joseph was exalted out of the dungeon to be a prince and a ruler over all the land. So Christ was exalted from being a prisoner of vindic[a]tive justice out of the grave, and as it were out of the pit of

hell, to be a prince, and to have all things put under Him. Pharaoh set Joseph over his own house. So God exalted Christ, and set Him over His Church, which is the house of God, (Heb. iii. 6,) and made Him King of heaven itself, which is the place of God. According to Joseph's word Pharaoh's people were to be ruled, only on the throne Pharaoh was to be greater than he. So Christ is made *the* head and ruler of angels and men; but yet God the Father is greater than Christ as Mediator; as Christ says, "My Father is greater than I," He is greater in His economical office than the Son, in that He is the person that sustains the dignity and maintains the right of the Deity. Pharaoh took off his ring from off his hand and put it upon Joseph's hand. So God the Father invested Christ with His own honour and dignity, that all men should honour the Son as they honour the Father, and they cried before Him, "Bow the knee," as it is said concerning Christ, "Let all the angels of God worship Him;" and agreeable to this it is said, Phil. ii. 8-10. . . . . Joseph was thus exalted as a reward for his being the means of saving the people from famine and death. So Christ is exalted to God's right hand, and all things put under His feet in reward for His working out the work of redemption. Pharaoh exalted Joseph and made him head over Egypt, and put the people and all the land into his hand, that he himself might have the immediate disposal and ordering of that office of saving the people from famine that he had laid the foundation for. So Christ is exalted to be a Prince and a Saviour, to dispose of the affairs of the actual applying and accomplishing that redemption that He had purchased; all things were committed to Him of the Father, that He might give eternal life to as many as God had given Him. The food of the land by which the people were to be saved from famine was committed to Joseph's hands, that he might be the immediate dispenser of it. So the purchased blessings are committed to Christ. He has received gifts for men. When He ascended on high, He had the purchased blessings given to Him, that He Himself might bestow them on those that He purchased them for. He received the promise of the Father, even the Holy Ghost, without measure, to shed down on believers, as Joseph had corn brought into him in immense quantities, (ver. 49.) Joseph had a vast flock in his hand. This signifies the sufferings of Christ for the supply of the wants of His people. Joseph was advanced thus to be a saviour to his brethren and kindred. So Christ was exalted to be the Saviour of men, whom He became related to by His incarnation, becoming the brother of believers. The saints are Christ's near relations. He that hears the word of God and keeps it, the same is His mother, and sister, and brother. Joseph, by his exaltation in Egypt, made way for his brethren's reception there. He there prepared a place for them in Goshen, and made way for their reception there, by taking his brethren and presenting them to the king, and interceding with him for them, (chap. xlvii.) Pharaoh gave them the best of the land by giving it to Joseph for them, (chap. xlvii. 6,) and Joseph nourished his brethren in Egypt. So Christ, by His exaltation in heaven, made way for their coming there, prepared, &c. Joseph saved his brethren, though they had been enemies, yea, though they had been his mortal enemies, though they would have put him to death, though they "sold" him. He saved them, by his banishment [and] those very sufferings which their sin, their enmity, brought upon him, as it was with Christ; and he saved them from famine. He first humbled them before he made himself known to them; he exercised them with a variety of dispensations, hopes, fears, disappointments, confusions, perplexities, to humble them before he made himself known to them. They bring their money with them to buy corn, whereas that was not their way to obtain it of Joseph; he would not accept of their money. So we must come to Christ for spiritual food, without our own righteousness, "without money and without price." Joseph at first made himself strange unto them, and spoke roughly to them; charges them with not coming as friends, but as enemies, and thereby he makes them sensible of their guilt in their former treatment of him. So when the elect are under convictions, and are first stirred up to seek to God for salvation, God is wont, as it were, to frown upon them, to express His anger, as though He looked upon them as enemies; thereby to bring their sins to remembrance, and make them sensible of their guilt in their former treatment of Him. Joseph insists on it that he should look upon them as enemies till they delivered up their younger brother, that one brother that they kept back; that they were tender of as a child; that they pitied and spared, and looked upon it that it would be too hard for him to be brought out of the family, and rent from the arms of his father and delivered up to another lord. So oftentimes sinners, when they begin to seek salvation, keep back something that is dear and tender in their eyes, and flatter themselves that they are not obliged to deliver it up; they think it is too hard and cruel for them so to expose such an enjoyment or possession; but God will surely look upon them as enemies till all is delivered up and nothing kept back. Joseph put them all together in ward three days. So God for a while holds sinners prisoners under conviction; they are shut up as condemned creatures; exposed to the execution of God's wrath. Joseph pities them, and weeps with compassion for them at the same time that he treats them thus roughly. So God oftentimes pities sinners under conviction at the same time that He seems terribly to frown on them. While they were backward to deliver up Benjamin, Joseph took from them Simeon, and bound him before their eyes. So while persons keep back some dear lust, God takes away some of their enjoyments from them. Before Joseph made known himself unto them, they did not understand his language; for he spoke to them by an interpreter. So sinners before their conversion don't understand God's language, and they therefore need the help and advice of ministers under their convictions, as interpreters for them. For a while they seem to have obtained their end; to have obtained food for their money; but this food lasts them but a little while before it was spent. So the false comfort that sinners obtain under conviction by their own righteousness lasts them but a little while before it is all spent. For a while they hoped their money was accepted ; but they soon find it rejected, to their great disappointment and confusion. They come back to their father in the land of Canaan, who in this case represents the first Adam, or [the] nature which men have from him by their parents; the father whose tenderest and dearest child Benjamin was that was kept back; they consult with their father under this difficulty, as men under convictions in their difficulties are wont to consult nature. Their father blames them for yielding to the lord of the land so far as they had done, and greatly objects against delivering up Benjamin. He cries out, "All these things are against me," as persons under convictions often do in a kind of discouragement; but, however, he at length is forced to it by sore famine. So men are, as it were, forced to deliver up their dearest lusts, that it grieves them to part with, by sore famine, by a sense of the extreme necessity of their case. He is brought to it by the possessions of Reuben and Judah. Reuben here represents the family of reason, which is the eldest child of man's nature. Jacob in his blessing calls Reuben "excellency of dignity," and the "excellency of power." The standard of the camp of Reuben bore the image of a man. Reuben never consented to the selling of Joseph. Man's reason never consents to his sin. Judah, the progenitor of Christ, the Word of God, the other brother that persuaded Jacob to deliver up Benjamin, signifies the word of God: or Judah represents the ministers of the word who preach the word of Christ; and therefore he rehearses the words of Joseph, and particularly declares his threatenings and solemn declarations, to persuade Jacob to deliver up Benjamin. Jacob, after disputing with Judah, delivers up Benjamin, the right-hand son, as the name signifies. So nature, after it has long hung back, and much disputing with the word of God, and objecting against it, by the word being earnestly set home, at last yields to cut off and deliver up the beloved lust and right-hand sin. Jacob, being at length forced by the extreme necessity of the case, delivers up that one son that he was most fond of, [if it must be so now, says he;] he is brought, as it were, to yield up the case as to the enjoyment of his children. "If I am bereaved of my children, I am bereaved." So sinners must be brought, as it were, to yield up the case as to the enjoyment of their sins. Nature must be brought to yield up the case as to the enjoyment of natural enjoyments. But now although the former price that Jacob sent to Joseph for corn was rejected, yet he, having delivered up Benjamin, is still for purchasing corn with his own price, and therefore sends the best fruits that his land afforded and double money. So sinners under conviction, after they have been seeking salvation by their own righteousness, and have trusted in it for a while, have had comfort in it, and then are disappointed, and find to their surprise that God rejects the price they have offered before their thorough reformation ; yet after they have more thoroughly reformed and proceeded further in religion, they make a new attempt, though the price they offered before failed : yet they hope, by doubling their price and offering the best fruits of nature's land, and by delivering up Benjamin, to prevail. Now again Joseph's brethren have new perplexities and discouragements, they are ready to look on their case as desperate; they thought they were taken prisoners, (Gen. xliii. 18.) So it often is with sinners under convictions. After this distress they had a great deal of comfort and peace in hope of the acceptance of their present. The steward, who here represents conscience, says to them, "Peace be to you, fear not." They seem to be well accepted and very kindly treated in Joseph's house, and they enjoyed a feast. But this peace and joy of theirs soon vanishes again and comes all to nothing, and, to their great confusion, their double money is found rejected. For now Joseph, that they thought had accepted them, and treated them so kindly for their present, appears more angry than ever with them, and sends a dreadful messenger after them, and lays a heavy charge upon them; fastens the imputation of being enemies more fully than ever upon them, lays their vile treatment of him upon them as deserving death; yea, and by opening their sacks to their view makes the justice of the charge to appear, after they themselves had acknowledged that, if they were guilty as they were charged, death was a just punishment, (chap. xliv. 9.) So sinners under conviction oftentimes, after going far in religion, and after many perplexities and troubles, have at last great peace and joy in their own righteousness, vainly thinking that God accepts them and loves them for their presents that they offer; and they have a feast of false joy: but all soon vanishes, and God appears more angry than ever with them, and a messenger of death is as it were sent to seize them, even Conscience. He that before said to them, "Peace be to you, fear not," and that invited them into Joseph's home, and there made a feast for them, now charges them with enmity and treason, and condemns them to death; and their hearts are laid open by conscience to let them see what is there, even as the steward opened the men's sacks to shew them the stolen cup and money; and they are made to own that the crime deserves death. Upon this Joseph's brethren are seized and carried before Joseph, the lord they had sinned against, and there their lord sets the heinousness of their crime before them, and they are brought down to his feet, to lie on the ground before him. Their mouths are stopped, and they confess their iniquity, (chap. xliv. 16,) and are brought to resign themselves into Joseph's hands, to yield that he should be their sovereign and they his servants, but yet to plead for mercy, and then they were prepared for comfort; then Joseph reveals himself to them as their brother; then they are received indeed as friends and brethren, with great and lasting comfort. Then Joseph reveals to them the whole mystery of their salvation from famine, by their selling him, and his humiliation and exaltation in Egypt. And Joseph gives them an inheritance in Goshen, and then they see that it was their brother, and understood his voice, (chap. xlv. 12.) And hereupon they are accepted of Pharaoh, whose deputy Joseph was in the kingdom; and he, even Pharaoh, the original king of Egypt, gives them inheritance in the land, and Joseph bids them not regard their stuff, their former possessions, for all the land of Egypt (in this case a type of heaven) was before them ; and now they are all clothed with changes of raiment, and they had sufficient provision given them to support them by the way till they came to Egypt, to Goshen, their inheritance, and he charges them not to fall out by the way. When the king exalted Joseph, he gave him a new name. So Christ in the Revelation speaks of His "new name," by which is meant that new honour and glory which He received at His exaltation. Joseph's new name, Zaphnath-paaneah, signifies "revealer of secrets." Christ was the greater revealer of secrets (John i. 18) who came out of the bosom of the Father, and was the great prophet of God to bring to light mysteries that had been kept secret since the world began. Some translate Joseph's new name "the saviour of the world," [see POOL, Syn.] Joseph was in some respect exalted over the whole world ; the whole earth was brought into a dependence on him for life. For it is said, (verses 56, 57,) all came bending to him, as Joseph's brethren did. So Joseph was in a sense the saviour of the world, and to him every knee bowed, not only in Egypt, but throughout the whole earth. Men were saved by Joseph's word, as we are saved by the word of Christ. It was his predictions, his warnings, his counsels that saved Egypt, and saved the world.

31. Gen. xliii. 34.] Thus he that is last is first, and the first last ; the last is the greatest. He that is but as a little child, is most exalted ; so he that is spiritually least, and most like a little child, is greatest in the kingdom of heaven, (Matt. xviii. 4.)

32. Gen. xlvii. 31.] The bowing here spoken of is a bowing of adoration, or a bowing to worship God, as is confirmed by what is said of David, parallel to this, 1 Kings i. 47, 48, and also by Heb. xi. 21.

33. Gen. xlviii. 22—"Which I took out of the hand of the Amorite."] This he speaks in the language of a prophet, according to which a prophet is often said to do that which he foretells shall be done, (see Jer. i. 10.) And they often speak of future events in the past tense ; or he may speak of himself as taking the land by conquest, because his posterity should do it. To call them himself is agreeable to the language of almost all his own prophecies. This passage is much illustrated by the next chapter, ver. 7, and chap. xxvii. 37.

34. Gen. xlix. 22—"Joseph is a fruitful bough, even," &c.] The word which is translated "branches," properly signifies "daughters," and the word which is translated "wall," signifies both a "wall" and an "enemy ;" so that the words may be translated either, "whose branches run over the wall," or, "whose daughters go over to the enemy." But let it be translated either of the ways, the event referred to, doubtless, is the tribe of Benjamin's being supplied with wives. For their wives that they were supplied with from Jabesh-Gilead were of this tribe, for Jabesh-Gilead was in the half-tribe of Manasseh ; and the daughters of Shiloh, which they catched when they came out

in dances, were of the tribe of Ephraim, for Shiloh was in that tribe. Thus their daughters went over to the enemy, or tribe of Benjamin, who were enemies to the other tribes of Israel, in that war in which their women and most of the men were destroyed. Thus, also, the branches or daughters of this fruitful bough or vine ran over the wall. As the whole people of Israel are several times in Scripture compared to a vineyard, so here a particular tribe in Israel seems to be compared to a distinct enclosure of fruit-trees or vineyard that was walled in, (as vineyards were wont to be,) and so separated from other vineyards. Joseph is compared here to an exceeding flourishing bough or vine, whose daughters or branches run over the wall and get out of the enclosure and run into another vineyard. In that it is said his branches run over the wall, and the same word that signifies branches, also signifying (and more properly signifying) daughters; it seems to shew which way his branches shall run over the wall—viz., by his daughters breaking over the enclosure or limits of the tribe and going to another tribe.

35. Gen. xlix. 24—"But his bow," &c.] This was remarkably verified in Joshua and Gideon, who were of this tribe, as appears with respect to Joshua by Num. xiii. 8, and with respect to Gideon by Judges vi. 11, with Joshua xvii. 2, and Judges vi. 35. They were wonderful instances of those whose bow abode in strength, and the arms of whose hands were strengthened by the hands of the mighty God of Jacob, who were strengthened, and succeeded by immediate help from God, as appears by their whole story. Jephthah the Gileadite was also of Joseph, being of the tribe of Manasseh:—["from thence is the Shepherd, the stone of Israel."] These words seem to have a remarkable fulfilment in Joshua, who was, as it were, the "shepherd of Israel," who led them into Canaan to their pasture, and conquered their enemies for them, and was, in a subordinate sense, the "rock" of Israel's salvation, who bore the name of Christ. Joshua is Jesus or the Saviour, and was a remarkable type of Christ, and who had Christ with him, and acted by His influence, and fought by His strength, and had His Spirit to guide him. It may also have respect to the ark and tabernacle being kept at Shiloh, as it was till the days of Samuel, for Shiloh was in the tribe of Ephraim, (Ps. lxxviii. 60, 67.) The ark was the type and symbol of Christ, the Shepherd and Rock of Israel; and the Tabernacle and the mercy-seat over the ark was the place of His presence. ["From thence," &c.]—*i.e.*, from the mighty God of Jacob, mentioned in the immediately preceding words. It seems, evidently, to be explained by the words immediately following—"From the God of thy father, and He will help thee." For so the words are, literally translated: "The arms of his hands were made strong" (thus He *helped thee*) "by the hands of the mighty God of Jacob," (who was Joseph's father:) "from thence is the Shepherd, the stone of Israel: even from the God of Jacob thy father, and He" (the Shepherd, the stone of Israel) "will help thee, and by Him shall the arms of their hands be made strong." He the Messiah, the hand or the

arm of the Lord, (as He is sometimes called,) which shall strengthen thine arms. [See POOL, Synop., on ver. 25.]

EXODUS.

36. Exod. iii. 2, 3—"And the angel of the Lord appeared," &c.] That is, Christ—who is often so called—appeared, &c. This bush represents—

(1.) The human nature of Christ, whose name is "the branch." This bush well represented the human nature of Christ, because it was the growth of the earth. Though Christ, with regard to His Divine nature, be the Lord from heaven, yet, with respect to His human nature, He was the growth of the earth; He was of earthly descent, of the race of mortal mankind. And upon the account of its low and humble stature; it was a bush or bramble, as the word in the original signifies. This well represented Christ's state of humiliation, and also His meekness and lowliness of heart. And also upon the account of its tenderness and liableness to be destroyed. What more easily crushed or consumed than a bramble-bush? This bush, upon each of these accounts, well represented what is spoken of Christ in Isa. liii. 2. This bush was "a root out of a dry ground," (see Hosea xiii. 5; Deut. viii. 15,) for it was a bush that grew on Mount Horeb, as ver. 1, which was so called from the remarkable dryness of the place, for the word Horeb signifies dryness. The Son of God, the Second Person of the Trinity, His appearing in this bush is a type of His being manifest in the flesh. Christ is said (Deut. xxxiii. 16) to have dwelt in the bush; hereby was typified His dwelling in flesh. As the bush burned with fire and was not consumed, so Christ, in the human nature, suffered extremely; He endured the wrath of God, but was not overcome, perished not, was not consumed, He rose again from the dead, and did not see corruption. Though His human nature was but a bush or tender plant, in itself easily capable of being consumed, and though the fire spent all its force upon it; yet, because of the Divinity that dwelt in it, it was impossible that it should be consumed. The power of God "was made perfect in weakness." Satan could not prevail against Christ; though he cast Him into the fire, yet he could not destroy Him.

(2.) This bush represents the Church, the mystical body of Christ; as it was with Christ, so it was with the Church. It is a tender plant. It is a branch of the earth; and oftentimes is in the fire. But God will not suffer it to be consumed; but it always survives the flames; the gates of hell never prevail against it; her enemies are not suffered to swallow her up; God has promised that, when she goes through the fire, she shall not be burnt, neither shall the flames kindle upon her. But, doubtless, a special respect is herein had to the Church, now in her suffering state in Egypt, where her enemies had laboured to destroy her, but were not able; the more they afflicted them, the more they multiplied. God always carried them on eagle's wings out of their enemies' reach, and when they had well-nigh swallowed them up at the Red Sea, God delivered them.

37. Exod. iii. 3—"Moses said, I will now turn aside, and see this great sight, why the bush is not burnt."] The great sight that Moses here said he would turn aside to see, and that he did turn aside to see as he said, as we have an account in next verse, was not that the bush was not burnt, for this Moses had seen already, which was the occasion of his earnestly desiring to know further, and his turning aside to see something further. But what the great sight he turned aside to see was, why the bush was not burnt, or upon what account, or for what reason, as the word in the original signifies. Moses seems to have spoke these words after he had stood a while with astonishment beholding the bush burn, and when he after a while perceived the bush notwithstanding was not burnt, he then considered it must be some great and very extraordinary thing that must preserve the bush as in the midst of the flames. By the sight is meant the thing to be seen: it is as much as if he had said, "I will turn aside and see this great thing, on the account of which the bush was not burnt." This great thing was that God dwelt in the bush, (Deut. xxxiii. 16.) It is probable Moses was sensible that there was something divine in the case ; he might probably see some token of Divine glory there present, some extraordinary lustre or effulgence that had an appearance of exceeding awful majesty, and also surprising sweetness and pleasantness,—like that which Peter describes, (2 Pet. i. 16, 17,) speaking of what he saw on the Mount of Transfiguration,—which Moses saw in the time that the bush was burning, and also said to continue there after the flame was out, and concluded that the bush's being preserved was by reason of that divine thing that he there beheld. This Moses seems to have respect to when he says, "I will turn aside and see this great sight." This appearance was so divinely excellent and ravishing, that it seems to have left an everlasting impression on Moses's mind, and probably made him the more earnestly desirous to see God's glory afterwards, (Exod. xxxiii. 18,) and he remembers it when he blesses Joseph, (Deut. xxxiii. 16.) And Moses had now a mind to come nearer to behold this great and sweet and wonderful sight, the glory of God united to and dwelling in the bush. This great sight that Moses speaks of represents two things,—(1.) The Incarnation of Christ, which was represented by God's dwelling in the bush ; (2.) The death and sufferings of Christ, which were represented by God's appearing and dwelling in the burning bush, and in the bush when all on fire ; which two things were the greatest sight that ever was seen by angels or men.

38. Exod. iii. 13—"And they shall say to me, What is his name? what shall I say unto them?"] They would be the more apt to enquire this, because they had now been so long in Egypt, where they had served other gods, that they had in a great measure forgotten the God of their fathers. Had it not been for God's mercy to them in thus renewedly making Himself known to them, the

case would soon have been with them as it was with other nations, who soon after the Flood forgot the true God and degenerated to the worship of idols, (see Ezek. xx. 5.) God chose them, they did not choose Him. He remembered them, and His covenant with their fathers when they had forgot Him. Israel was a people that God formed for Himself; He took them when they were (the body of them) idolaters and ignorant of Him, and made them His people. He redeemed them from the gods of Egypt, from their idolatry as well as from their taskmasters; and that was the most glorious redemption. Here is a notable instance of the Church's being hidden and obscured, as it was under antichrist before the Reformation. There were, doubtless, left amongst them some true worshippers of God thinly sown among them, as it was under the tyranny of that city which is spiritually called Sodom in Egypt. The Church was now in the wilderness as it was then, (see Ezek. xx. 7–10; 2 Sam. vii. 23; Levit. xvii. 7; Joshua xxiv. 14; Ezek. xxiii. 3–8, xix. 21-27.) We have another remarkable instance of the like nature in the time of the Jews' captivity in Babylon, another great type of the Antichristian Church, (see Jer. xvi. 13.)

39. Exod. vi. 3—"And I appeared," &c.] God Almighty= all-sufficient, (see Gen. xvii. 1, xxviii. 3,) ["but by my name Jehovah," &c.]. God, when He appeared unto Abraham, and promised that He would do such and such things for his seed, He appeared as God all-sufficient, a God sufficient to accomplish the things that He then promised. Now the time is come for the accomplishment of them, now He appears as Jehovah, as He that *is* what He *was*, or "*is that He is*," not only sufficient to fulfilling, but actually fulfilling; the same in accomplishing, that He was in promising.

40. Exod. vii. 5—"The Egyptians shall know that I am the Lord, when I stretch forth My hand."] The first time that Moses and Aaron went to Pharaoh, they told him that Jehovah, the God of Israel, commanded that he should let His people go, as in the beginning of chap. v. Pharaoh then took it in great disdain to be told of such a command from Jehovah the God of Israel, a poor abject people, a company of slaves; and, by the character they bear, he concludes that He made no better figure among the gods than His people did among the nations. He makes answer, "Who is Jehovah, that I should obey His voice to let Israel go? I know not Jehovah." *Jehovah* was a hard name to him that he never heard of before, but he resolves that it shall be no bugbear to him. Jehovah! who is that? says Pharaoh in disdain. Now God tells Moses that He will make him know who He is—"He shall know that I am Jehovah when I stretch forth mine hand upon Egypt, and bring out the children of Israel from among them."

41. Exod. viii. 1—"Let My people go, that they may serve Me."] As the children of Israel were redeemed out of Egypt that they might serve God, so are we redeemed by Jesus Christ, not that we might be at liberty to sin, but that we might serve God. They were

delivered from serving their old masters the Egyptians, that so they might serve God. So we are redeemed from the service of sin, that we might henceforth serve God; being made free from sin, we are become the servants of righteousness, as Rom. vi. throughout; Gal. ii. 17-20. "Christ gave Himself for us, that He might redeem us from all iniquity, and purify unto Himself a peculiar people, zealous of good works," (Tit. ii. 14; Heb. ix. 14; Luke i. 74, 75; 2 Cor. v. 15.)

42. Exod. ix. 10.] The Egyptians had oppressed Israel in the furnaces in which they burnt their bricks, and now the ashes of these furnaces were made as much of a terror to them as ever they had been to the Israelites. These furnaces were a type of hell. God sends upon the wicked those plagues that are some participation of the misery and destruction of hell, are as a sprinkling of the ashes of that furnace upon them. Their consciences are scalded with the hot embers of hell-fire. Their boils and blisters were exceeding grievous, probably attended with extreme smart, like the continual scalding of the hot embers of a furnace. Therefore it is said the magicians could not stand before this plague. This sort of boil is called the botch of Egypt, (Deut. xxviii. 27.)

43. Exod. xi. 2, 3.] With so high a hand did God bring out the children of Israel, that He did not only set them at liberty from their slavery to the Egyptians, but He also took care that they should be well paid by the Egyptians for their first service as they went off. So that, after all the Egyptians' obstinacy in refusing to part with their future service, God at last made them in effect part with the benefit both of their future service and past service too, (chap. xii. 36.)

44. Exod. xii. 22.] The striking or sprinkling the blood of the lamb with a bunch of hyssop on the two side-posts and lintel of the door signifies the cleansing of our conversation by the blood of Christ, which is, in the language of Sacred Scripture, called "our going out and coming in," (1 Sam. xxix. 6.) Surely, &c.: 2 Sam. iii. 25. Thou knowest, &c.: 2 Kings xix. 27. I know, &c.: Isaiah xxxvii. 28; Ps. cxxi. 8. The Holy Spirit probably has respect to this very type of the going and coming being cleansed by the blood of the Paschal Lamb in 1 Pet. xviii. 19, where the Apostle speaks of our being redeemed from our vain conversation by the precious blood of Christ, as of a lamb without blemish and without spot. The destroying angel passed by none but those who had the blood of the Lamb on their door-posts, signifying that when God comes to proceed with men as a judge He will judge every one according to his works, and will save none but those whose conversation has been cleansed by the blood of Christ, [see ver. 7.]

45. Exod. xii. 35, 36.] The Hebrew word which our translators have rendered "borrow" is *shaal*, which does not signify to "borrow," but to "ask one to give." It is the very word used: Ps. ii. 8—"Ask of me, and I will give Thee the heathen for Thine inheritance," &c. [Shuckford's "Connection," vol. ii. p. 340.] The

same word is used in chap. iii. 22, xi. 2. That to "ask to give," or to "beg," and not to "borrow," is the proper English of the word according to the sense in which it is commonly used in Scripture, is abundantly evident by Buxtorf, (Lexicon, *sub voce.*) To lend is to "give" in 1 Sam. v. 28. It is probable that when the Egyptians urged the people to be gone, they mentioned to them their poverty, and the difficulty of undertaking such a journey without such and such supplies, particularly that they should need many things to offer to God and serve Him with. The Egyptians were not unacquainted with costliness in worship, and therefore would not think it strange that the great God that had wrought such wonders among them required a lasting service. The Egyptians were now made sensible how much it concerned them to reconcile themselves to this God, and so to obtain the favour of this people who were such peculiar favourites of His, and whom they had heretofore so greatly injured, and thereby so much provoked their God; even Pharaoh himself is now brought to desire their prayers. The wills of the king and people were now broke, and their frame now was to be kind to them, as heretofore it had been to afflict and destroy them. They were now engaged with vehemence of spirit to counteract their former ill-treatment of the people. They were brought to be willing, as it were, without hesitation or delay, to yield and resign up anything to save their lives, fearing they should very speedily be all destroyed. They were in a great terror and great conviction of mind, and like the sea, which after a very high and strong flood, when it comes to ebb, returns with the greater impetuosity. Mr Henry observes, "The Egyptians by their gifts probably intended to make atonement that the plagues might be stayed, as the Philistines when they returned to the ark sent a present with it for a trespass-offering, having an eye to this precedent," (1 Sam. vi. 6, taken with the context.)

46. Exod. xiii. 21—"And by night in a pillar of fire, to give them light; to go by day and night."] Here in the camp of Israel was something of a resemblance and image of what is said of new Jerusalem, (Rev. xxi. 23.) The glory of the Lord did lighten, for here the Shekinah, which was commonly called the "glory of the Lord," gave them light; and in ver. 25—"There shall be no night there," the like of which was said of Zion, (Isa. lx. 20,) and of the Church in her glorious state, (Zech. xiv. 6, 7.) Here is some resemblance, for the camp of Israel had always light, both day and night; nor was it a dim light that they had in the night, but a light sufficiently clear well to direct that vast multitude in travelling in the wilderness, so that night was, in a great degree, turned into day amongst them, (see Num. ix. 21; Deut. i. 33; Neh. ix. 12, 19; Ps. lxxviii. 14, cv. 39.) The congregation of Israel, in all their travels, were in the form of an army. They went up by their armies, (chap. xii. 51,) and they went up harnessed, (ver. 18.) They were in military order in their camp and in their marches, and the pillar of cloud and fire was their grand "ensign," lifted up in the view of the whole army as the ensign which

they should follow and the standard by which they should abide; and as the pillar of cloud and fire was the symbol of the presence of Christ, so here was represented that which is spoken in Isa. xi. 10. As here this "ensign," the pillar of cloud and fire, was to lead the people to their rest, so ver. 12—"And He shall set up an ensign for the nations." . . .

47. Exod. xiv. 20—"And it was a cloud," &c.] In like manner as the gospel and the discoveries God makes of Himself in and by Christ are a mere cloud, and darkness and foolishness, "a stone of stumbling and rock of offence," a "snare and gin," "a savour of death unto death" unto some, while it is a most glorious light, the "power of God and the wisdom of God," a "savour of life unto life" unto others.

48. Exod. xiv. 30—"Dead upon the sea-shore."] The Egyptians were very nice and curious in embalming and preserving the bodies of their great men, [and erecting stately sepulchres and monuments for them;] but here the utmost contempt is poured upon all the grandees of Egypt. See how they lie heaps upon heaps, as the dung upon the face of the earth. The beasts and birds of prey are called to eat the flesh of captains and mighty men, (Isa. lxvi. 24.) Probably the Israelites stripped the slain and now got arms from them.

49. Exod. xvi. 10—"The glory of the Lord appeared in the cloud."] The Shekinah that now appeared, and that appeared afterwards in the Tabernacle and Temple, was called the "glory of the Lord," not only because of that outward brightness that appeared, but especially because that brightness was the symbol of the Son of God as there manifesting Himself, who is the brightness of God's glory. The Glory of God is spoken of as a Person in Isa. iii. 8. See Rev. xxi. 23.

50. Exod. xviii. 2–5.] What is here related, if that clause in 2d verse, "after he had sent her back," had not been inserted, would have been much such a difficulty as there is in some other parts of the Scripture history through the brevity of the relation. We have an account that Moses, when he went from Jethro into Egypt, took his wife and his children with him; and yet here we have an account of Jethro's bringing of them to him in the wilderness *from his own house*, as if Moses had not taken them with him when he went away. We should have been ready to suspect that this was a blunder in the Historian, had it not been here hinted that Moses had at some time sent her back, for we have no account of her being sent back anywhere else. We may here observe the remarkable self-denial Moses subjected himself to, whereby he was fitted for those privileges he afterwards received of God, and which was rewarded by these privileges. First, he refused to be called the son of Pharaoh's daughter; he renounced the wealth and glory and pleasures of the kingdom of Egypt, that he might have had as the heir of Pharaoh's crown, choosing rather to suffer affliction with the people of God. All this he forsook for a share with God's people. And then he met with another great trial; he was banished away from those whose company he preferred to all the glory of Egypt; yet he might not

enjoy that, but was driven away alone into the wilderness, wandering in a poor disconsolate, desolate condition, he knew not whither; and now, after he had dwelt forty years in the land of Midian, in the family of Jethro, into which he had married, and had a family and a place of rest there, he was called on God's errand to forsake his wife and children without ever expecting to see them any more, and once more to leave all that he had to follow Christ.

Corol. Hence we may learn that ministers, in order to fit them for the service of Christ, should be brought to be willing to be cast off even by their own people, by saints, by those to whose good especially they are ministers. Moses was cast off by his brethren the Midianites.

51. Exod. xix., xx.] As there was a trumpet at the giving of the Law, so a great trumpet will sound when the Law comes to be executed at the day of judgment. As then Mount Sinai was in a conflagration, [so] at the day of judgment the whole earth will be in a conflagration, and the other appearances will be proportionably greater, the trumpet louder, the appearing majesty of God greater, the fire more terrible, the thunder and lightning more dreadful. How miserable will those be that then shall feel the Almighty vengeance of that Being whose wrath will be proportionable to those appearances of His dreadfulness! See Ps. lxviii. 8, 9.

52. Exod. xix. 10, 11—"Sanctify them to-day and to-morrow," &c.] The third day here spoken of, or the day on which God came down on Mount Sinai, was the first day of the week, as is evident, because the feast of Pentecost, which was appointed in commemoration of this, was appointed to be always on the first day of the week, as appears by Lev. xxiii. 15, &c., so that the days wherein the Jews were to sanctify themselves in order to this day were the sixth and seventh days of the week; but chiefly the seventh, for there was only a part of the sixth remaining when God gave the order; and probably but a little part, considering the antecedent transactions of the day which we have here account of. So that the Jewish sabbath was to be spent in preparing themselves for the day following—viz., the first day of the week, the day on which God descended and gave the Law on Mount Sinai in honour to this day, being the day on which Christ was to rise from the dead and on which God would descend more gloriously on His Apostles, to reveal the glorious gospel. Thus this day is, by God's own direction, set above the day of their sabbath; the day of the Christian is honoured above the Jewish sabbath by God's appointing the Jewish sabbath to be a day of preparation for it, as the Jewish Dispensation was a preparation for the Christian. The Law is a handmaid to the Gospel, and is "our schoolmaster to bring us to Christ," (Gal. iii. 24.)

53. Exod. xx. 3–7.] The three first commandments. The first commandment respects the object of worship; and especially forbids those things in worship that are against *God the Father*. The second commandment respects the means of worship; and especially forbids those things in worship that are against *God the Son*, that it should

not be by other lords and mediators instead of Christ, the Lord our God, who is, as it were, the husband of His people, and is a jealous God, a jealous husband, that will not bear spiritual adultery. This commandment forbids our making use of other images in our worshipping God besides Christ, who is "the image of the invisible God, the brightness of His glory, and the express image of His person," by which image alone God makes known Himself and sets forth Himself, and shews His glory as the fit object of our worship; for we behold "the glory of God *in the face of Jesus Christ.*" The Heathen had images that they might have something present with them as representatives of the Deity that was absent; but Christ only is our Immanuel or "God with us." The third commandment forbids those things in worship that are especially against the *Holy Ghost,* even the unholy manner of worship. We ought, when we come to God to worship Him, to come by the Son, that we may come by right means; and we ought to come by the Holy Spirit, that we may worship with a right spirit and in a holy manner. These sins against the Holy Spirit are represented as peculiarly exposing persons to Divine vengeance without forgiveness, agreeable to what we are taught in the New Testament.

54. Exod. xx. 4—"Any likeness of any thing that is in heaven above"]—*i.e.*, the likeness of sun, moon, or stars, or any bird; [or "that is in the earth beneath"]—*i.e.*, of any man, woman, beast, or creeping thing; [or "that is in the water under the earth"]—*i.e.*, any fish. This interpretation is evident from Deut. iv. 16–18. That the second commandment has respect to worshipping the true God by images, see Deut. v. 7, 8.

55. Exod. xx. 8—"Remember."] This expression "remember" was probably the rather used because this was not the first institution of the Sabbath; it had been too much forgotten, especially while the children of Israel were in Egypt. The Sabbath had also been renewedly commanded, (chap. xvi.) God here charges them to take notice of His institution of the Sabbath, and not to forget it as they formerly had done.

56. Exod. xxiii. 20–23.] God says of this Angel, "My name is in Him." God had a little before, from this same Mount Sinai, declared to Moses with very great solemnity that He might thereby make Him known to the children of Israel (who were become very ignorant of Him) what His name was—viz., "I Am that I Am," and "Jehovah," (Exod. iii. 13, 14, and again chap. vi. 2, 3;) and again, very lately after the children [of Israel] were come to that Mount Sinai where God revealed Himself to Moses and told him His name, to declare it to the children, the people heard God speak from thence Himself in a most solemn and awful manner, with a great voice declaring the same name, chap. xx. 2—"I am Jehovah," &c., which were the first words of God that they heard from Mount Sinai when He spoke to them from thence, when "the mountain burnt with fire," &c. This was at most but a few days before God said this that He does concerning His Angel, and perhaps it was the same day. So that when

He says, "My name is in Him," they would naturally understand no other than that name that He had lately revealed Himself by, which was in an eminent manner His name, even "I Am that I Am," or "Jehovah," which being in an eminent manner God's name, above all other names expressing His nature; and it having been a common thing in those days from the beginning of the world to give names to express the nature of things, they naturally must understand it that God's nature was in Him, and that as His name Jehovah belonged to Him, they must naturally understand it that the thing expressed by that name was in Him. And that the children of Israel understood it so, is also confirmed by this—that here God commits the care of the congregation to this His angel, that He might go before them as their Captain, and lead them and bring them into the land of Canaan, and fight for them and possess them of the land; and therefore when the Angel appeared to Joshua with a sword drawn in His hand, (Joshua v. 13,) and told them that as the Captain of the Lord's host He was come, Joshua seems to understand Him to be this Angel, and therefore immediately falls on his face, and the Angel teaches Joshua to pay Him divine respect by taking off his shoes because the ground was holy, as Moses was commanded when Jehovah appeared to him at the Bush, and he obeyed; and afterwards in the process of the story this Angel is called Jehovah, as in the next chapter, ver. 2., by the penman of the history. What is said of the Messiah, Micah v. 5, is parallel with this—" And He shall stand," &c.; Prov. xxi. 24—" Proud and haughty," &c.—*i.e.*, that is His true nature and character. The saying, "My name is in Him," evidently implies as much as that my Divine essence and character is in Him. By God's name is plainly meant His internal nature and essence, in Prov. xxx. 4. Why should it be there represented that none can tell what God's name is when God had so plainly and expressly declared it to Moses, and told him that His name was Jehovah and I Am that I Am? Therefore the meaning might be that none could comprehend that infinitely perfect nature signified by that name. "None by searching can find out God;" His nature "is high as heaven; what can we do? deeper than hell; what can we know," (Job xi. 8)

57. Exod. xxviii. 15—"Of judgment."] So called because they were wont to make use of it to inquire of God in judgment, or in determining causes and controversies. For when the people had controversies among themselves, or causes to be judged, they were wont to come to inquire of God. See Exod. xviii. 15, 16; Lev. xxiv. 12; Num. xv. 34; Deut. xvii. 8, 9, &c.

58. Exod. xxxii. 19—"And brake them."] Moses's breaking the tables seems to signify the following things:—

(1.) That sin breaks the Law, and particularly that it breaks it as a covenant of works. The tables were the tables of the Covenant. The ten commandments contained a new revelation of the covenant of works, of which two ways of fulfilment were proposed. One was by mere man, the other was by Christ. These tables of the Law were the workmanship of God, without any hewing of Moses's, as the tables of the heart of man in innocency, wherein the Law was written, were already prepared by God, and needed not any work of the Law or hewing of legal conviction to prepare it.

(2.) Another thing signified by Moses's breaking the table was God's breaking His Covenant between Him and the people, and so were threatened to be cast off from being His Covenant people, (for there were the tables of the Covenant between God and the people,) agreeable to God's threatening, (verses 9, 10 ; see chap. xxxiv. 1.)

59. *Ibid.*] God, as it were, brake the tables in pieces, as disannulling all hopes of men's ever obtaining life in that way. Now this second time the tables are made by the ministration and instrumentality of Moses, who herein is a type of the gospel ministry. God commanded that the second tables should be committed to the ark to preserve them, that they might not be broken as the first were, (compare Deut. ix. 16, 17, with x. 1, 2.) Thus the affair of the preservation of the hearts of God's people in holiness is committed to the keeping of Christ. The delivering of the tables of stone this second time is spoken of as the making of a New Covenant, (Exod. xxxiv 10.) When Moses came down from the Mount with these new tables it was with his face shining, and not with wrath in his face as before. It was this Covenant that was renewed in Deuteronomy. This was a lively type of what we read of in Jer. xxxi. 31, 32, (see place, and Heb. viii. 9.) What is said in these places would lead one to think that Moses's breaking these tables signified the breaking or God's setting aside, not only the Covenant of works, but that old federal Dispensation by which God was as a husband to that people Israel, because of its proving insufficient through their sins to make way for a better Covenant ; a federal Dispensation to be introduced by Christ, and in Him to be fulfilled and confirmed, and made an everlasting Covenant, as the second tables made instead of these were secured and kept safe in the ark.

60. Exod. xxxiv. 1.] Moses was commanded to hew two tables of stone like the first that were broken, signifying that after man had broken the Law which God wrote at first on the tables of his heart in innocency, which was God's own workmanship, that in order to the Law's being written on the table of the heart again after the Fall, the heart needs to be first prepared by being hewed by Moses —*i.e.*, hewed by the Law of Moses, or by legal convictions, but that the Law can go no further than this. It can prepare the heart, but it is Christ's work, and His only, to write the Law in the heart : Rom. viii. 3, 4—" What the law could not do," &c. Moses was commanded to prepare these second tables to bring them with him that He might write the Law on them, when He should cause all His goodness to pass before him, and proclaim His sovereign mercy in forgiving iniquities, &c., which should preserve these tables from being broken as the first were, would prevent a final breach of Covenant between God and the people, (compare chap. xxxiii. 19, xxxiv. 1–7, 10 ; Jer. xxxi. 31–33, and 32, 40.) There is this in the nature of the case

that confirms that the breaking of the first table was a type of the breaking of the first Covenant, and the utter impossibility of men's obtaining life by the Law. Moses himself in all probability cast away the tables and broke them beneath the Mount when he came to see the golden calf, under a strong apprehension that was impressed on his mind by what he then saw, that it was not worth the while to carry this holy Law to such a people under any notion of the keeping it, and so obtaining God's favour by that means. The ten commandments at first were given with thunder and lightning and earthquake; but now the second time with a gracious proclamation of mercy, long-suffering, abundant goodness and truth, and forgiveness of iniquity, transgression and sin, yet mercy perfectly consistent with infinite holiness and strict justice, "which will by no means clear the guilty." When the children of Israel had broken the Covenant, Moses cast it away and broke the tables in pieces, which represents God's utterly casting away that Covenant made at first with mankind as now entirely useless, the obtaining life in that way being now utterly and everlastingly to be despaired of, (see chap. xxxii. 19, and xxxiv. 1.)

LEVITICUS.

61. Lev. i. 9.] The inwards and the legs were to be washed to represent purity of heart and "walk."

62. Lev. x. 1, 2.] This awful destruction of two of the priests, the sons of Aaron, happened on the eighth or last day of the consecration of Aaron and his sons, by which the Levitical priesthood was first introduced, or on the first day of Aaron and his sons officiating as priests. That it was on this day appears, because it was on this day they offered the goat (Lev. ix. 3, 15) which was burnt, because on this day such things had befallen Aaron that he was not fit to eat thereof, as in the 16–20 verses of this chapter. Thus the service of the Levitical priesthood was begun with the woeful death of two of the priests that were consumed by the Divine wrath, [and] thus it pleased God to shew the insufficiency of the Levitical priesthood at the first setting of it up. He observed that they were so insufficient to make atonement for others that they were liable to the Divine wrath themselves for their own sins, [see Pool, Synop. *in loc.*;] and this was also so ordered to impress on the minds of the priests a sense of the sacredness of their work, and the infinite holiness and majesty of that Being with whom they had to do in their office, as ver. 3. . . . There is no temptation visible that Nadab and Abihu should have to offer "strange fire" rather than the "holy fire" that had descended from heaven. But the case with them seems to have been this—that day being the first day that ever they had officiated in the priest's office, and a day of rejoicing and feasting, wherein they fed on their

peace-offerings; and it seems that these two young men had in this Feast in a measure intoxicated themselves with strong drink, whereby they either became unable to keep exactly to the points of the Law in the execution of their office and to distinguish between holy and profane, or at least made less careful so to do; so that while they were elevated with drink they did not distinguish between holy fire and common fire, which seems to be the special reason of God's appointing that Law, which he does in verses 8-11; for that Law seems to be given on this occasion. It was given on the same day that Nadab and Abihu died, as appears on comparing the beginning of the IXth chapter with the latter end of this; and it was immediately upon it, for it was while the affair of their offering the sacrifices of the day were under consideration, as appears by ver. 12 *seq.*—Corol. By this it is manifest that persons are responsible before God for those crimes they commit when drunk.

Another thing observable concerning Nadab and Abihu's death is this. We have an account in the latter verse of a fire coming out from before the Lord and consuming the sacrifices on the altar. Here we have an account of fire in like manner coming out from the Lord and consuming not the sacrifices offered, but the persons that offered, because they had not respect to and did not trust in that fire from the Lord consuming the sacrifice, but offered strange fire, fire of man's kindling, whereby we seem to be taught that they that come to God and do not trust in the Atonement for sin, made by Christ's being consumed in the fire of God's wrath, shall be consumed by that fire of God's wrath themselves. They that come to God offering strange fire, and dare to appear before Him in their own righteousness, He will be a consuming fire to them. They will be exposed to all the fierceness of the flame of God's vindictive justice, having no benefit of the execution of it on Christ the great sacrifice for sin.

63. Lev. xiv. 12-18.] The sacrifice was to be offered to God with oil. They were to be waved together before the Lord, and after the Lamb was slain, and his blood shed before the Lord, the Priest was to sprinkle of the oil seven times before the Lord. So the sacrifice of Christ was offered up to God with the Spirit, with Divine love, love to God and love to men, which sanctified the sacrifice and made it effectual. Both the blood and the oil were first offered to God before they were applied to the leper. So not only is Christ's blood first presented to God before it is applied to the sinner, but the spirit of love that He had without measure first flows out to God, before it flows out to the sinner, and be communicated to him in sanctification. In the application, both the blood and oil are applied to the right ear of him that was to be cleansed, to cleanse the ear, by which men hear and listen to the commands and counsels of God, and the offers and invitations of the gospel; and the thumb, the chief part of the right hand, to cleanse the hands by which we work; and to the chief part of the right foot, to cleanse the feet by which we walk. The application of the blood is to cleanse from the guilt of sins of the ear or heart, and of the hands or works of the hands, and of the feet

as the way to walk. The application of the oil which followed signifies the sanctification of them by the Holy Spirit. The blood and oil were first applied to the ear, hand, and foot, and then afterwards oil was poured on the head of the leper, to signify that persons are first justified, then sanctified, and then glorified, as pouring oil on the head was used as a token of initiation to some high and honourable office and great dignity, as that of prophet, priest, or king, as the saints when glorified are made kings and priests unto God; and as the ear is sanctified to hear God's commands, and the hands to do God's work, and the feet to walk in God's way before the pouring oil on the head, it shews that a holy conversation is the only way to glory.

64. Lev. xix. 14.] Though the fear of these deaf and blind will not restrain you, because they cannot hear or see you, yet God hears and sees. . . .

65. Lev. xxiii. 3—"Convocation."] By this it appears that although the children of Israel were obliged to meet together at the Temple but three times in the year, yet the weekly sabbath among them was from the beginning a day for their meeting together for some sort of religious public worship, which is confirmed from 2 Kings iv. 23; Isa. lxvi. 23; Ezek. xlvi. 3. Whence it may be argued that the people had something like synagogues among them long before the captivity in Babylon, which is confirmed by Ps. lxxiv. 8. The word translated "synagogue" signifies a convention, congregation, or meeting together. See also Ps. lxxxiii. 9.

66. Lev. xxiii. 10.] The sheaf was to be offered to God on the first day of the week after the Passover, on the same day that Christ rose. It was the first-fruits of all the seed sown. So Christ was "the first-fruits of them that slept." The body that dies and is buried is compared to the seed of bread, corn sown in the earth, (1 Cor. xv. 36, 37;) and Christ's resurrection in particular is compared to this, (John xii. 24,) and the end of the world, the time of the resurrection, is represented by the harvest, (Matt. xiii. 39.) Things rising in the Spring, after all seemed to be dead in winter, is a lively image of the resurrection. This sheaf was the first-fruits of the earth that they had in the Spring; and it is to be noted that the time when this sheaf of the first-fruits was offered was not only on the same day of the week, but at same time of year, the first day of the week after the Passover, as that was.

NUMBERS.

67. Num. x. 35, 36.] The ascending of the ark out of the wilderness into Canaan, "the land flowing with milk and honey," typified the same thing with the ark afterwards ascending into Mount Zion, even the ascension of Christ into heaven; and there-

fore the same words were uttered by David on that occasion that were uttered by Moses on this, (Ps. lxviii. 1,) and therefore also, David on that occasion speaks of this marching of the ark through the wilderness, (Ps. lxviii. 7.) In these words that Moses spake on the occasion of taking up the ark in order to its ascending into Canaan,—viz., "Rise up," &c.,—respect seems to be had to the glorious victory and triumph Christ had over His enemies that He had been conflicting with, in His resurrection and ascension spoken of, (Ps. lxviii. 18;) and in those words which Moses uttered when the ark rested,—"Return, O Lord," &c.,—respect is had to Christ's returning again to the earth, after His ascension, by His Spirit, (agreeable to His promises, John xiv. 18–23, and xvi. 16,) whereby the number of His people was so vastly increased, agreeable to Ps. cx. 1-3.

68. Num. xi. 29.] This wish of Moses was fulfilled in the Christian Church, after Christ's ascension; according to the prophecy of Joel; (chap. ii. 28, &c.,) God put His Spirit in His extraordinary gift upon the saints in general throughout the world.

69. Num. xiii. 30.] According to Caleb's faith so was it done unto him. The people were discouraged with that report of the spies, that there they saw giants, the sons of Anak, and that they were in their own sight as grasshoppers, and so they were in their sight, (verses 28, 33.) Caleb was confident that they were well able to overcome them, and therefore God gave Caleb Hebron for his possession, which was the chief seat of these giants, as appears by ver. 22; (Joshua xi. 21, and xiv. 12, 15.) God enabled Caleb himself to drive the giants thence, (Joshua xiv. 12, and xv. 13, 14.)

70. Num. xxvii. 18, 19, 23.] By what is here said it is manifest that it is proper, in ordaining or appointing a person to an office in the name of God, to give a charge with the laying on of hands.

DEUTERONOMY.

71. Deut. iv. 21, 22.] In this Moses was a type of Christ. God was angry with Moses for their sakes. So God was, as it were, angry with Christ for our sakes. He bore the wrath of God for our sakes. Our iniquities were laid upon Christ. Our guilt lay upon Him, and so He in some respect partook of our guilt. So Moses partook of the guilt of the children of Israel when by their rebellion they provoked his spirit, so that he "spake unadvisedly with his lips." And Moses was, as it were, a sacrifice for them; he died in the wilderness, and they lived and went out to possess the good land, as in ver. 22. Moses mentions this as an instance of God's mercy to the people, as is evident by the foregoing verse, and by ver. 22—"But *ye*," &c. God was pleased so greatly to testify His displeasure against Moses's sin, though he but lightly partook of the

sin of the congregation, as utterly to refuse to suffer him to go over and possess the good land, and yet to suffer them, the children [of Israel] of that evil generation, who partook more largely of their fathers' sin, to go over. God insisted on having a great outward manifestation of His displeasure against the sin of that congregation. The death of so great a person and so holy a person as Moses, the head of the congregation, (who only was nearly related to them, and lightly partook of the evil of that degenerate time,) was so; as God, in a time of public judgment, is pleased sometimes to slay the righteous with the wicked, whereby there is so much greater and more awful testimony of His displeasure to the world, (Ezek. xxi. 3, 4.) God thus slaying Moses and not suffering him to go in to the good land, God looked on the outward manifestation of wrath by this means to be sufficient without slaying the congregation, and so the younger generation were spared, and suffered to go in to the good land. Thus Moses's death was a kind of atonement for the congregation as to temporal judgment and manifestation of God's wrath in this world, and so he was an eminent type of Christ.

72. Deut. iv. 32–34.] That which is here mentioned is spoken of as the wonder of wonders—that a people should hear God speaking to them out of the midst of the fire, such a devouring fire that was so terrible to behold, that had such peculiar manifestations of God's awful majesty and His consuming justice and vengeance, (see chap. v. 25,) and "yet live." It is not to be supposed that God would speak of this as so exceedingly and beyond all parallel wonderful, but that He had in His eye that which is indeed the wonder of wonders, and which is often spoken of as such by the prophets, which God's people are the subjects of through Jesus Christ. Through Him we hear God speaking to us out of the midst of the fire. God manifests Himself to us in all His dreadful majesty and most terrible and strict justice, and yet we live; we are safe; God appears to us as a strict judge and terrible revenger of all sin, and yet as our Saviour and a fountain of life to us. God is just, and yet the justifier of him that believes on Jesus. Although this that the children of Israel were the subjects of at Mount Sinai is here spoken of as so exceeding wonderful, yet this which is accomplished by Christ is spoken of as so much more wonderful. These things which God did for the children of Israel, when He brought them out of Egypt, are represented as no more worthy to be mentioned or remembered after God had wrought this, (Jer. xvi. 14, 15, and xxiii. 7, 8; and Isa. xliii. 18, 19.) Balaam does in effect say that these things that God wrought for Israel, when He brought them out of Egypt, are typical of that wonderful, astonishing thing which He would work for them in the latter days: Num. xxiii. 23—"According to this time [or agreeable to what God has done at this time] it shall [hereafter] be said of Jacob and of Israel, What hath God wrought!' See also Micah vii. 15. The context is a full proof that this was what God had in His eye when God spake to the children of Israel from Mount Sinai in so terrible a manner. It was in giving the Law; and thus God's people

hear God speaking to them from Mount Sinai in all ages; for they all hear God's voice in His holy, strict Law. God's appearing at that time as a "consuming fire," without doubt was a representation of the thing spoken of here in ver. 24—"The Lord thy God is a consuming fire, even a jealous God;" and the words of the text we are upon are brought in as an evidence of what is spoken of in the immediately preceding verses—viz., God's forbearing to execute justice on the people for their wickedness and His forgiving their iniquities, in the exercise of His great mercy, and His faithfulness to the Covenant of grace made with their Fathers.

73. Deut. v. 7, 8.] That this first commandment has respect to worshipping other gods; but the second has respect to worshipping the true God by images, is confirmed by chap. iv. 16–18. The people were in danger of representing God by some image of bird or beast, or some other animal, because the Egyptians, that were a neighbouring nation, and a people among whom they had dwelt, represented all invisible things by images or hieroglyphics.

74. Deut. v. 26.] These words, with the context, lead us to suppose that the apprehension that seemed to be so generally fixed in the minds of God's people of old came from a tradition handed down from the ancient patriarchs, that sinful man could not have immediate access to God, and intercourse with Him who is a consuming fire; and that the presence of God, and to have to do with Him directly without a Mediator, would be the sinful creature's immediate destruction. See Exod. xxxiii. 20; Gen. xxxii. 30; Exod. xxiv. 11; Judges xiii. 22, 23. See POOL, Synop. on Exod. xxxiii. 20. See ver. 24 of this chapter, and Deut. iv. 33; Judges vii. 22, 23. From Judges xiii. 22, 23, . . it appears that this notion was not from an apprehension that death would be the natural consequence of so great and terrible a sight, but that sinful men in such a case would be exposed to be slain by the anger of God.

75. Deut. ix. 21—"And I cast the dust thereof into the brook that descended out of the mount."] This brook in all probability was the water out of the rock, for that rock was in Mount Horeb, (Exod. xvii. 1–8,) the mount that is here spoken of in ver. 8. If there had been any other brook there before, it would not be said that there was no water to drink, as Exod. xvii. 1. There would have been no such murmuring for want of water, nor would there have been occasion to fetch water out of the rock. From the dryness of the place the mountain was called Horeb, which signifies dryness. This brook that came forth out of the rock, and that descended out of the mount of God, was a type of the Holy Spirit; the same with Ezekiel's waters that came out of the Temple, and the same with the pure river of water of life that proceeded out of the throne of God and the Lamb, and the same with those rivers of "living water" spoken of, John vii. 38, 39, which, we are there told, is meant of the Holy Spirit. The idol of the children of Israel is ground to powder, and the dust of it cast into this brook, to signify that it is by God's Spirit that God consumes idols and destroys the kingdom of Satan. The same seems to be sig-

nified by Hezekiah's casting the idolatrous altars into the brook that watered Jerusalem, God's holy city, (2 Chron. xxx. 14, and also 2 Chron. xxix. 16.) We are told (Exod. xxxii. 20) that Moses made the children of Israel drink of the water; but that was no otherwise than as he strewed the dust on that brook which the congregation wholly depended on for drink, and so were obliged to drink of it. Their drinking that water in which their idol was consumed was a type of repentance, in which men are made partakers of, and have the influences of that Spirit that destroys those sins and consumes those idols that they formerly were devoted and addicted to. There is another thing also, that perhaps is more especially intended by that which we have here an account of. There seems to be a special respect to this (Ps. xcix. 8) speaking of Moses and Aaron—"Thou answeredst them, O Lord our God: Thou wast a God that forgavest them, though Thou tookest vengeance of their inventions," which is agreeable to the history of this affair in chap. xxxii. of Exodus, where we have an account of God's pardoning the people on Moses's intercession; but vengeance was taken on the calf they had made. The idols of the people are called "their inventions," so Ps. cvi. 28, 29, and verses 38, 39. They sacrificed unto the idols of Canaan, and the land was polluted with blood. Thus they were defiled with their own works, and went a-whoring with their own inventions. God's fierce wrath and vengeance was typically executed to the full on the golden calf; three things were done to it that are made use of to signify the merciless executions of God's wrath in the perfect destruction of him that is under guilt. Moses burnt it with fire, and stamped and ground it to powder, beat it very small, even till it was as small as dust; and that brook that this dust was mixed with signified the blood of Christ, for it was as it were the bleeding of the Rock that had been wounded by the rod that smote it, and "that rock was Christ." The calf, in thus having vengeance executed upon it, being cast in its utter destruction into this brook, signifying that the sin of those who are pardoned of God has full vengeance taken on it in the blood of Christ. Their calf is here called "their sin." The water of this brook was the drink of the children of Israel, with this destroyed and ruined calf in it; and thus it is that believers do by faith drink the blood of Christ—viz., as an atonement for their sins, or as that in which their sin is fully punished and perfectly destroyed, and justice fully satisfied.

76. Deut. xi. 24.] The land was not given in this extent, but a small part of it, till David's time. Then first the people had given them the promised land fully, though the people probably expected immediately upon their entry into the land [to "possess" it.] This is an instance of the gradual fulfilment of the promises that God makes to His Church. So the promises made to God's people when they should return from Babylon, in the main things contained in them, were not fulfilled till Christ came, and will not have their fullest accomplishment till the last calling of the Jews. So the blessings that are so often promised should come by the Messiah are principally deferred till after the destruction of Antichrist.

77. Deut. xii. 5.] God forbore to choose Him a place in Israel for His settled habitation to place His name there till the days of David, which was a manifestation of the displeasure of God against that people for their frequent transgressions and apostasies. He refused to settle His abode among them as long as they remained so unsteady in His service and so perverse in their ways; but walked in a tent and in a tabernacle as ready to depart, or at least undetermined whether to stay with them or not, and yet in His great goodness loath to leave them; but at last He did actually depart from them, when He forsook the tabernacle of Shiloh. But remembering His covenant with Abraham, Isaac, and Jacob, He returned again, but then stayed in the border of the land, as though it were to see whether they would reform or no before He would again enter in amongst them. But when on long trial it proved that they never were like to appear worthy that He should be with them, at length David, a great typical Mediator, appeared. God for his sake came into the midst of the land, and chose Him a place in Israel "to put His name there," and took up His settled abode there, and instead of a tent dwelt in a temple. God speaks of it to David as an instance of His peculiar favour to him, that He now at length consented to settle His abode; that He had never moved any such thing before. David had spoken of having a house built for him, (2 Sam. vii.,) and God there declares that for his sake He would shew favour to Israel, and would plant them that they might dwell in a place of their own, &c.; and it is often mentioned afterwards as the reason why He did not cast off Israel. This is another instance of God's deferring the accomplishment of that which, by the manner of prediction, was expected to be accomplished immediately upon their being settled in their own land, (see note on chap. xi. 24, *supra*,) for David seemed to expect an immediate accomplishment of the glorious things that were to be brought in by the Messiah on the return of the Jews from Babylon, (see Deut. ix. 23, 24.) So the primitive Christians seemed to expect Christ's last coming to accompany the destruction of Jerusalem.

78. Deut. xv. 9—"Sin unto thee."] Sin here is put for calamity, misery, or ruin, because that is the consequence of sin. Thus the word sin is often used in Scripture. So Deut. xxiv. 15, xxiii. 21, 22; 1 Kings xii. 30, xiii. 13, 34; Ps. cix. 7; Prov. x. 16. So probably it is to be understood, Prov. xxiv. 9; see also Hosea viii. 11. So *iniquity* is a word often used in like manner in Scripture to signify both sin and its punishment, both moral evil and natural evil, or misery and destruction.

79. Deut. xvii. 14, 15.] In what is said here about a king we have a plain instance of God's suffering the people to do that which yet He did not approve of, parallel to the instance Christ mentioned, Matt. xix. 8. For when the people did the very thing here spoken of, when they said, "*I will set*," &c., God manifested His great disapprobation of it, (1 Sam. viii. 6–8, and xii. 16–19.)

80. Deut. xx. 19—"For the tree of the field is man's life," &c.] It might have been rendered much more agreeable to the original, "For

man is a tree of the field." It was God's will that a fruitful tree should not be cut down, but only trees that yielded no meat. Because trees with respect to their bareness or fruitfulness represented man, and therefore he would have men deal with them as He deals with men. This is an argument in the Law of Moses itself, that its commands were given from some typical respect.

81. Deut. xxi. 23.] The manner of the Israelites in pursuance of this institution used to be to let them hang till the sun was down, and then to take the bodies down and bury them, as is evident by Joshua viii. 29, and x. 26, 27. God did not see meet that that which was a curse and execration should remain in open sight for an abomination to the pure eyes of the God that dwelt in that holy land. They were therefore to remove such abominable things out of God's sight, that God might dwell and walk in the land, and not withdraw from it, (see Deut. xxiii. 13, 14.) But it is very probable that one reason why those that were hanged and accursed were to be taken down and buried as soon as the sun was down, was that the sun was a type of Christ, and in setting was a type of that death of Christ, (Luke xxiii. 44.) The curse was to be removed and buried as soon as the sun was set, to signify that the curse is removed by the death of Christ; for He in dying was made a curse for us, and that curse by His death is taken from the earth, or at least from the land of Israel, or the land of the Church, so that that land is not defiled. God's people have not the curse remaining amongst them to render them abominable to God, and to cause Him to depart from them. Their sins and abominations are buried for ever out of His sight by Christ's death. Indeed it was so ordered that the body of Christ, though it was hanged on a tree, was taken down and buried before sunsetting; the Jews took it down before, that it might not remain in the open air on the sabbath-day, (John viii. 31.) This seems to be so ordered, because Christ, though made a curse, was not such a curse as was removed by what was typified by the setting of the sun, but He was the antitype itself.

82. Deut. xxxii. 2.] God here speaks to the people quite in a different manner from what He did at Mount Sinai, when He spake to them out of the midst of the fire, with a great and terrible voice that was not suited to their tender frame, and that exceedingly terrified them, and was ready to destroy them. God's word then was like thunder and lightning and devouring fire, overbearing and consuming so frail and tender a creature as man, who is like the grass and flower of the field. God's voice is now gentle, delivered in a pleasant song; and instead of being like lightning to destroy and consume, is like the gentle showers and refreshing dew to the tender grass, instructing, reproving, warning, revealing not only His will, but His great mercy, in a manner adapted to man's tender frame. There is much of the glorious gospel in this song, and even the warnings and threatenings that are in it are delivered in an evangelical manner, much in the same way that they were delivered by the gentle voice of the glorious Messiah. All the songs of Scripture are the voice of the gospel. The glorious things of the gospel are

their foundation and subject-matter, and therefore in them God's word drops as the rain, &c.

83. Deut. xxxii. 5—"Their spot," &c.] In all probability here is a reference had to those spots mentioned in Lev. xiii., where are rules for the trials of spots, whether they were leprous spots or no. There are many spots there mentioned that something resembled the leprosy, notwithstanding which the diseased person was to be pronounced clean, and might still be looked upon as of the congregation of Israel, and allowed the privileges of such. But if the spot was upon trial found to be a leprosy, he was to be separated from the congregation,—his spot was not the spot of God's people, and he was not to be looked upon as one of them.

84. Deut. xxxii. 14.] It is a further evidence that God intended wine, which is the juice of the grape squeezed or pressed out, to be a type of the blood of Christ shed under His extreme sufferings as a sacrifice, that the word used in Gen. xl. 11 for pressing grapes in order to get thence wine, is the same that is used for killing or sacrificing. The chief butler, relating his dream, says he sweated or pressed the grapes into Pharaoh's cup. Thus the word שָׁחַט signifies to sacrifice, or to cut the throat, as they did in sacrificing, and is everywhere so used, as appears by the Hebr. Con., and this text is mentioned as the only exception where it is used to squeeze or press grapes, which is a good argument that the pressing of grapes was a type of the sufferings of Christ, [which were] the antitype of the sufferings and deaths of their sacrifices of old.

85. Deut. xxxiii. 2—"From His right hand went a fiery Law for them."] The words seem to be something wronged in the translation. The word 'went' is not in the original, but is supplied, and if the word 'proceeded' or 'come' had been supplied, it might more naturally have led us to what Moses had respect, which seems to be God's writing the Law with His right hand on the two tables of stone, and then delivering them with His right hand thus engraven, to be for the people, as He did the two first tables that were the workmanship of God; and also the other two that Moses had made were delivered to Moses out of God's hand after He had written the Law on them. But the sense seems to be wronged in the translation more in rendering the words, a "fiery Law for them:" the words in the original are "a fire of Law for them"—*i.e.*, to be for a light to them, or as a fire to enlighten, as the pillar of fire was for a light to them in the night; for "the commandment is a lamp, and the Law is a light." The same seems to be meant here as is expressed in Isa. li. 4—"For a Law shall proceed from me, and I will make my judgment to rest for *a light* of the people." This last agrees with the foregoing words, wherein it is said that God "shined from Mount Paran;" and it is more natural to understand it thus, for it is said to be "for them." It was a light to enlighten them; it is more natural to say it is "for them" than if it were a fire threatening to consume them. And this sense much the best agrees with the following verses, and their evident connexion with these words which speak of God's great love and

grace in giving them this Law, and how it was given as an inheritance to them, and with what pleasure and delight they received it: "Yea, He loved the people; all His saints are in Thy hand: and they sat down at Thy feet; every one shall receive of Thy words. Moses commanded us a Law, even the inheritance of the congregation of Jacob."

86. Deut. xxxiii. 7.] So David was brought to his people as their prince after being driven out and banished by Saul, and again after he was driven out by Absalom. Solomon was brought to his people after he was excluded by Adonijah. Christ was brought to His people to be their King after the family of David had long been excluded from the throne by the power of the four monarchies and by other enemies. Christ, after He was thrown away by the Jews, was brought to have a place in the building, and to be the head of the corner. He will be brought to His people again, after He has been long as it were driven away by Antichrist, and He will come to His people at the end of the world for their most complete and eternal salvation, after being driven out by Satan operating on Gog and Magog, and after all the instances of His expulsion and exclusion by all His enemies through all ages of the world.

87. Deut. xxxiii. 8.] Here Christ is evidently called Levi's "holy one." Aaron, the high priest of that tribe, was Levi's holy one in some sense; but it was not Aaron but Christ that was tempted at Massah and Meribah. (1 Cor. x. 9.) Moses was of that tribe, and might also be called their holy one; but neither was he the person there tempted, yea, both Moses and Aaron there rather concurred in the temptation, (Num. xx. 10–13;) and the great antitype of Moses and Aaron, the true High Priest, that was the substance and end of all the ancient sacrifices and offerings, and of all the peculiar ministrations of the high priest of the tribe of Levi, according to Jer. xxxiii. 17–22. Christ may well be called Levi's "holy one;" for it is there represented as though the great honour and privilege of Levi, in its having the office of the priesthood, should be upheld and completed in Christ. For all the honour and privilege which there ever was in having the priesthood of their tribe, arose from the relation of that priesthood to Christ, and the glorious things which He should accomplish in His sacrifice and intercession, and the eternal benefits He should procure; and therefore the actually existing and appearing of Christ, the great and true High Priest, and actually accomplishing those glorious things, and procuring those eternal benefits, are the sum and substance and perfection of all the honour and privilege which belonged to their office. And therefore this is properly mentioned in Moses's blessing of this tribe. For it shews this privilege above all other things, inasmuch as herein it appears that their priesthood was no vain thing. It was unspeakably valuable, and of infinitely good effect, as it stood in relation to the priesthood of Christ, and should be brought to its glorious and infinitely blessed effect in Him. It was by the Thummim and Urim that the high priest was especially furnished with to enter into the holy of holies, to make atonement and intercession for the people there once a year, and was enabled

to teach the people, and reveal the mind and will of God to them. But this typical Thummim and Urim were nothing but as they relate to and were typical of the perfections, merits, light, and glory that were in Christ. In Christ having this perfection, glory, and merit, and this sufficiency to be the light of the world, Levi's Thummim and Urim were fulfilled, and so honoured and magnified. That spoken of and promised concerning the priests, the Levites, in Jer. xxxiii. 17–22, is manifestly the chief of all blessings of God's Covenant with that tribe; as that which was promised in the first place concerning the house of David is the chief thing promised in God's Covenant with David, which is a thing that much confirms that this is the great thing here intended in Moses's blessing of this tribe.

88. Deut. xxxiii. 12.] *i.e.*, Benjamin, being the beloved of the Lord, shall dwell in safety by the Lord. Paul the great Apostle was of this tribe, who perhaps was above all mere men the beloved of the Lord.

89. *Ibid.*] Which seems to allude to a custom of parents carrying their children on their backs or between their shoulders, agreeable to the custom of the Indians here in America. The same thing seems to be alluded to again in Isa. xlix. 22, and perhaps also in the parable of the lost sheep in Luke xv. 5.

90. Deut. xxxiii. 18, 19.] This seems to have respect to the calling of the Gentiles by the preaching of the Apostles, who were of Galilee, and probably chiefly of the tribe of Zebulon, which was that part of Galilee where Christ was chiefly conversant. It is evident the mountain here meant is the mountain of the House of the Lord, the place of offering sacrifice; and the event referred to by their calling the people to the mountain seems to be that prophesied of, Isa. ii. 2, and xxvii. 13. The great trumpet shall be blown, and the offering sacrifices of righteousness, &c., is the same with that spoken of, Isa. lx. 7, 20; and this seeking the abundance of the sea and treasures hid in the sand, seems to have reference to what is foretold in Isa. lx. 5, 9, 16, and lxvi. 12. The success of the Apostles was chiefly in gathering the people that dwelt in the sea, or beyond the sea, called in prophecy the islands of the sea; and therefore as they were fishermen before their calling, and gathered the fulness of the sea for their food, so Christ, when He called them, told them He would make them "fishers of men" to gather the multitudes of men, that were, as it were, the inhabitants of the sea.

91. Deut. xxxiii. 26.] The universe is the chariot in which God rides and makes progress towards the last end of all things on the wheels of His providence; and the place of the chariot on which God has His seat is the highest heavens, as in Ps. lxviii. 33, and also ver. 4; the pavement of the chariot, above which God's throne is, is the firmament or the sky, as Ezek. i. 25, 26. Therefore this verse signifies as much as that God governs the whole world for the good of His Church; the wheels of the chariot of the universe move for them, and the progress that God makes therein on His throne above the firmament, the pavement of His chariot, is for them, and every

event in the universe is in subserviency to their help and benefit.—Corol. Hence it was meet that Christ, when He came to be invested with the government of the universe, as Head over all things to the Church, to govern the motions of this chariot, and make progress on it for their help and salvation, should ascend into the highest heavens above its pavement, to sit on the throne of this chariot; and therefore in Ps. lxviii., which is on the subject of Christ's ascension, mention is made once and again of God's riding on the heavens, as in verses 4 and 33. The underpart of the wheel of a chariot seems to run backward, but it is not so; the whole machine is constantly moving forward towards the journey's end. So when the Church of God is brought low in the world, it is like that part of the wheel that is brought next the ground. The course of things seems to be backward and away from the proposed and promised end; but it is a mistake, God is still constantly making progress towards the Church's promised glory.

92. Deut. xxxiii. 29—"Thine enemies," &c.]—*i.e.*, liars in their boastings and menaces; ["and thou shalt tread," &c.]—*i.e.*, their fortresses built upon high rocks and steep places—that is, thou shalt conquer and take their strongest places, and take possession of them. God is said to be a high place, (Ps. ix. 9, and xlvi. 7,)—*i.e.*, a fortress or refuge.

93. Deut. xxxiv. 5.] Moses brought the children of Israel into the wilderness and to the very border of Canaan, but carried them no further; there he left them, and it was not Moses, but Joshua or Jesus, that carried them over Jordan and brought them into Canaan, to the promised rest, and gave them possession of the land flowing with milk and honey, which seems to signify to us that we can never obtain heaven or saving blessings by the Law. Moses, who gave the Law, seems here to signify the Law; the Law brings persons into the wilderness,—that is, can bring souls under conviction,—and so leads them on into the wilderness. It carries along in that work—that is, preparatory to saving grace and comfort—even till they are brought to a next preparation for conversion and comfort, but there it leaves them. It can bring them no further; it cannot bring them over Jordan into a state of salvation, that must be done by Jesus or the spiritual Joshua. All the use of the Law is to lead men on in their wilderness travel, and when it has done that, and brought them to the border of Canaan, and to a next preparedness for a state of salvation, there it dies. John says, "The Law was given by Moses, but grace and truth came by Jesus Christ." (John i. 17, and Heb. vii. 19.)

JOSHUA.

94. Joshua i. 2.] As soon as ever Moses is dead, God commands Joshua or Jesus to lead the people over Jordan. So as soon as ever

men through the Law are dead to the Law, they are fitted for the comforts of Canaan. When Moses or the Law, our first husband, is dead, we are at liberty to be married to a risen Saviour, and so to be brought to the possession of Canaan, that is His inheritance.

95. Joshua ii. 18, 19.] Faith is made the condition of Rahab's kindred, as well as her own. They were to retire to Rahab's house, and not stir out, which they would not have done unless they had believed that God would indeed deliver that city and Land into the hand of the children of Israel as He had said, and would destroy their enemies and save their friends. As in the old world they that believed that God would destroy the world as He had said, fled to the ark; and in Egypt they that believed that God would accomplish what He had said concerning the hail and fire, retired to their houses beforehand and were saved. And in Jerusalem they that believed what Christ had said about Jerusalem's destruction fled out at the signal that Christ gave them, and were saved. And in Jerusalem's first destruction they that believed that God would destroy the city, as He had said by the prophet Jeremiah, went and submitted themselves to the king of Babylon, and were saved. Rahab, as she was the [type of the] mother of Christ, so her house in this case was a type of the Church, or of the house, the habitation and fortress of the Church, Christ Jesus, where the righteous dwell in safety, and where they must hide themselves till the indignation be overpast, and from whence they must not depart, but must be found in Him at the hour when judgment comes, in order to their being saved. Ver. 20. It was needful that Rahab should keep counsel in this matter, lest they should be betrayed when they were gone, or lest others should tie scarlet lines in their windows.

96. Joshua iv. 16.] The Lake of Sodom, into which Jordan emptied itself, was a type of hell on many accounts. The fire by which Sodom and Gomorrah and the neighbouring cities were destroyed is expressly called eternal fire. The river Jordan, (that was a swift river,) whose waters were constantly and swiftly flowing into that Lake, represents the continued flowing of multitudes (that are in Scripture often called 'waters') into hell. The Lake of Sodom was never full though these waters incessantly flowed into it. So hell is never satisfied. The waters must be supposed to have some subterraneous passage from that Lake, by which they were, as it were, sucked down into the lower parts of the earth, and, as it were, into hell, which makes the type more lively. These waters shall be in a great measure cut off when our Jesus or Joshua comes to bring His spiritual Israel into Canaan at the latter day, by that work which was an antitype of this work of Joshua that we have an account of in this Book. Then shall the great stream that constantly flowed down to hell fail. This shall be at the time of God's spiritual harvest, spoken of in Rev. xiv. As Joshua's bringing the people through Jordan was at the time of harvest, just before the waters were thus cut off by Joshua, [when they] flowed in more than ordinary plenty, it being a time when Jordan overflowed all its banks. So just before

Christ shall do this for His Church in the latter day, it will be a time of great wickedness and depravacy. Secondly, These sweet waters of Jordan represent the means of grace, which was one thing represented by Ezekiel's waters of life. So [also] the waters of Jordan represented [this] in healing Naaman's leprosy. And the Lake of Sodom in this case represents the same as those 'miry places and marshes' in Ezekiel's vision that were given to salt, never to be healed by the living waters, however constantly and plentifully flowing by them. Therefore the waters being cut off when Joshua comes, represents the awful judgment of God on reprobates who had long abused means of grace; when Christ shall come, these means which they have enjoyed shall be taken from them. They shall be miserably destroyed, and all streams of mercy shall be cut off from them. Lastly, This river flowing into the Lake of Sodom represents the supplies of the kingdom of Satan, and especially the Church of Rome, that is spiritually called Sodom, and so represents the same that the river Euphrates did in old Babylon. These shall be dried up when the spiritual Joshua shall come. Thus the sixth vial was poured out on the great river Euphrates, and the waters thereof were dried up, that the way of the kings of the East might be prepared. As there the river Euphrates represents two things that the literal river Euphrates was to old Babylon—viz., its supply and defence—so here Jordan, to Sodom and the Land about, used formerly to be a supply when it was well watered everywhere, as the "garden of the Lord," and now was a supply to the Lake of Sodom; but to Jericho, another type of the kingdom of Satan, it was a defence. It is evident that the destruction of Jericho was a remarkable type of the destruction of Satan's kingdom by the spiritual coming of Christ in the latter days. The dividing Jordan therefore, to make way for the enemies of Jericho to come from the East and destroy, was eminently a type of the same thing that is accomplished by pouring out the sixth vial.

97. Ver. 17—"And the city shall be a thing devoted, even it and all that is therein, to the Lord."] So the words might have been rendered. This was the first city that was taken, the first-fruits of their conquest, and therefore fitly devoted to God. Hereby the whole land was consecrated to God. For "if the first-fruits be holy, the lump is also holy," (Rom. xi. 16.)

98. Joshua v. 2.] This was the second general circumcision of the congregation. The first was probably before the Passover they kept in Egypt while they had peace in Egypt, (as Mr Henry says, "They doubtless," &c., down to "was interrupted.") But before the Passover, the night before they went out of Egypt they were doubtless generally circumcised, because it was then most strictly commanded that no uncircumcised person should eat the Passover. As now, this general circumcision in Gilgal was at the same time of year, just before they kept the Passover. (See chap. iv. 19, and the 10th verse of this chapter.)

99. Joshua v. 4, 6, 7—Concerning their not circumcising the chil-

dren, that were born in the wilderness.] Considering the plainness of the precept of circumcision and the strictness of the injunction, and that no great stress was laid upon it, and that it was so expressly commanded that no uncircumcised person should eat of the Passover, which was with great strictness and often commands required most watchfully and diligently and without fail to be kept every year, and considering that the congregation in the wilderness was under Moses's government,—I say, considering these things, it is unaccountable that all the children that were born for thirty-eight years together should not be circumcised, unless it was omitted by Divine direction. Some think God favourably dispensed with the omission on consideration of the unsettledness of their state and their frequent removes, and that stirring the children might be dangerous to them while they were sore. This reason is generally acquiesced in, but does not seem to be satisfactory. For sometimes they stayed a year in a place, (Num. ix. 22), if not much longer, and in their removes their little children though sore might be wrapped so warm and carried so easy as to receive no damage, and might certainly be much better accommodated than the mothers in travail or lying in. Therefore it rather seems to have been a continued token of God's displeasure against them. Circumcision was originally a seal of the promise of the land of Canaan. But when God had sworn in His wrath concerning the men of war that came out of Egypt that they should be consumed in the wilderness and never enter Canaan, as that sentence is here repeated, (ver. 6,) relation being thereunto had, (it seems to be here brought in as giving the reason of the omission.) As a further ratification of that sentence, and to be a constant memorandum of it to them, all that fell under that sentence and were to fall by it were forbidden to circumcise their children; (or rather, I should think, Moses, as the prophet of God, immediately under the Divine direction, was restrained from putting them upon it, was ordered to let them alone and leave them to their own negligent and disobedient hearts in this affair.) "This was such a significant indication of God's wrath as the breaking of the tables of the Covenant was, when Israel had broke Covenant by making the golden calf," [HENRY.] It is probably they who generally omitted keeping the Passover from the pronouncing of the sentence in Num. xiv. until now; for they never would have been tolerated in keeping the Passover from year to year in uncircumcision. The keeping of the Passover here seems to be mentioned as being now a new thing among them as well as circumcision. This gives light unto what is said in ver. 9. God suffering them judicially to continue in uncircumcision for so long a time like the Egyptians, where their fathers for a long time had many of them lived in uncircumcision for their hankering after Egypt, and going about to make them a captain to return to Egypt, was a continuing of them under the reproach of Egypt, which reproach was now rolled away. Moses had told them, while they were in the plains of Moab, (Deut. xii. 8,) that when they came into the land of Canaan they should not do as they did then, every man what was right in his own eyes, which confirms that the omission of circumcision, the Passover, and other Divine institutions, was not from a Divine prohibition, but rather from a judicial leaving them to themselves, (Amos v. 25.)

100. Joshua vii. 12.] God had often made absolute promises of the Land of Canaan, but yet here the fulfilment of these promises is suspended upon the condition of obedience. So eternal life is absolutely promised to believers, but yet we often find the fulfilling of that promise suspended on their persevering obedience.

101. Joshua x. 12.] Gibeon was the place that the sun appeared to stand over at that time in the place where Joshua then was; and the valley of Ajalon the place which the moon, which was also then visible, appeared standing over. Now was a remarkable fulfilment of those words of Job, chap. ix. 7—"Which commandeth the sun, and it riseth not, and sealeth up the stars;" which words are a confirmation that the sun, moon, and stars all stopped as to their diurnal motion by the staying the revolution of the earth about its axis. In the song of Deborah it is said the "stars in their courses fought against Sisera." The angels are called stars. Christ is often compared to the sun. Here we have all the heavenly hosts—the sun, moon, and all the stars—standing still to fight against the enemies of God's people, representing that Christ and all the heavenly host of saints (constituting the heavenly Church represented by the moon) and all the angels are fighting against the enemies of the Church. Hereby is typified that which is represented in prophecy. (Rev. xix.)

The moon's standing still. This proves the truth of the history, for a circumstance of the sun's standing still being caused by staying the earth's diurnal revolution is mentioned, though the occasion of such a circumstance must be wholly unknown in those days to the Jews, which argues the truth of the fact; for nothing but the real fact (the means of which was wholly unknown) could have put this into the head of the historian.

102. Joshua xv. 32.] And yet here are thirty-eight names. The probable reason why in the summing them up they are reckoned but twenty-nine is this:—The other nine were afterwards set off to another tribe—viz., the tribe of Simeon—viz., Beersheba, Maladah, Hazar-shual, Azem, Eltolad, Hormah, Ziklag, Remmon, and Eder or Ether.

JUDGES.

103. Judges v. 14.] This shadows forth the great hand that authors shall have in the great and last battle that the Church shall have with her enemies, of which that about which is this song, was a type.

104. Judges ix. 45.] The end of sowing the place with salt was not to make it barren, for it was a city not a field that is spoken of.

But this action seems to have been used in those days as symbolical to signify the curse of being perpetually desolate. It was an open solemn declaration that they devoted the place thus sowed with salt to everlasting desolation and emptiness. Probably it came to be thus used from what was observed of the providence of God with respect to Sodom and the cities and country round about, that were effectually devoted to perpetual desolation by being covered with the Dead Sea.

105. Judges xi. 24.] The land which the Amorites now possessed was a land that they had taken from others—viz., from the Zamzummims. (Deut. ii. 20, 21.) They had been extraordinarily assisted to prevail against and drive out this people, though a very mighty and gigantic people. This they ascribed to Chemosh their god, and they therefore thought they had a good title to the land, seeing their god had given it to them.

106. Judges xiii. 18—"Why askest thou thus after my name, seeing it is secret?" (=wonderful.)] This argues that this is the same person spoken of in chap. ix. of Isa. ver. 6—"To us a child," &c., "*Wonderful*," which is the same word in the original that is here rendered 'secret;' and what is said in ver. 20 further argues it. [See note on Isa. ix. 6.] What is here said about the name of this person, compared with Prov. xxx. 4, argues that it was the Son of God. (See also Rev. xix. 12; Gen. xxxii. 29.)

RUTH.

107. Ruth iv. 14—"Kinsman."] The kinsman here meant is the child now born, as appears by this and next verse, especially the last word of the next verse, and by the name they gave the child—Obed, (ver. 17,) signifying *serving*.

I. AND II. SAMUEL.

108. 1 Sam. ii. 8.] It is probable that what was especially called the throne of glory was the throne of God in the Tabernacle and Temple, on which the glory of the Lord abode and where it appeared. Christ who dwelt there was the glory of the Lord, and was called simply 'glory,' (1 Sam. iv. 21, 22; Ps. lxxxv. 9; Haggai ii. 7; Jer. xvii. 12.) In the original it is "a high throne of glory."

109. 1 Sam. iii. 1.] HENRY *in loc.*, "There." From this time it began to be otherwise. There was "open vision." "And all Israel, from Dan even to Beersheba, knew that Samuel was established to be a prophet of the Lord," (ver. 20, chap. iv. 1.)

110. 1 Sam. v. 4.] The Bible and other remains of the true religion that were kept in the Church of Rome, the Antichristian Church, will at length be the occasion of the fall of their Dagon and of the breaking of his head and hands. When Antichrist falls there will be a remainder of him yet; but he shall be utterly despoiled of strength and glory. He will be like a stump without head or hands.

111. 1 Sam. xii. 11.] This Bedan seems to be the same with Jair the Gileadite of whom we read, (Judges x. 3, 4,) for this Bedan was a Gileadite, as appears by 1 Chron. vii. 17. But Jair was the only Gileadite that judged Israel, except Jephthah, who judged Israel next to him, and is mentioned next to him in this verse.

112. *Ibid.*, ver. 15.] There is in this and the foregoing verse an opposition between *being after the Lord*, as in the foregoing,—*i.e.*, having God going before them and leading them as their Captain and Saviour,—and God's being their enemy, or the hand of God, its being against them.

113. 1 Sam. xxv. 26.] The sense is, as the Lord liveth, and as thy soul liveth, seeing the Lord Himself hath withholden thee from coming to shed blood, and from avenging thyself with thine own hand, God Himself will certainly avenge thee and will take him away, as I desire that God would take away all thine enemies. It is a strong expression of assurance concerning a future event such as we have in the next chapter ver. 10.

114. 2 Sam. i. 17.] David's behaviour on occasion of the death of Saul his (see verses 11, 12) grand persecutor, who long sought his life, and whose death was so much to his advantage, together with the spirit he shewed on other occasions of love and meekness and forgiveness towards those that injured him, do greatly confirm that the imprecations we have in his Psalms on his persecutors, of whom Saul was the chief, are not the expression of a spirit of private revenge, but imprecations he put up in the name of Christ as Head of the Church against His and His Church's enemies, and what he spake as a prophet in the name of the Lord. Observe, also, his behaviour with respect to the death of Abner and Amasa. By this also we may see what is the spirit of true religion, how it disposes persons to overlook and hide the worst faults of their worst enemies, and [to] speak the best of them and lament their calamities. See note on Ps. lix. 13, and on Job xxxi. 30.

115. 2 Sam. vii. 10.] God's ceasing to walk in a tent and tabernacle, and dwelling in a temple, was a great token of mercy to the children of Israel; for while God dwelt in a movable tabernacle, He dwelt as a wayfaring man, as one that was not fixed in His abode, was ready to depart, that is, to stay but a little while, or that is undetermined whether to stay or no. But when He came to dwell in a temple,—that is, a fixed habitation,—it was a token for good several ways. It was a token that God would dwell among them, and make His settled abode among them, and that He would not lead them forth out of the Land, but continue them in the possession of it, for they were to go where the tabernacle went before them; but now dwelt

in an immovable temple, it was a token that they should no more be removed. It was a token that God would not cast them off from being His people ; for if He should do so, He would remove them out of that Land, for the Land was His Land, a Land that He had chosen to be a holy Land.

116. 2 Sam. vii. 20.] *i.e.*, What can he desire more of Thee, or pray for more to Thee?—that this is the meaning is evident by 1 Chron. xvii. 18, where it is thus expressed, "What can David," &c.,—[" for Thou, Lord," &c.]—*i.e.*, Thou hast chosen Thy servant. God's knowledge is here put for election, as often elsewhere. God's election is mentioned as the ground of these great and admirable favours. The words that follow in the next verse confirm this verse.

117. 2 Sam. vii. 21—" For Thy WORD's sake, and according to Thine own heart."] In 1 Chron. xvii. 19 it is, " For Thy servant's sake, and according to Thine own heart," which confirms that by the " word" here is meant Christ, who appeared in the form of a servant, and is often, by way of eminency, called God's ' servant.' [See POOL, Synop. *in loc.*]

118. 2. Sam. x. 16.] Which armament is 7000 men, ten to a chariot, so this place is reconciled with 1 Chron. xix. 18, (see POOL on 1 Chron. xix. 18.)

I. AND II. KINGS.

119. 1 Kings ii. 37.] This may help us to understand God's threatening to Adam, when He said, " In the day," &c. When Solomon thus threatened Shimei, we cannot naturally understand any more by it than that death should be certain to him from that day: he should stand guilty of death, obliged to die by a fixed unalterable establishment. We cannot suppose that Solomon concluded that, if he did go over the brook Kedron, he should hear of it so as to execute this threatening on that very day. As it proved that he did not, it seems to have been some time after before the threatening was executed. See note on Gen. ii. 17.

120. 1 Kings viii. 56.] So long was it before God fully gave Israel that rest in Canaan which He had promised them by the hand of Moses, which may make us the less to wonder that many of those great things that were promised by Christ to His Church, and spoken of by His Apostles relating to the kingdom of heaven, and the glory that Church should receive at Christ's coming in that kingdom, as to their more full accomplishment should be so long delayed.

121. 1 Kings xi. 5–7.] It does not appear that Solomon did himself worship these strange gods. But what his wives persuaded him to, was to build high places for them to worship their gods in: he probably went after other gods only as he honoured them so far as to build places for their public worship in the land of Israel, wherein

his wives and their attendants might worship them. For it is said in ver. 8 he did this "for his wives," &c. He might possibly think it but reasonable that his wives should be allowed the exercise of their own religion and the worship of their own gods, and might think it hard, seeing he had brought them out of their own country, to deny them high places and altars at which they might worship them in his country.

122. 1 Kings xiii. 31, 32.] The old prophet orders that his corpse might be laid in the sepulchre of the man of God, and his bones by that prophet's bones, that so they might not be disturbed, and burnt on the altar of Bethel by Josiah. This is implied as the reason he gives himself in ver. 32, and so the event was: the bones that were laid in that sepulchre were not disturbed by Josiah, (2 Kings xxiii. 17.)

123. 1 Kings xiv. 14, 15.] It is God's manner in Scripture, when threatening the wicked for their sins, to pass from those judgments that are soon to be inflicted, and are the more immediate, and which are the occasion of God's sending a messenger to threaten them, to some great remote judgments, of which perhaps the judgments more immediately threatened are images or forerunners. Thus when God first sent Moses to Pharaoh, He sent him with a threatening of the last and greatest plague; and the other foregoing plagues are all omitted. (Exod. iv. 22, 23.) So in chap. ix. ver. 15, God again threatens the last plague and Pharaoh's own destruction, that was accomplished in the Red Sea; though there was the plague of hail, and locusts and darkness afterwards, before the plague of pestilence. So here, when the wife of Jeroboam comes to the prophet to enquire whether her son shall live, the prophet passes from a threatening of his death and judgment suddenly to be inflicted on his family, to the captivity of the ten tribes, though it was to be long after Jeroboam's death. So also it is the manner of the prophets, when sent on some particular occasions to promise some mercy to God's people, to insist on some greater mercy that is remote, and that is to be bestowed on God's people in after generations. Thus when Isaiah was sent to Ahaz, when Rezin, king of Syria, and Pekah, son of Remaliah, were combined against him, to comfort him by foretelling the disappointment of their enemies and deliverance of Judah, he comes to Ahaz with Shear-jashub, his son, that signifies the "remnant shall return," to foretell the return from the captivity to Babylon, as in Isa. vii. And it is very frequent with the prophets, when foretelling lesser mercies that God has to bestow on His people, to pass to and insist upon that greatest of all mercies, the coming of Christ. So did Isaiah, when He came to Ahaz on the forementioned occasion. (Isa. vii. 14.) So the prophets, when foretelling the return from the Babylonish captivity, often insist on the redemption of Christ, of which this is a type. So do the prophets Haggai and Zechariah, when sent to encourage the people to build the Temple, with promises of mercies therein, insist chiefly on the prosperity that God will give the Church in the times of the gospel.

124. 1 Kings xviii. 33–35.] Elijah's sacrifice, in the time wherein it was offered, was attended with the greatest obstacles to its being consumed by fire. God, who has more ends than one in what He does, probably did not only intend by this to shew His power beyond that of Baal, but to represent what came to pass with respect to the sacrifice of Christ, the great antitype of all the ancient sacrifices, Whose last Suffering was attended with such circumstances as seemed to tend in the highest degree to hinder His going on to offer Himself, in the heavenly flames of Divine charity, and voluntarily presenting Himself to suffer the flames of Divine wrath. Such was God's hiding of His face from Him, and dealing with Him in some respects as if He had been an enemy, which was a great trial of His love to the Father, and tending like floods of water to quench the fire of Divine love in His soul, and to prevent that great degree of it which was necessary to carry Him through the extreme sufferings that were before Him; and also the extraordinary view which Christ had then given Him of the unworthiness of mankind for whom He died, the hateful nature of their sin that He was about to expiate by His extreme sufferings, and their great enmity against Him, which was then set before Him and exercised towards Him, in the contempt and cruelty of His enemies. And some of them the very persons that He was about to die for; and the ingratitude of His own disciples, that had already received the saving benefits of His death, in their coldness towards Him in the times of His agony,—their being unwilling to watch with Him one hour—their all forsaking Him when He was apprehended—Peter denying Him with oaths and curses. These were like floods of great waters that were then thrown upon Him to quench His love, and to prevent His going on to endure those extreme torments in the fire of God's wrath; as was also that extraordinary view that was given Him beforehand of the cup He was to drink, which made His soul exceeding sorrowful, even unto death. But "many waters could not quench His love, nor could the floods drown it." (Song of Solomon viii. 7.)

125. 1 Kings xix. 20, 21.] See Matt. xxiv. 17, 18. The truth with respect to what is related in these verses probably was thus:—Elijah was directed by the Spirit of God to cast his mantle on Elisha; but Elijah had not the design of God in it fully made known to him, supposing it to be intended as a sign that Elisha should be a prophet after him, agreeable to what God had said to him at Mount Sinai. But God had a further meaning in it, which was intimated by His Spirit, which went with Elijah's mantle to Elisha—viz., that he should immediately forsake all and follow him, and devote himself to the work of the ministry in the business of a prophet. Elisha, supposing Elijah had this design of God made known to him, and had been directed to cast his mantle on him with this view, and finding at first a reluctance and desire of Elisha that he by his prayers would obtain leave of God that he should first kiss his father and mother; Elijah, surprised at this request, as is natural, supposing him thus ignorant, says, "Go back: for what have I done that should hinder

it?" However, Elisha, who understood the mind of God, soon recovered from his reluctance and went no further back than to his oxen, and took them and the instruments and offered up all to God, signifying by this action his full consent to forsake all and make a sacrifice of all this world's possessions and concerns to the great and infinitely important designs of his ministry.

126. 1 Kings xxii. 19—"And all the host of heaven standing by Him."] Here we may observe that they under the Old Testament were sensible of a multitude of inhabitants in the heavenly world as well as now, since another world has been more fully revealed by the gospel.

127. 2 Kings ii. 9.] Elijah was now about to leave the world, and as parents, when they are leaving the world, are wont to bequeath portions to their children, so Elijah asks Elisha what *he* shall bequeath to him. Elisha was as it were his child, and calls him father. (Ver. 12.) That portion that he desires to inherit from his father is his spirit, and he desires a double portion of it—*i.e.*, a much larger portion than the rest of his children, as it was ordained that the eldest son should inherit a double portion. (Deut. xxi. 17.) It was his birthright to have the best share of his father's estate. Elijah had many other children besides Elisha. There were many sons of the prophets that were under Elijah's care and instruction, so that he was as it were a father among them as afterwards Elisha was, as is evident by chap. iv. 38, and chap. vi. 42. Now what Elisha desires is that he may be distinguished from all the rest of the children by having a double portion of his spirit bequeathed to him. For Elijah's estate did not consist in silver and gold, but in those gifts of the Spirit which he possessed. So that he was about to give something he might say of as Peter. (Acts iii. 6.) He asked a double portion of this, and to be made the main heir of those blessed spiritual gifts which he had, which was accordingly granted him.

128. 2 Kings v. 17—"Two mules'," &c.] See BEDFORD, "Scripture Chron.," p. 627. Thus though he would not allow before that the waters of Israel were better than the waters of Damascus, yet, having been convinced by experience of his error in that, he now easily conceives that the *earth* of the land of Israel is better than that of Damascus.

129. 2 Kings xxi. 10–15.] It is evident by this, and many other passages of Scripture, that the first destruction of Jerusalem was principally for the sins of Manasseh and the wickedness that the people were guilty of in his reign, (see chap. xxiii. 26, 27, and xxiv. 3, 4, and Jer. xv. 4;) and yet the first captivity in Jehoiakim's time was not till about forty-four years after Manasseh's death, and the total destruction of Jerusalem in Zedekiah's time not till about fifty-five years after his death. Hence I would observe that it is no argument against the dreadful destruction of Jerusalem by the Romans, its being an evident token of God's wrath against the people for their rejecting and crucifying Christ, that that destruction happened about forty years after Christ's crucifixion.

I. AND II. CHRONICLES.

130. 1 Chron. xi. 39—"Zelek the Ammonite."] Here one of David's worthies is said to be an 'Ammonite,' and another of them (ver. 46) a Moabite, and yet in Deut. xxiii. 3 it is forbidden in the Law of Moses that an Ammonite or Moabite should ever enter into the congregation of the Lord. So Ruth was a Moabitess, but yet was received. By this it appears that evident piety prevailed for persons' admission notwithstanding the Law. When the case was so, they were no longer Ammonites or Moabites in the eye of the Law. By these things and many others, it appears that evangelical qualifications always prevailed over legal ones. So in the case of them that were legally unclean, that yet kept the Passover in Hezekiah's time. (2 Chron. xxx. 17–20.)

131. 1 Chron. xxiii. 26.] Thus the Ceremonial Law was in part altered before Christ's time. The service of the Levites by the Law of Moses consisted much in carrying the tabernacle, and vessels and instruments of it, (Num. iii. and iv.;) but when the Temple was built this service ceased, and was abrogated by David, there then ceasing to be occasion any longer for that work, and therefore David gave them new ordinances, and appointed them new work, which shews that the Ceremonial Law was alterable. If it may be altered in part, it may be altered in the whole; if David might abrogate some ordinances, Christ, the true David, might abrogate all, (Jer. iii. 16, 17, and Isa. lvi. 3, 4.) In 2 Chron. xxiii. 18, the ordinances of David are mentioned as of parallel validity with those of Moses, as a rule for their public worship. See note on Isa. li. 4.

132. 2 Chron. xii. 8.] *i.e.*, That they may know the difference between my service and theirs. So the forbidden tree in Eden was called the tree of the knowledge of good and evil, because the experience of the one illustrated and shewed the value of the other. God would hereby let Judah know by their experience how much better His service was that they had forsaken and cast off, than the service of the kingdoms of the countries whose gods they had chosen.

133. 2 Chron xv. 17—"But the high places were not taken away."] *i.e.*, Those that were used in the service of the true God, for Asa took away those which were used in idolatrous worship. (Chap. xiv. 3, 4.)

134. 2 Chron. xxxii. 31—"That He might know all that was in his heart."] By this, together with verses 25, 26, it appears that Hezekiah had much sin in his heart, though, as he pleads with God in the time of his sickness, he had walked before God in truth and with a perfect heart. See also 2 Kings xviii. 3, 5, 6.

ESTHER.

135. Esther v. 2—"Sceptre."] Favour was offered by the king by holding out to her the golden sceptre; but it was expected that she, in order to a title and interest in the offered favour, should draw near and touch the top of the sceptre as an expression of her joyful acceptance of the favour, submission to the royal dominion and power, of which the sceptre was the ensign, and her dependence on the king's free, sovereign but offered favour. The acts and benefits of saving faith in Christ may be compared to this act of Esther towards Ahasuerus, her king, her husband, and in this affair, and in what followed, her saviour.

JOB.

136. Job vi. 6.] Job was reduced to such necessity that he was forced to content himself with such insipid unsavoury morsels. This is the meaning, as appears by the next verse.

137. Job xiv. 22.] It is not unlikely that the Spirit of God in this has some respect to the misery of wicked men in a future state, when both soul and body shall be cast into hell. See Eccles. xi. 10.

138. Job xix. 25—"I know that my Redeemer liveth."] Though I shall die, and my flesh shall be destroyed with worms, [and that He shall stand at the latter day upon the earth.] In the original it is, 'He shall stand over the dust,' עַל-עָפָר The word 'earth' is very often used in the Book of Job, and the word is everywhere '*eretz,*' and nowhere this word that properly signifies 'dust.' And it is not true that at the day of judgment Christ will properly stand on the earth. The meaning is this:—Christ will stand over the dust of the dead saints. ["My Redeemer."] The word also as it was used among the Hebrews signified 'near kinsman,' as in Ruth iii. 12—"And now it is true that I am thy near kinsman, [Goel,] howbeit there is a kinsman [goel] nearer than [I] [Goel.]" Ver. 13, "Tarry this night, and it shall be in the morning, that if he will perform unto thee the part of a kinsman, [or if he will redeem thee,] well; let him do the kinsman's part: but if he will not do the part of a kinsman to thee, then I will do the part of a kinsman to thee." So the word is the same, 1 Kings xvi. 11—"As soon as he began to reign, he slew all the house of Baasha; he left none of his kinsfolks." There were four things the 'goel' was to do for his kinsman unable to act for to himself: (1.) He was to marry the widow of the deceased kinsman raise up seed to his brother, as Christ marries the elect Church that was left a widow by the first Adam, the first surety, and by the Law or first covenant, the first husband, having no seed, (Rom. vii. 3, 4.) (2.) He was to redeem the inheritance of his poor kinsman, (Lev.

xxv. 25.) So Christ redeems the inheritance which we sold. (3.) He was to ransom his poor kinsman in bondage, paying the price of his redemption. (Lev. xxv. 47, 48, 52.) Thus does Christ redeem us from bondage after we have sold ourselves. (4.) He was to avenge the blood of his slain kinsman on the slayer. Thus does Christ avenge our blood on Satan.

139. Job xx. 11.] Both these expressions import the same thing, and are as much as to say the sins of his youth remain with him after he is dead: his sin shall lie down with him in his grave, and shall remain in his dead corpse there when his flesh is putrefied and turned to dust. Then his iniquity shall still remain in his bones: his bones shall be full of them; which signifies that his sins shall for ever remain with him after he is dead: he shall never get rid of them, but they shall to all eternity lie upon him. (See Ezek. xxxii. 27.

140. Job xxiv. 23.] The words more literally translated are, "Though it be given him to be in safety, and he depends upon it, yet his eyes are upon their ways"—*i.e.*, though God gives those wicked men that are so unjust to be in safety, and they, because God protects and preserves them for the present, depend on future safety, as though God took no notice of their wickedness and would never punish it, yet God's eyes are upon their ways.

141. Job xxvi. 13—"His hands have formed the crooked serpent."] It might have been translated, "His hands have wounded or tormented the crooked serpent"—*i.e.*, the devil. The word translated "formed" is the same that is used in ver. 5—"Dead things are 'formed' from under the waters," [see *in loc.*] That the devil, that old serpent, that great leviathan, should be meant, agrees with the foregoing verse—"He divideth the sea with His power; by His understanding He smiteth through the proud," which was remarkably fulfilled in dividing the sea and destroying Pharaoh, compared to leviathan, the water-monsters that are especially to be found in the waters of Egypt: Ps. lxxiv. 13, 14—"Thou didst divide the sea by Thy strength: Thou brakest the heads of the dragon in the waters. Thou brakest the heads of leviathan in pieces," where he is spoken of as the image of the devil; and this leviathan is called the "crooked serpent" in Isa. xxvii. 1—"In that day," &c., "the piercing serpent," [as the serpent lying across like a bar, *nahash bariach*, the very same name used here,] "even leviathan that crooked serpent; and He shall slay the dragon that is in the sea." This is fitly subjoined to the former part of the verse—"By His Spirit He hath garnished [or beautified] the heavens." For at the same time that God cast Satan down to hell He purged and also beautified heaven, increasing the holiness and happiness of His elect angels; and at every time of Christ's remarkably overcoming Satan and bruising his head, is a beautifying heaven and advancing His holiness and happiness, as when He rose from the dead and ascended into heaven, and when He shall destroy Antichrist, and at the end of the world; and it is not incredible that Job should here speak of such mysteries, for it is evident he now

speaks under the influence of the Spirit of prophecy, by what he says in the preceding verse concerning the dividing of the sea, &c., fulfilled afterwards. This interpretation is confirmed by ver. 5—"Dead things," &c. Mr Henry observes that some ancient versions render the words thus: "Behold, the giants groan under the waters, and those that dwell with them;" or the words ought to have been rendered: "Rephaim are wounded and pierced through under the waters," agreeable to the original. (See BUXTORF.) "From under the water" seems to allude to the waters of the Flood, under which the giants were destroyed in God's terrible wrath, which deluge of water was a remarkable type of the deluge of God's wrath which comes on the ungodly in another world. The observing this is to Job's purpose, for, as Mr Henry says, "is there anything in which the majesty of God appears more dreadful than in the eternal ruin of the ungodly, and the groans of the inhabitants of the land of wickedness?" Ver. 12 confirms this interpretation, and also ver. 13.

142. Job xxviii. 5—"Under it is turned up as it were fire"]—*i.e.*, that which shines like fire, as in Deut. xxxiii. 2. The Law of God, because it, as it were, shines and gives light, is called a "fiery Law."

143. Job xxx. 24—"Howbeit He will not stretch out His hand to the grave"]—*i.e.*, to rescue men from death. Every man must die and be retained in the grave,—"the redemption of the life is precious, and it ceaseth for ever;"—God will recover man from thence to live again in this world, [though they cry in His destruction,] though they dread death never so much when death comes, and would never so earnestly cry to be delivered from the grave.

144. Job xxxi. 34—"Did I fear?" &c.] In these early days great account was made of men's pedigree, and they were kept with care; and when men's lives were so long, great numbers of the dependents of one living ancestor were alive at once, so that those who were called a family were commonly a great multitude. Job declares that he was not deterred from doing justice in his office of a judge through fear of the great multitude that were of the family of him that was to be condemned or displeased in the judgment.

145. Job xxxiv. 20.] Remarkably fulfilled when the first-born were slain: as there are several things in this Book in which the Spirit that in the general directed in the forming of the speeches of Job and his friends,—either in them or others, which they answered these sayings from,—had respect to those great things which were accomplished when the children of Israel were brought out of Egypt and led to Canaan, (see chap. xxvi. 12, xxxviii. 22, 23, ix. 7.) [At midnight,] (see ver. 25, and chap. xxxvi. 20, xxvii. 20; Matt. xxv. 6; 1 Thess. v. 2.) . . .

146. Job xxxvi. 27, to end of the next chapter.] Elihu concludes his discourse with observations and improvements of God's wondrous works in the clouds—rain, lightning, and thunder. It appears to me probable that the occasion of it was the appearance, at a distance, of the clouds and lightning and thunder of the storm that was then approaching, out of which God spake to Job. There was nothing in Elihu's foregoing discourse that seemed to lead him to it. It is true

that he was, in the foregoing verses, speaking of the greatness of God and His works; but there seems nothing that led him thus suddenly to begin about the clouds and rain in this 27th verse. But if there then appeared to them a thunder-storm arising, that will easily account for it, why he, when speaking of God's greatness, should insist on this rather than any other of God's works. The 30th verse of the XXXVIth chapter seems to confirm this—["Behold," &c.] The manner of expression, his calling on Job to 'behold,' agrees with the supposition that the thing was then appearing that he was speaking of, and the description here given, 'He spreadeth His light upon it, and covereth the roots of the sea,' as it is in the original, agrees exactly with the appearance of a thunder-storm appearing as arising above the horizon; for the top of the clouds, in such cases, is commonly all spread over with an exceeding bright light. Thus God spreads His light upon it; and the lower part of a storm that appears thus rising, seems to cover the utmost confines and extreme parts of the sea that are next the horizon, that are here called the "roots of the sea," which may elegantly be so called according to the notion they then had of the world as being a flat, and that there was first the land and after that the sea, which they supposed was bounded by the horizon, or at the meeting of the firmament with the waters. He certainly here speaks of a thunder-storm as it is [seen] when rising and approaching, whether there was then one approaching or no. By the 30th and also the 32d and 33d verses, having first observed how the cloud appears on the top of it covered with light, and how the bottom covers the roots of the sea, he next observes how it is, as it advances higher and comes nearer, how the cloud interposes between the sun and the earth and hides its light, and how the thunder-storm grows louder, and the notice the cattle seem to shew of it; and in the beginning of the next chapter, Elihu seems to speak of what then appeared—"At this also my heart trembleth, and is moved out of its place," &c.; and it was not the only instance of God's speaking out of a storm of thunder, for so He did at Mount Sinai, (Ps. lxviii. 8.) POOL, Synop. on chap. xxxviii. 1.

147. *Ibid.*, ver. 29, 30.] Here the clouds are represented as being spread out over the concave of the heavens as the covering of a tabernacle, which come down as curtains and cover the utmost edge of the sea, which is the uttermost part of the pavement or ground of the tabernacle. Here the clouds are represented as one covering and the light another, spread out upon it, as in the Tabernacle built in the wilderness there were various coverings one without another. Elihu probably has respect to the cloud as it now appeared. The clouds of a thunder-storm, when rising, appear at top spread over with a bright light, and at the bottom covering the utmost ends of the earth or sea.

148. Job xl. 2–4.] Since Job had undertaken to find fault with God and His dispensations, and to desire an opportunity to dispute with Him, that he might argue the matter of the erroneousness of His dispensations with him, he is now called upon by God to

'answer' to what He had said, and speak in his turn. But now Job declines it and owns he has nothing to answer—"Behold, I am vile," &c.

149. Job xli. 11—"Who hath prevented Me, that I should repay him?"] These words are a great evidence that leviathan is here spoken of as a type of the devil. For no other leviathan was ever subject to God's moral government, or ever rebelled against Him, that God should repay him.

PSALMS.

150. Ps. xi. 6—"Snares."] *i.e.*, This destruction shall come suddenly and unexpectedly upon them, while they are saying peace and safety, while they are eating and drinking, marrying and giving in marriage, and gratifying their lusts—as a bird that is securely feeding on the sweet bait, suspecting no harm nigh, and is suddenly caught in the snare. (Luke xxi. 34, 35; see also Matt. xxiv. 36–39, and 1 Thess. v. 6, and Eccles. ix. 12.)

151. Ps. xxiii. 6—"I will dwell," &c.] Being there not merely as a servant, or as a guest kindly entertained for a little while, but as a child adopted into the family. For, as Christ says, "The Son abideth in the house for ever."

152. Ps. xxxix. 12.] David asks mercy as a stranger, having reference to the Law often repeated in the Pentateuch, of shewing mercy to strangers, ("a sojourner with Thee,") alluding to that which is said in Lev. xxv. 23.

153. Ps. lix. 13—"Consume them," &c.] The title of the Psalm shews that the occasion of David's penning this Psalm was Saul's persecuting of him. Here seems, therefore, to be an imprecation of God's wrath on Saul to consume and cut him off from the earth; and yet, when Saul was cut off from the earth, how did he rend his clothes, and mourn and weep and fast for Saul as well as Jonathan, [2 Sam. i. 11, 12,] and how did David revenge his death on the Amalekite that slew him, and how did he lament Saul's death as the death of one that he greatly loved and [who] was very dear to him, in his elegy; which is a great evidence that David's imprecations of God's vengeance on his enemies, in the Book of Psalms, are not the expressions or breathings of his own spirit, but prophecies uttered; prophetical curses denounced by the Spirit of God. (See note on David's Elegy, 2 Sam. i. 17.)

154. Ps. lxxii. 15.] It might have been rendered—"Prayer also shall be made *through* Him continually, and daily shall He be blessed." The word rendered 'praised' is that which is commonly rendered 'blessed,' when speaking of an act of worship towards God; and the word translated 'for' is sometimes used for 'through,' as

Joshua ii. 15—"'Through' the window." If we hold the translation 'for Him,' then it must be understood of the saints praying for the Father's accomplishment of His promises made to the Son in the covenant of redemption, that His kingdom may come, His name be glorified, and that He may see His seed, and that the full reward may be given Him for His sufferings, and so that He may receive the joy that was set before Him.

155. Ps. lxxiv. 25—"Flood."] God, in dividing Jordan, did not only divide the water that ordinarily belonged to the river, or the water which came from its fountains, but also the extraordinary additional waters by the great rains a little before harvest. So God cleaved both the fountain—*i.e.*, the fountain water—and the flood.

156. Ps. lxxxiv. 9—"Behold, O God, our shield."] [For this use of the] word 'behold,' see 2 Chron. vi. 42, and Ps. cxxxii. 10.

157. Ps. lxxxix. 15.] There is the dreadful and there is the joyful sound. The dreadful sound was at Mount Sinai. The joyful sound is from Mount Sion. When the people heard the former they were far from beholding the glory of God's face. Moses only was admitted to see His 'back-parts;' the people were kept at a distance, and the light of God's glory that they saw was so terrible to them, that they could not abide it. But they that know the "joyful sound," they shall be admitted near, nearer than Moses, so as to see the glory of God's face or brightness of His countenance, and that not only transiently, as Moses saw God's back-parts, but continually. The light of God's glory shall not be terrible to them, but easy and sweet, so that they may dwell in it and walk in it; and it shall be to them instead of the light of the sun; for the sun shall no more be their light by day, nor the moon by night, but God shall be their everlasting light. Compare this with Isa. ii. 5, and Rev. xxi. 23, 24, and xxii. 4, 5.

158. Ps. cxvi. 10, 11—"Spoken; was greatly afflicted; I said in my haste, All men are liars."] The meaning seems to be this—I spake as I have declared, (ver. 4,) because I trusted in God. I was greatly afflicted, I was in extreme distress, (as I declared before;) I was in great astonishment and trembling, (as the word rendered 'haste' signifies trembling as well as haste, as it is rendered in Deut. xx. 3;) and in these circumstances I did not trust in man; I said, all men are liars—*i.e.*, not fit to be trusted in; those that will fail and deceive the hopes of them who trust in them, agreeably to Psalm lxii. 8, 9. See POOL, Synop. on ver. 11.

159. Ps. cxxxvi.] This Psalm confirms me that an ultimate end of the creation of the world, and of all God's works, is His goodness, or the communication of His good to His creatures. For this Psalm sufficiently teaches that all God's works, from the beginning of the world to the end of it, are works of mercy to His people, yea, even the works of His vindic[a]tive justice and wrath, as appears by verses 10, 15, 17–22.

160. Ps. cxliv. 5—"Bow thy heavens, O Lord, and come down."] This was never so remarkably fulfilled as in the incarnation of Jesus

Christ, when heaven and earth were as it were brought together. Heaven itself was as it were made to bow that it might be united to the earth. God did as it were come down and bring heaven with Him. He not only came down to the earth, but He brought heaven down with Him to men and for men. It was a more strange and wonderful thing. But this will be more remarkably fulfilled still by Christ's second coming, when He will indeed bring all heaven down with Him—viz., all the inhabitants of heaven. Heaven shall be left empty of its inhabitants to come down to the earth; and then the mountains shall smoke, and shall indeed flow down at His presence, as in Isa. lxiv. 1.

PROVERBS.

161. Prov. xi. 18—"The wicked worketh a deceitful work"]—*i.e.*, a work that will deceive him, or that he is greatly deceived in the consequences of. The work that he does, as he views it, seems to promise fair for happiness: his work looks to him as that which yields him a great benefit; but his work deceives him, and he will find himself miserably deceived in it. From the seed that he sows he promises himself a crop of pleasant fruit; but it will deceive him, for the fruit that it will yield will be gall and wormwood, and will prove the most deadly poison. That this is the sense is evident by the words that follow in the latter part of the verse.

162. Prov. xvi. 4.] The wise man, in the expression, "hath made all things," has not respect merely to the works of creation, but also to the works of Providence: making and creating is commonly understood in this large sense in Scripture for bringing to pass; yea, bringing to pass, though not by an immediate effecting, but only by permitting, ordering, and disposing, is called 'making' in Scripture. The making the wicked, here mentioned, is a work of Providence. God makes men wicked in the same sense as He is said, in Rom. ix., "to make them vessels of wrath," to "harden them," and "fit them to destruction"—viz., by so disposing and ordering things in His providence, that they, in consequence of His disposals, especially in His permission, or withholding restraints, do continue in wickedness or are hardened in it. They are distinguished from others in being impenitently and obstinately wicked, and are suffered to multiply wickedness and heap up wrath; and God's end in it is to glorify Himself in the day of their evil or ruin. God makes wicked men in no other sense than He creates darkness, which is not by any positive efficiency, but only ordering, withholding light; for darkness is only a negative. (Isa. xlv. 7.) These things that are here said to be formed, made and created, are all works of Providence; and some of them brought to pass by no positive efficiency, because negative only.

Works of Providence are said to be created, (Num. xvi. 30; Isa. lvii. 19, and xli. 20, and xlv. 8, and xlviii. 7, and liv. 16; Jer. xxxi. 22,) so that it does not appear that this Scripture will justify such an expression as that God made some men to damn them. It is most probable that the wise man, by "making the wicked," has respect to something that God doth respecting the wicked or reprobates, that is distinguishing and peculiar to them. God's distinguishing dealing towards mankind might be expressed thus—that God maketh both the righteous and the wicked in the same sense—*i.e.*, whom He will He has mercy on and makes righteous, and whom He will He hardens and leaves to wickedness. But if the wise man had respect only to the bringing men into being, having guilt and corruption, this is common to all. All, in this sense, are made wicked alike. It is probable that by making the wicked, here is intended the same as is expressed in Rom. xi. 7–10; 2 Thess. ii. 11, 12; Ps. lxxxi. 12; Isa. vi. 9, 10, which is a judicial proceeding and a punishment of sin, though it be a mere sovereign proceeding in God that He distinguishes some by not executing this punishment upon them.

163. Prov. xxv. 25.] Good news from our friends at a distance, who have been gone long from us. Heaven is a far country—a far country especially to sinners, who have gone far off from God to the very borders, and seems to be a far country indeed to an awakened convinced sinner. The gospel is "glad tidings" from thence. Abraham's servant brought to Rebekah good news from a far country. Joseph's brethren, when they returned to Canaan, to their kindred there, after Joseph had made himself known to them in Egypt, and Joseph sent by them an account of his being alive, and his riches and glory, and plentiful supplies for them, and invited them to come down to him and partake of his wealth and glory, they brought good news from a far country to them who before were sorrowful, and ready to perish with famine. Moses brought to the children of Israel in Egypt, who were in great affliction there, and almost worn out with cruel bondage, good news from Mount Sinai, near the land of Midian. The spies, when they brought an account of the exceeding fertility of the land of Canaan, brought good news from a far country to them that were faithful in Israel. Cyrus sent good news from the Persian court to the poor captive Jews in Chaldea, as we have an account in Ezra i. Darius's messengers brought good news from the same court to the Jews in Judea, (Ezra iv.) Ezra came with good news to Jerusalem, when he brought from thence Artaxerxes's commission and decree, (Ezra vii.) Nehemiah came to Jerusalem with good news from the same court, (Neh. i.) Esther's messengers brought good news from Shushan to the Jews in Judea and in all the distant provinces of Esther, and Mordecai's advancement, and of great salvation for the Jews. Naomi, when in the land of Moab, heard good news from Canaan, when she heard how the Lord had visited His people in giving them bread, (Ruth i. 6.) All these are types of the good news sent us from heaven in the gospel of Jesus Christ, which gospel was good news from a far country;

also, in another sense—viz., it is preached to the Gentiles who were far off—aliens and strangers—far off from the Church of God and sent from Jerusalem and the land of Canaan to the remote parts of the world.

164. Prov. xxvii. 7.] This is to shew that there is not so much difference between the rich and the poor, as to comfort in outward enjoyments, as the world is ready to imagine. (Eccles. v. 12.)

165. Prov. xxx. 19, 20.] The way of a man with a maid, and the way of an adulterous woman, are here distinct instances. In the criminal intercourse of a man with a maid, the maid was liable to a discovery by some effects that were left in her body, at least it is so generally. But the man might conceal his wickedness—it might be hid as much as the way of a serpent on a rock; and when a married woman is guilty of adultery, then the woman may conceal her wickedness, as well as the adulterer his. See POOL, Synop.

ECCLESIASTES.

166. Eccles. iii. 11.] Instead of heart, it should have been translated *middle.* God hath set the world in the middle of things. God has not set us at the beginning, nor at the end of things. We see but the middle of God's works, not the beginning of them; we should have seen how wisely and beautifully they were contrived in the Divine counsels—how He made everything beautiful in its time. We see not the end and final issue of things. Then we should see the excellent and glorious issue; that all was order, most fitly and beautifully. The same word is used for middle or midst: Jonah ii. 3—"Midst of the sea." So again the same word for the midst of the sea in Exod. xv. 8, and the same word is used in 2 Sam. xviii. 14—"In the midst of the oak."

167. Eccles. vi. 10—"That which hath been is named already, and it is known that it is man."] There is a certain sphere in which God hath placed man, certain limits by which his attainments in the world and the degree of his worldly happiness are circumscribed, which limits men have come to in time past, and it is a vain imagination for any to expect to exceed those limits. Whatever men attain to, still they are but *men.* He that made him gave him his name, 'Adam,' which implies that he is dust; and let him be never so greedy, aspiring, busy, and restless and grasping in his pursuits, and vast in his expectations, he never will be any more. Man in his first transgression was ambitious of getting above his limits, of being as a god; and this disposition is common among men: but He that is mightier than man hath set his limits, and it is in vain to contend with Him, as it follows—["Neither may he contend with Him that is mightier than he."] God will make it to be known that men are but men, (Ps. ix. 20.)

168. Eccles. viii. 1—"Who is a wise man? and who knoweth the

interpretation of a thing?"] The word translated 'thing' is *dabher*, which previously signifies 'word.' The meaning seems to be—Who is a wise man? A man who has a right understanding of the Word of God.

169. Eccles. viii. 2–5.] There is a remarkable agreement between what is said in these verses and that which is said by the Apostle in Rom. xiii. 1–5. Here ver. 2 agrees with Rom. xiii. 5; verses 3 and 4 agree with Rom. xiii. 2 and latter part of ver. 4; and here the former part of ver. 5 agrees with Rom. xiii. and the former part of ver. 4.

170. Eccles. x. 5.] *i.e.*, To Jerusalem, eminently called the City: the city to which all Israel was to go three times a year to worship God, and wait on Him for His blessings in the Temple. The meaning of the Spirit of God probably is this—that although there be innumerable kinds of sinners that are intending to go to heaven, and endeavouring to find out ways of their own thither, consistent with their wickedness and the folly that reigns in them, and innumerable such ways are invented, yet they all labour in vain. "Strait is the gate," &c. "Many there be that seek," &c.

SONG OF SOLOMON.

171. Sol. Song v. 2—"I sleep, but my heart waketh."] It may be well explained by these words of Christ to His disciples: Matt. xxvi. 41—"The spirit indeed is willing, but the flesh is weak."

ISAIAH.

172. Isa. iii. 10, 11.] What is contained in these two verses seems to be an introduction to what follows. Through the former part of this book, Isaiah proceeds in his preaching, to the end of chap. xxxv., agreeably to the direction given him of God in this verse,—interchangeably threatening terrible judgments to the wicked that were in Israel, and revealing glorious promises to the righteous among them; as from hence to the end of this chapter the prophet says to the wicked it shall be ill with him; in the next chapter he says to the righteous it shall be well with him. In the first twelve verses of the VIth chapter he again says to the wicked it shall be ill with him; and chap. vi. 13, and vii. 1–16, he says to the righteous it shall be well with him; but ver. 8 is a threatening to the wicked, ver. 17 to end to the wicked; chap. viii. 1–8, to the wicked; verses 9, 10, the righteous; ver. 14, part to the righteous and part to the wicked; ver. 15, to the wicked; verses 16, 17, to the righteous; from thence

to end, to the wicked; chap. ix. 1–7, to the righteous; ver. 8 to end, and chap. x. 1–6, to the wicked; ver. 6 to end, and chaps. xi., xii., xiii., and xiv., to the righteous; chap. xxii. 1–19, to the wicked; ver. 20 to end, to the righteous; chap. xxiv. 1–12, to the wicked; ver. 13 to end, and chap. xxv. and xxvi. 1–9, to the righteous; verses 10, 11, to the wicked; ver. 12 to end, and chap. xxvii., to the righteous; chap. xxviii. 1–4, to the wicked; verses 5, 6, to the righteous; verses 7, 8, to the wicked; verses 9, 10, to the righteous; verses 11–15, to the wicked; ver. 16, to the righteous; verses 17–22, to the wicked; ver. 23 to end, to righteous; chap. xxix. 1–4, to the wicked; verses 5–8, to the righteous; verses 9–16, to the wicked; ver. 17 to end, to the righteous; chap. xxx. 1–7, to the wicked; ver. 18 to the end, to the righteous; chap. xxxi. 1–3, to the wicked; ver. 4 to end, and chap. xxxii. 1–8, to the righteous; verses 9–14, to the wicked; ver. 15 to end, and chap. xxxiii. 1–6, to the righteous; verses 7-14, to the wicked; verses 15-17, to the righteous; verses 17, 18, to the wicked; ver. 19 to end, and chap. xxxiv. and xxxv. to the righteous.

173. Isa. ix. 6—"Counsellor."] Not only because He is man's Counsellor, but God's. See Gen. i. 26.

174. Isa. ix. 6.—"Wonderful."] Which shews that this child that was to be born is the same person with the Angel that spake to Manoah, that ascended in the flame of the altar; for He tells Manoah that His name is 'Secret,' (Judges xiii. 18.) The word is the same in the original that here is translated 'Wonderful,' and that person was God, for He is there spoken of as being God, (verses 22, 23;) so that here is a prophecy of God's being born, which agrees with the names that follow—'The mighty God,' 'The everlasting Father,' and to the name that He is called by in the last preceding chapter but one, in the 14th verse—viz., 'Emmanuel.' And it also confirms that the child here intended is the person that was to be a sacrifice for sin, because this person, whose name was Secret and Wonderful, ascended before Manoah in the flame of the altar; and so it argues it to be the same person that wrestled with Jacob, for when Jacob enquired after His name He answers, "Wherefore enquirest thou after my name?" in like manner as He answered Manoah when he enquired after His name. It argues it also to be that Son of God spoken of in Prov. xxx. 4; see also Rev. xix. 12.

175. Isa. xvi. 2.] The comparison is to be understood of such birds as the children of Israel used to keep, as doves particularly, which, if they were turned and shut out of their dove-houses, would not know what to do nor where to go, no more than Noah's dove when sent out of the Ark. As to wild birds, the difficulty was not such with them which had no particular house or certain fixed home, and if they were turned out of one nest could make another. See Hosea vii. 11, and xi. 11.

176. Isa. xxx. 8–10.] Such passages as these are a notable evidence that these books of the prophet were not forged by the Jews, and were not received with such respect and made so much of by them, but because they were of Divine authority.

177. Isa. xxxiii. 21.] Jerusalem had no considerable river running by it, as the royal cities in Egypt and Assyria and Chaldea and most great cities had; nothing but the brook Kedron, upon which account their enemies despised them: nor did the children of Israel deal much in ships, as Egypt and Assyria and Chaldea did, and carried on their wars in considerable measure by them. (See chap. xliii. 14.) But in God there shall be more than an equivalent; the glorious Jehovah will be to Jerusalem a "place of broad rivers and streams." Thus we read of a river running through the New Jerusalem. But if there be "broad rivers" and "streams" in Jerusalem may not these yield an easy access to the fleet of the invader? No! These are rivers and streams in which shall go no galley with oars or gallant ship. If God Himself be the river, it must needs be inaccessible to the enemy. God's people need not fear though the earth be removed, for there is a river that makes glad the city of God. (Ps. xlvi.) [See HENRY.]

178. Isa. xxxiv. 5.] Reference to the terrible destruction of the angels in heaven.

179. Isa. xxxiv. 16.] The book of the Lord here meant is this Book, or the book of this prophecy wherein the things in the two foregoing verses are mentioned, as appears by comparing these words with the foregoing and following. When it is said here, "Seek ye out of the book of the Lord," &c., the meaning is, hereafter, when the event shall prove whether this prophecy be true or no, then read this book and examine this prophecy and compare it with the event and see if anything fails. See if any one of these "doleful creatures" fails of posessing Idumea and Bozrah, and every one with their mate—*i.e.*, see if the prophecy be not most exactly fulfilled.—Corol. Hence the Books of the Prophets should be regarded by the Church of God as part of the Canon of Sacred Scriptures as well as the Books of Moses. They are the "books of the Lord," or Biblia.

180. Isa. xxxvii. 38.] God pours contempt not only on this great king, but on his god. He had cast great contempt on the God of Israel, and made as though He were unable to defend Jerusalem from his power, as chap. xxxvi. 18–20, and in verses 10–13 of this chapter. This God of Israel that he so despised, as though much inferior to his god, now shews how unable his god is to defend him, by ordering it so that he should be slain in the very temple of his god in whom he trusted, in his sanctuary and in the secret of his presence, and that while he was there worshipping of him and imploring his help under his present low and distressed circumstances, and slain, too, by his own sons.

181. Isa. xxxviii. 18, 19—"For the grave cannot praise Thee," &c.] The death that is here spoken of is that which is death indeed, or is properly so called. The state of death is here spoken of as it is originally, and as being still a state of death, and not as it is changed by redemption from a state of death to a state of life, or so as to be made a more glorious rest of life. Hezekiah speaks of

that death wherein men do really die or are truly dead, and not that improperly so called, wherein men are a thousand times more alive than they were before, and are immortal and beyond a possibility of dying. Death as it is originally, and when it is properly death, is a state wherein men cannot "praise God" nor "celebrate Him," nor "hope for His truth." It is a state of evil without any good: it is, Job says, "A land of darkness as darkness itself, and the shadow of death without any order, and where the light is as darkness." It is a state wherein there is no good done, no good enjoyed, no good hoped for. It is a state of absolute emptiness of any good or principle, happiness or hope. They that are in hell are in such a state of death. Such was death originally. Such was death as it was threatened to our first parents; and very commonly when death is spoken of in the Old Testament it is in this notion of it. For the change of a state of death into a state of more glorious life was not fully revealed under the Old Testament. "Life and immortality are brought to light *in the gospel*." It is under this notion that death seems to be spoken of in Eccles. ix. 4-6, where it is said that "a living dog is better than a dead lion," and that "the dead have no more a reward," and that "they have no more a portion for ever in any thing done under the sun." Hezekiah did not mean that they that are redeemed from the power of the grave, they that get the victory over death and shall never die, (as Christ promises to believers,) "shall not praise God, nor hope for His truth." We see in this instance that the better men are the more terrible would it make death if there were no future state. For the better they are the more they love God. Good men have found the fountain of good. Those men who have a high degree of love to God do greatly delight in God. They have experience of a much better happiness in life than others, and therefore it must be more bitter to them to have their being eternally extinct by death. Thus this seemed to be above all other things the sting of Hezekiah's affliction in his expectation of death, that he should no more have any opportunity of communion with God, and of worshipping and praising Him, as appears by these two verses, together with the 11th and 22d verses, there not being at that time a clear and full revelation of a future state. Hence we may strongly argue a future state, for it is not to be supposed that God would make man such a creature as to be capable of looking forward beyond death, and capable of knowing and loving and delighting in Him, as the fountain of all good, and should make it his duty so to do, which will necessarily increase in him a dread of annihilation, and an eager desire of immortality, and yet so order it that that desire should be disappointed, so that his loving his Creator should in some sense make him the more miserable.

182. Isa. xli. 8—"Chosen."] This epithet especially belongs to Jacob rather than to Isaac or Abraham, because God 'chose' him before Esau his brother, though they were children of the same parents and twins in the womb together, and though Jacob was the

youngest; and chose them before they were born, or either of them had done good or evil.

183. Isa. xlii. 10-12.] The songs of the Lord of old were very much confined to the Temple at Jerusalem. When the Jews were in a "strange land" they hung their harps on the willows, and could not sing the Lord's song. (Ps. cxxxvii. 2-4.) Now the songs of holy joy and praise shall be sung all the world over. The Gentile nations shall share equally with the Jews in their testament blessings, and therefore shall join in the New Testament praises and acts of worship. The conversion of the Gentiles is often foretold under this notion of their singing praises with God's people, as appears by Rom. xv. 9-11. See Isa. xxiv. 16.

184. Isa. xliii. 21-28.] In this prophecy of the great gospel salvation, the freeness of God's grace in it, as not being at all for our righteousness, is largely insisted on here in the 21st verse, and also in the 4th and 7th and 25th verses, and beginning of chap. xliv. The sovereign good pleasure of God and His electing love is represented as the grand original of all those blessings, and in the 22d and following verses is particularly shewn how it is not and cannot be for any sacrifice offered by those that are the subjects of these blessings, or any righteousness, or anything given, offered or done by them, or anything whatsoever of their own, (ver. 26,) and it is particularly shewn that they have nothing of their own but sins either in themselves or in their ancestors. When the children of Israel were redeemed out of Egypt, and had corn given them, which was a great type of the gospel redemption, and care was taken to instruct the people that it was not for their righteousness. So here when the redemption of the children of Israel out of Babylon is spoken of, (ver. 14,) another great type of gospel redemption, and that redemption is prophesied of under that type; great care is also taken to inform the Church that it is not for their righteousness. Thus the doctrine of justification by free grace without the works of the Law, or our own righteousness, is the doctrine both of the Old and New Testament, and this confirms it that when the Apostle so much insists on justification without the works of the Law, he means without any moral goodness of ours whatsoever. Justification is the thing here especially spoken of, as appears by verses 25, 26. See chap. xlviii. 9-11, with the context.

185. Isa. xlvi. 1-7.] Bel and Nebo, the gods of Babylon, were first carried by men on their shoulders, (ver. 7,) and then afterwards when Babylon was destroyed they were carried by the beasts. When the Medes and Persians destroyed Babylon they took the cattle of Babylon, and made them carry the gods of Babylon away into captivity, and they were a great burden to the poor cattle, for the images were made of gold and silver, (ver. 6,) and they were very great and heavy, and these gods of Babylon were not able to deliver either the men or so much as the beasts of the city. They were called the protectors of both. [But yet they] must go into captivity; yea, they themselves must go into captivity. They not only could not preserve the cattle

from being led away captive, but they could not deliver them from that grievous circumstance of their captivity, of carrying them who were so heavy a burden to them. It was quite otherwise with the God of Israel. He did not need to be supported and borne by His people, much less by their beasts. But, on the contrary, His people were supported by Him. He carried them from the womb, and even to hoar hairs. (Verses 3, 4.)

186. Isa. xlix. 23—"And kings," &c.]—*i.e.*, to nurse thy children, thy sons and daughters, (spoken of in the foregoing verse,) that the Gentiles shall bring in their arms, and upon their shoulders. It is not meant that kings shall stand in the relation of nursing-fathers, and queens be nursing-mothers to thee. For that hardly will agree to what follows—"They shall bow down," &c., which does not so well suit with the relation of fathers and mothers as of servants. It is meant they shall be thy nourishers and nurses, not *to* thee, but *for* thee, to thy children. Tutors and nurses are a sort of servants in great houses; and that a sort of servants or ministers are meant here is confirmed from chap. lx. 10, 16.

187. Isa. lii. 15—"The kings shall shut," &c.]—*i.e.*, they shall be silent, attending to His wonderful doctrine and instructions as it follows, "for that which had not been told them," &c. They shall shut their mouths as learners, in acknowledgment of His superior wisdom, and as a testimony of their desirousness to hear and learn, as Job says, chap. xxix. 21, 22. They shall be silent also in token of their admiration [= wonder.]

188. Isa. liii. 11—"By His knowledge."] The word for 'knowledge' here is very often used for 'righteousness,' 'holiness,' and 'piety.' See Job xxi. 22, and xxxiii. 3, and xxxvi. 12; Ps. cxix. 66; Prov. i. 4, 7, 22, 29, and ii. 5, 6, 10, and v. 2, and viii. 9, 10, and ix. 10, and x. 14, and xi. 9, and xii. 1, and xiii. 15, 16, and xiv. 7, 18, and xv. 7, 14, and xviii. 15, and xix. 25, 27, and xx. 15, and xxi. 11, and xxii. 12, and xxiii. 12, and xxiv. 5, and xxx. 3; Eccles. ii. 21, and vii. 12; Isa. v. 13, and xi. 2, and xxviii. 9, and xxxiii. 6; Jer. iii. 15, and xxii. 16; Hosea iv. 1, 6, and vi. 6. Besides, many places where the verb this noun comes from, is used in an agreeable sense, concerning which I have not examined the Concordance; and other words of like signification. But Isa. xlii. 19–21, is particularly worthy of observation.

189. Isa. li. 4—"Hearken," &c.] Here seems to be a prophecy of a new revelation to be made of God's mind and will, and a new dispensation or establishment of religion, for any constitution or establishment by Divine revelation is called a Law in the Old Testament. So that gracious Covenant, and these free promises established to Abraham, is called a Law. (Ps. cv. 8, &c.) So the whole of the revelation of God's will is called a Law throughout the 119th Psalm. Counsel and advice is sometimes called a Law: Prov. i. 8—"Forget not the Law of thy mother," and vi. 20, and chap. xiii. 14—"The Law of the wise is a fountain of life." As the first Law went out of Mount Sinai, so the second went out of Mount Sion; Isa. ii. 3, and

Micah iv. 2, speaking of gospel times—"For out of Zion," &c. It might as well have been translated "a Law shall go forth out of Zion," as here it is said, a Law shall proceed from Me; for the word in both places is without any diversity; and when it is said, the Law shall proceed or go forth out of Zion, it is meant that a Law shall be given at Mount Zion in the same manner as it is said in Deut. xxxiii. 2. As there it is said, "The Law shined forth from Mount Paran, and that from His right hand went a fire of Law for them," (for so it is in the original)—*i.e.*, to enlighten them. (See note *in the place.*) So here it is said, "A Law shall proceed from Me, and I will make My judgment to rest for a light of the people." We find that Mount Sinai and Mount Sion are opposed one to another by the Apostle in this respect, that as the Law went forth out of the one, so the glorious gospel went forth from the other. (Heb. xii. 18–22 and 25–27.) This new Law went forth out of Mount Sion or Jerusalem in two respects —(1.) As it went forth from the spiritual Mount Sion, from heaven and the Church of God, (Heb. xii. 25;) and also as it first went forth from Jerusalem when the Spirit was poured out on the Apostles on the day of Pentecost, which was the same day that the Law was given at Sinai, and a day kept in commemoration of that event. See 1 Chron. xxiii. 26.

190. Isa. liii. 2.] This verse has respect to Christ's appearance in mean and low circumstances, without outward pomp and splendour. Great outward glory is in Scripture often compared to a tree growing high and large, and flourishing in its pride, (Ps. xxxvii. 35; Dan. iv. 10, &c.; Isa. x. 33, 34; Ezek. xxxi. 3, 4, &c.; Isa. ii. 13 with context, and Job xxix. 19, 20;) and therefore Christ's being destitute of earthly glory, is [represented] by His being "a root out of a dry ground," not like a tree planted on a fat soil or by streams of water, that flourishes and grows large, and makes a great show. Christ is in Scripture often compared to a root, plant, or branch. The Jews expected such a branch as this; but, on the contrary, He is a root out of a dry ground, that grows low and spreads but little and makes no gay appearance. It was a low bush, and not a mighty tree, that was seen burning on Mount Sinai and was not consumed, which was a type of Jesus Christ. The same thing is signified by His being "without form, or comeliness, or beauty." Earthly pomp and glory of wealth, power, and magnificence is called 'comeliness' in Scripture, as Ezek. xxvii. 10, and so it is called 'beauty,' (2 Sam. i. 19; Isa. xiii. 19, xxviii. 1; Ezek. xxvii. 3, 4, 11, xxviii. 12, 17.)

191. Addition to Isa. liii. 2.] Particularly we find the pomp and magnificence of great earthly princes is compared to the stateliness and beauty of a great, tall, spreading, flourishing tree in a fruitful soil, with a multitude of waters at the root, (Ezek. xxxi. 2–10; compare Deut. iv. 12; Isa. x. 33; Ps. xxxvii. 35,) and this stately flourishing appearance of such a tree, called its beauty or comeliness, (verses 3, 7–9;) and therefore here, when the Messiah is spoken of as being not like such a stately flourishing tree, with many waters at the root, but as a low tree or bush, and weak tender plant, and root out of a

dry ground, or having no waters at the root, it is natural that we should understand that the Messiah should come without this pomp and glory of earthly princes; yea, in a state and with an appearance that should be the reverse of it.

192. Isa. lvi. 3, 4, &c.] Here is plainly a prophecy of the abrogating of some of the Law of Moses. In gospel times [this shall be,] or particularly those in Deut. xxiii. 1–3. See 1 Chron. xxiii. 6; Jer. iii. 16, 17.

193. Isa. lxv. 20—"Child . . . hundred years"]—*i.e.*, though it dies in childhood, shall die with the attainments of one a hundred years old—a great happiness to be old—the child shall be fully happy. "Accursed,"—*i.e.*, though he live till he be a hundred years old, though he seems to prosper and be let alone, yet the curse shall overtake him. (See Eccles. viii. 12, and vi. 3–6.)

194. Isa. lxvi. 1—"The heaven is my throne, and the earth is my footstool."] The mercy-seat in the Temple is no longer God's throne; but heaven and the ark and temple are no longer God's footstool, as they used to be called. (1 Chron. xxviii. 2; Ps. xcix. 5, cxxxii. 7, 8; Lam. ii. 21; Isa. lx. 13.) The glorious times shall come wherein the whole habitable world shall be blessed with as honourable tokens of God's presence, not only as the Land of Canaan, but as the Temple; yea, as the holy of holies and the ark that had God's glory upon it. See Jer. iii. 16, 17; Isa. lx. 2, ii. 5, 6; Rev. xxi. 23, 24; also compare Haggai ii. 7; Isa. vi. 1, 3.

JEREMIAH.

195. Jer. xvii. 16, 18.] What we find in these verses is a confirmation that when the prophet Jeremiah, and other inspired penmen of the Old Testament, imprecated judgments on their enemies, those parts of their writings are not of private interpretation, or that they did therein express their private inclinations and desires; but spake prophetically the mind [of God;] cursed them in the name of the Lord, or foretold that these judgments should come. For here Jeremiah, in ver. 16, solemnly appeals to God that he had not desired the woeful day. But yet, in ver. 18, he prays that the evil day might be brought on his enemies.

196. Jer. xxvi. 9.] That which they persecute the prophet Jeremiah for, is the same thing that they charged as a great crime upon Stephen, and for which they put him to death. (See Acts vi. 13, 14.)

197. Jer. xx. 14, &c.] How great an evidence is to be gathered from this, and other like passages of the Old Testament, of a future state of reward to the saints. Jeremiah was a man of affliction in this life. It is evident that as long as he lived he met with opposition, hatred, and continual affliction, so that he was heartily weary of life

and wished he had never been born. This affliction was followed with no remarkable alteration from affliction to prosperity, as it was in Job; but while he lived, he lived to see nothing but those things that were most grievous to his heart, which made his being in this world far worse than no being. Now, if there be no future state, how is this consistent with the frequent declarations of God in the Old Testament, that those that fear Him are blessed and happy; and His promises, that it shall be well with them, that He will be their defence and exceeding great reward, &c., which the Old Testament is full of; and with what God said and promised to Jeremiah in particular, (chap. i. 8, 18, 19, xv. 11;) and also with the promises God makes by Jeremiah to the righteous, which he applies to him in this very context, (verses 11–13)?

EZEKIEL.

198. Ezek. vii. 12—"Let not the buyer rejoice, nor the seller mourn."] Here it may be asked, What occasion would the seller here have to mourn more than the buyer, if there had been no captivity approaching? When men make bargains, both buyer and seller aim at their own advantage. Answer: The prophet here has respect to buyers and sellers of inheritances. Inheritances were not wont to be sold in Israel, unless a man was become poor and was obliged to sell his inheritance, and it was looked upon as a great calamity to a man when he was thus obliged to sell his inheritance; and therefore God, in mercy and tenderness to them, required that the land should not be sold for ever, but that a redemption should be granted. (Lev. xxv. 23–25.) But at this time, neither had the seller any occasion to mourn nor the buyer to rejoice, for it made no alteration in the circumstances of one or the other, because the whole Land was about to be broken up and left desolate, and they were all to be carried away out of it into captivity.

199. Ezek. ix. 5, 6.] It is a great evidence that infants are guilty of sin,* that when these destroying angels were sent on that errand to execute God's fury upon the people, (ver. 8,) and that reason was given for it, that their iniquity required such terrible vengeance, and that it was a just recompense of their sin, (ver. 10,)—I say that when these angels came on such an errand, and also had express direction to spare some, to avoid them with great care and not come nigh them, yet they are directed to smite and slay utterly without pity all the rest, young and old, and even little children. Those that they are with such great care to except and not come near, are excepted expressly because they had approved themselves not partakers in the sins of the city; and therefore who can imagine that at the same time orders

* Query: Rather involved in the guilt and penalty of the Fall?—G.

should be given to smite and slay utterly, without their eye sparing or having pity, those that were a great deal more evidently free from having any share in the sin of the city, because they are not capable of sinning, which is the case of little children if they have no original sin? This order would never, surely, have been given with such circumstances, merely for the sin of the parents, if they had no sin that was properly their own, as we may be the rather assured, because God Himself did so fully and largely declare to this prophet that children would not die for the iniquity of the father, nor for any iniquity that they were not properly guilty of, in chap. xviii. of Ezekiel.

200. Ezek. x. 19.] The *Shekinah* or 'glory' of the God of Israel made four removes: first, to the threshold of the house or Temple, (chap. ix. 3;) secondly, to the east gate of the court of the Temple, which is mentioned here; thirdly, from hence to the top of Mount Olivet, (chap. xi. 23;) lastly, from thence into heaven, (ver. 24.)

201. Ezek. xiv. 14.] This shews that it is no new notion, lately first thought of in the world, that one may be favoured of God for the sake of another's righteousness. It was old at Ezekiel's time, and it is not spoken of here as a false or unreasonable notion, as though there were no such thing as one's being accepted for the sake of another's righteousness; but only the wickedness of the Land was so great that the righteousness of these eminently holy men would not be sufficient to avail for them, or at most, that the righteousness of men is of so little worthiness that it is not sufficient to recommend any more than themselves. But the righteousness of Christ is sufficient. It is so excellent and worthy in God's account, that it is sufficient to procure favour for the vilest of sinners. Herein is Christ a more excellent and sufficient Mediator than Noah, Daniel, or Job, or the most holy and eminent of mere men. Noah was in the old world, but saved only himself and his family. Daniel was in Babylon when it was destroyed, and only saved himself. Job saved only himself by his righteousness, when all his children were destroyed. Each lived in a very degenerate time. Noah in the old world. Job when all nations were falling away to idolatry. Daniel in a most degenerate time in Israel.

202. Ezek. xvi. 6.] Doubtless it is something very remarkable and wonderful that God would here signify by this emphatical repetition; and the emphasis lies partly in these words, "when thou wast in thy blood," the circumstances that she was in when God shewed mercy on her; and partly in these words, "I said unto thee, Live," shewing the wonderfulness and excellency of the favour God shewed her in these circumstances. The thing that God would have so much remarked, and to have such special notice taken of, is the absolute freeness and sovereignty of His grace in bestowing life upon her. He said to her, "Live," when she was polluted in her blood, while she was in her sin, and so not for her righteousness, or in anywise moved by her moral purity. God is not moved by this either in converting or justifying the sinner, for He both renews and justifies the ungodly. (Titus iii. 3-7; 1 Cor. vi. 11; Eph. ii. 1-13; Rom. iv. 5.) This also signifies

God's shewing mercy to the sinner when he is helpless, for what is more helpless than an infant cast out in its blood? ["I said unto thee, Live."] This signifies that life in her was wholly the effect of God's power, and wholly the fruit of His mere good pleasure, which is further signified by ver. 8—"Thy time was the time of love."

203. Ezek. xvi. 49—"Poor and needy."] Hence we learn that the poor, though wicked, are the objects of our charity. For it is not probable that the poor and needy in Sodom here spoken of were only godly persons, where there were scarce any who were righteous, and not ten in the whole city, and it may be none but Lot; who was not poor but rich.

204. Ezek. xxiv. 6, 7.] The Law required that they should not eat flesh with the blood, but that the blood should be poured on the ground and covered with dust. (Lev. xvii. 13.) Flesh dressed and eaten with the blood was polluted, abominable flesh. The people of Jerusalem are here compared to such flesh in the caldron. Her blood is in the midst of her; she is like a pot where scum is in the midst of it. When bloody flesh is boiled in a pot, the blood rises in a scum. The sin of the people is compared in these words to two things: (1.) To the blood and scum, which is the pollution and abomination of bloody flesh. (2.) To the wickedness of those that shed blood of men, and did not cover it with earth, as they were required to do the blood of beasts, but were so open and daring in it as to set it on the top of a rock.

205. Ezek. xlvi. 15.] Here is mention made of a morning sacrifice, but no evening sacrifice; because in that glorious time here spoken of there will be a continual and unceasing day, but no evening: intimated by that in Isaiah—"Thy sun shall no more go down," &c.; and that in Zechariah—"It shall be one day; not day and night: but at evening-time it shall be light;" and typified by the sun's standing still in Joshua's time.

DANIEL.

206. Dan. vii. 5—"Three ribs in the mouth of it," &c.] These ribs seem to be the bones of his prey. The ribs rather than other bones were represented perhaps, because the ribs are those bones which are next the vitals, and the sight of them did naturally excite the idea of his tearing and devouring the vitals of his prey; not one rib, but three at once are seen in his mouth, the better to represent his extraordinary voraciousness.

NEW TESTAMENT.

ST MATTHEW.

1. ii. 10—"*When they saw the star*, they rejoiced with exceeding great joy."] The wise men that sought Christ travelled through a vast howling wilderness, full of pits and drought and serpents, hideous rocks and mountains, even the desert of Arabia, before they had this 'joy' of seeing that star; and soon after they enquired of the priests, the star arose—which well represents what commonly is before persons have that joy which arises from the discovery of the Person represented by this star, even Christ, "the bright and morning star." [Rev. xxii. 16, compared with ii. 28.]

2. ii. 11—"And when they were come into the house, they saw the young child with Mary His mother, and fell down and worshipped Him: *and when they had opened their treasures, they presented unto Him gifts; gold, and frankincense, and myrrh*."] Gifts proper to be offered to a King and a God: gold, such as was wont to be given to kings; frankincense and myrrh, the chief ingredients of the incense that was offered to God in the Temple. This was a specimen or earnest of the fulfilment of that prophecy, Isa. lx. 6—"The multitude of camels shall cover thee, the dromedaries of Midian and Ephah; all they from Sheba shall come: *they shall bring gold and incense;* and they shall shew forth the praises of the Lord." [By these 'gifts,' too,] the charge of their journey into Egypt was provided for. [See Matt. ii. 13.]

3. ii. 16—"Then Herod, when he saw that he was mocked of the wise men, was exceeding wroth, and sent forth, *and slew all the children* that were in Bethlehem, and in all the coasts thereof, from two years old and under, according to the time which he had diligently enquired of the wise men."] Herod's slaying all the young children: this was a just punishment of the people of Bethlehem for their treatment of the blessed Virgin and her young child, by inhumanly refusing to entertain her in their houses when her travail came upon her, thereby exposing the life of her child; and not only refusing to entertain the Virgin in travail, but suffering her afterwards to remain in the stable with her child. For this treatment of this Divine infant and His

mother, God, by a terrible judgment, destroys their infants, and dreadfully afflicts their mothers. They were inhuman and cruel to the blessed Virgin and her young child, and they are justly punished with the effects of dreadful inhumanity and cruelty executed on their young children.

4. v. 8, 9—" Blessed are *the pure in heart:* for they shall see God. Blessed are the peacemakers: for they shall be called the children of God."] Christians should be first 'pure,' then 'peaceable:' James iii. 17—" The wisdom that is from above is *first pure, then peaceable;*" . . . [*cf.*] St Mark ix. 29—" And He said unto them, This kind can come forth by nothing, but by *prayer and fasting.*" *

5. v. 9—" Blessed are the *peacemakers:* for they shall be called *the children of God.*"] Because they are therein like Christ, 'the child of God,' the Prince of Peace, and the great Peacemaker; and are of a peaceable spirit, as becomes those that are brethren in God's family.

6. v. 1–11—" And seeing the multitudes, He went up into a mountain; and when He was set, His disciples came unto Him: and He opened His mouth, and taught them, saying, Blessed are the poor in spirit: for theirs is the kingdom of heaven. Blessed are they that mourn: for they shall be comforted. Blessed are the meek: for they shall inherit the earth. Blessed are they which do hunger and thirst after righteousness: for they shall be filled. Blessed are the merciful: for they shall obtain mercy. Blessed are the pure in heart: for they shall see God. Blessed are the peacemakers: for they shall be called the children of God. Blessed are they which are persecuted for righteousness' sake: for theirs is the kingdom of heaven. Blessed are ye, when men shall revile you, and persecute you, and shall say all manner of evil against you falsely for My sake."] In these Beatitudes, Christ seems to have a special design to correct those corrupt notions the Jews entertained of the kingdom of heaven, or the kingdom that the Messiah was about to erect. As in ver. 3 He has respect to the expectation they had in the Messiah's days of enjoying great outward wealth, and being made much of by the Messiah, as more excellent and honourable and worthy than other nations, and so vaunting themselves in these things that should greatly gratify their pride and covetousness; in ver. 4 He has respect to their expectations of great worldly mirth and pleasure and festivity; in ver. 5, He has respect to an imagination that military courage and martial exploits, and fierce revenge on the Romans, and other Gentile nations that had injured them, were to introduce their glory under the reign of the Messiah; in ver. 5, (also,) He has respect to their carnal desires of worldly possessions and sensitive appetites, which they hoped would be abundantly gratified in the Messiah's days; in ver. 6, He has respect to their expectation of scenes of slaughter and desolation in the Gentile world, which they expected and hoped to see and have a hand in in the Messiah's day; in ver. 8, He has respect to those impure and luxurious delights which

* By a slip the reference is given to ver. 30.—G.

usually attend worldly victories, and princes' courts, and great and flourishing earthly kingdoms, which things they supposed the Messiah would introduce; in ver. 9, He has respect to those desolating wars and bloody battles with which they supposed the Messiah would set up and propagate His kingdom; in ver. 10, He has still respect to their expectation of nothing but pomps, pleasures, wealth, and triumphs in the kingdom of heaven, or of the Messiah; in ver. 11, He has respect to their expectation of being advanced to great honour, as a kind of priests and princes, under the Messiah their King, having the Gentiles their slaves, and even their kings and great men bowing down and licking up the dust of their feet. That Christ has a design in these Beatitudes to give them right notions of the kingdom of heaven is manifest, for He several times in them makes express mention of the kingdom of heaven, as ver. 3 and ver. 10; and ver. 5 speaks of inheriting the earth, which His hearers doubtless understood of that inheritance of the earth and reigning over the world that is promised to God's people in the days of the Messiah; and that being comforted which He promises, (ver. 4,) they doubtless understood Him of that ancient prophecy, such as Isa. xl. at beginning, and others, [which] was commonly called among them the consolation of Israel—viz., the comfort that should be introduced by the Messiah; and in the promise (ver. 6) of being filled Christ probably has respect to such promises made in the Old Testament, concerning what God would do for His people in the Messiah's days: that they should be filled as bowls and as the corners of the altars, (Zech. ix. 15;) that they should be abundantly filled or satisfied with the goodness of God's house, and that He would make them drink of the river of His pleasures, (Ps. xxxvi. 8, and lxv. 4;) that they should get that which is good, and delight themselves in fatness: Isa. lv. 2—"Wherefore do ye spend money for that which is not bread? and your labour for that which satisfieth not? hearken diligently unto Me, and eat ye that which is good, and let your soul delight itself in fatness." That they should eat when others were hungry, and drink when others were thirsty: Isa. lxv. 13—"Therefore thus saith the Lord God, Behold, My servants shall eat, but ye shall be hungry: behold, My servants shall drink, but ye shall be thirsty: behold, My servants shall rejoice, but ye shall be ashamed." That they should be satisfied with God's goodness, and their soul satiated with fatness: Jer. xxxi. 14—"And I will satiate the soul of the priests with fatness, and My people shall be satisfied with My goodness, saith the Lord;" and that He would replenish every sorrowful soul: Jer. xxxi. 25—"For I have satiated the weary soul, and I have replenished every sorrowful soul." That bread should be given them: Isa. xxxiii. 16—"He shall dwell on high; his place of defence shall be the munitions of rocks; bread shall be given him, his waters shall be sure." That their poor should be satisfied with bread: Ps. cxxxii. 15—"I will abundantly bless her provision: I will satisfy her poor with bread;" and many other parallel prophecies: and in the promise of obtaining mercy, (ver. 7,) Christ probably has respect to such promises made to God's people in the Messiah's time, as those in Isa. xlix. 10, liv. 10, and lx. 10, and in other parallel places; and in the promise of seeing God, in ver. 8, Christ probably has respect to such prophecies concerning the glory of the Messiah's times, as that then God's glory should be revealed. Their eye should see the King in His beauty. They should see eye to eye. That they should walk in the light of the Lord, and walk in the light of God's countenance, and the like; and God's being their light instead of the sun: and in the promise of being the children of God, (ver. 9,) there is great reason to think Christ has respect to the many prophecies of the Messiah's kingdom, that speak of God's people being then especially owned and treated as His children, His sons and daughters.

7. v. 18—"For verily I say unto you, Till heaven and earth pass, one jot or one tittle shall in no wise pass from the law, till all be fulfilled."] The manner and style in which Christ taught, as well as the way in which He wrought miracles, were different from that of other prophets. Other prophets were wont to say, "Thus saith the Lord;" but Christ used to express Himself thus, "Verily I say unto you," as became the Lord Himself, the Lord that sent and inspired the prophets, and in whose name they spake and whose word they delivered.

8. vi. 10, 11—"Thy kingdom come. Thy will be done in earth, as it is in heaven. Give us this day our daily bread."] The order of these petitions is agreeable to the direction given in ver. 33—"Seek ye *first the kingdom of God*, and His righteousness; *and all these things shall be added unto you.*" So here Christ directs, first, to pray for 'the kingdom of God,' and then to pray for other things.

9. viii. 21—"And another of His disciples said unto Him, Lord, suffer me first to go and bury my father"]—*i.e.*, let me stay till my aged father is dead. He was not willing to follow Him yet, and pleads this as an excuse, that his father was old and needed his care; or he was dear to him, and he was loath to leave him while he was alive: but after he should be dead, he would be willing to follow Him.

10. x. 17—"But beware of men; for they will deliver you up to the councils, and they will scourge you in their synagogues."] To understand how this comes in, and how the particle 'but' connects it with what went before, it must be observed that Christ here explains Himself in what He said in the preceding verse. There He told them that He sent them forth as sheep in the midst of wolves; but, says He, beware of men: these are the wolves that I mean. It is men, and not wolves, I bid you beware of.

11. xi. 5—"The blind receive their sight, and the lame walk; the lepers are cleansed, and the deaf hear; the dead are raised up, and the poor have the gospel preached unto them." *Τυφλοὶ ἀναβλέπουσι, καὶ χωλοὶ περιπατοῦσι, λεπροὶ καθαρίζονται, καὶ κωφοὶ ἀκούουσι, νεκροὶ ἐγείρονται, καὶ πτωχοὶ εὐαγγελίζονται.*] By the poor seems pretty evidently to be meant "the poor in spirit." In the last effect

here mentioned the poor are evangelised; the manner of speaking and connexion of the words lead us to suppose there is the like relation and opposition between the benefit and character of the subject of that benefit, as in the foregoing effects mentioned, such as between receiving light and darkness, a being raised up and death. The word εὐαγγελίζονται, 'evangelised,' implies not only being the subject of the preaching of the gospel, or the telling the good news, but a being encouraged, refreshed, and revived, and made joyful and happy by it; and between such a benefit and a being poor in spirit, of a broken heart, or heart mourning, humbled, being wretched, miserable, and undone in his own eyes, and despairing in the world and in himself. I say, a being evangelised in the sense mentioned has a like relation to such a qualification of the subject as sight has to blindness, light to darkness, walking to lameness, life to death. The poor's being evangelised is the last effect mentioned, it being that which crowns all, representing the main thing which Jesus comes into the world for, the blessed effect that He had respect to in all that He said and did, and the great thing of which the other things here mentioned were but types and representations. In these last words Christ has a plain reference to Isa. lxi. 1. In Luke iv. 18, Christ cites these words thus, "He hath anointed Me to preach the gospel to the poor."

12. xi. 30—"For My yoke is easy, and My burden is light."] These words have a relation to the words of the invitation. (Ver. 28.) The invitation is to them that labour and are burdened. A yoke is what is put on the necks of the cattle in order to their labouring, and when Christ says, "My burden is light," the word 'burden' is the noun of the verb or participle translated 'heavy burden.'

13. xii. 30—"He that is not with Me is against Me; and he that gathereth not with Me scattereth abroad."] The true reason of Christ's observing this in this place, where He is reproving the Pharisees' saying, that "He cast out devils by Beelzebub," is this, that these Pharisees, till now, appeared to exercise that kind of prudence, falsely so-called, which is commonly to be seen among them that count themselves wise and great men, who think it becomes them to let matters of religion much alone, and not to appear forward and zealous, or apt to shew their minds. When Christ appeared working great miracles, with which the multitude appeared much affected, and some appeared zealous to commence His disciples and followers, they thought it their prudence to hold their tongues till Christ proceeded so far in His wonderful works, and the esteem that He gained among the people, that they apprehended themselves in apparent danger of having their glory eclipsed, and of losing the esteem and honour of the people; and then they could bear it no longer. They openly shewed what was in their hearts before—viz., a bitter enmity against Christ, and that truly they had never been indifferent as they appeared.

14. xii. 49, 50—"And He stretched forth His hand toward His disciples, and said, Behold My mother and My brethren! For who-

soever shall do the will of My Father which is in heaven, the same is My brother, and sister, and mother."] The figure of speech Christ here uses will appear the more natural and beautiful, if it be considered that there were probably then sitting by, not only His male disciples, but also Mary Magdalene and Joanna (the wife of Chuza, Herod's steward) and Susanna, and many other women that were His disciples, who at that time attended Him, ministering to Him of their substance, as seems by Luke viii. 1-3, with ver. 21.

15. xiii. 32—"Which indeed is the least of all seeds; but when it is grown, it is the greatest among herbs, and becometh a tree, so that the birds of the air come and lodge in the branches thereof."] The least of the seeds that they used, or that they were wont to sow, in their land.

16. xiv. 24, 25—"But the ship was now in the midst of the sea, tossed with waves: for the wind was contrary. And in the fourth watch of the night Jesus went unto them, walking on the sea."] This which we are told of Christ shews what He was—viz., a Divine person. For it is spoken of in Job ix. 8, as a property or act of God, "that He treadeth on the waves of the sea." Christ here not only walks on the waters of the sea, but that when it is tossed with high waves, He treadeth on its boisterous waves. For it is said here that the ship was tossed with waves, and it is said in John vi. 18, that the sea arose by reason of a great wind that blew.

17. xiv. 24–27—"But the ship was now in the midst of the sea, tossed with waves: for the wind was contrary. And in the fourth watch of the night Jesus went unto them, walking on the sea. And when the disciples saw Him walking on the sea, they were troubled, saying, It is a spirit; and they cried out for fear. But straightway Jesus spake unto them, saying, Be of good cheer: it is I; be not afraid."] What we have here an account of seems livelily to represent what very frequently comes to pass to persons in the affair of their conversion. Christ did not appear unto them till they had been long tossed with a great tempest; the wind arose in the beginning of the night, and it was against them, and they had been rowing all night, and striving to get to the desired haven, and all to no purpose, so that by this time probably they were almost discouraged and just ready to yield the case, and see that it was utterly in vain for them to strive any more to reach their port. Then Christ in the latter post of the night appears to them, and comes to their help, and appears as one above their difficulties, walking in the boisterous waves that distressed and threatened to destroy them, treading them under His feet. So it commonly is with sinners under conviction before Christ appears for their help. They are first made sensible of their danger and brought unto great exercise and distress, and reduced to the last extremity, and to see that they can never reach the haven they seek of themselves. They are brought to yield their case as to their own strength, and then Christ appears as one that is above their guilt, and above all those evils that threaten to swallow them up, as it were treading under His feet those mighty waves that

encompass them on every side, that they are ready to sink in, and upon those raging waves that toss them and are ready to overwhelm them. These difficulties the disciples met with were in the night, a time of darkness, as Jacob's wrestling was in the night, signifying the darkness that persons meet with while under those convictions that are preparatory to conversion; and it is remarkable that the time when Christ appeared was near the breaking of the day, for it was in the fourth watch, which was the last post of the night. "Though weeping may continue for a night, yet joy comes in the morning." It seems to be an emblem of the light that arises to the soul after darkness, when Christ appears. This was the time when Christ arose from the dead, and this was the time when Jacob obtained the blessing after long wrestling. It is also worthy of notice that when Christ first appeared they did not know what it was, they were troubled at the sight, and said it is a spirit, and cried out for fear. So very often, at the first spiritual discoveries that persons have after great awakenings and distresses of conscience, they do not know what it is, they fear it is only a delusion, and are terribly afraid to receive it, as has been often seen in the time of the late extraordinary pouring out of the Spirit here in Northampton,

18. xvi. 23—"But He turned, and said unto Peter, Get thee behind Me, Satan; thou art an offence unto Me: for thou savourest not the things that be of God, but those that be of men."] We are not to understand it that Christ here calls Peter, Satan. No; Christ speaks to Satan, that He said had a hand in the matter, and that influenced Peter thus to think and speak. He speaks to Peter's indwelling sin, which was as it were the Devil in Peter. It was not an instance in Christ's severity towards Peter that He thus speaks, but His love and grace that He would not impute what Peter says to himself, but to Satan. He graciously makes a distinction between His disciple Peter and his indwelling corruption, as Paul says, Rom. vii. 20—"It is no more I, but sin that dwelleth in me."

19. xvi. 26.] Preciousness or value of the soul, or anything above other things, will appear by comparing it with other things, considering of it either as to be sold for them or to be bought with them. If it be considered as to be sold for them, then the preciousness of it above them appears in the unprofitableness of the bargain; if it be considered as to be bought with other things, then its superior value appears by their insufficiency to buy it. The preciousness of the soul is set forth in this verse both these ways, as being more precious than the whole world. It is first set forth by the unprofitableness of the bargain, in case that it should be sold for the whole world; and next it is set forth by the insufficiency of anything in the world, or of the whole world, to buy it or redeem it; and in that last expression —"What shall a man give?" &c. In the former part is set forth the insufficiency of the whole world to be received, in case that the soul be exchanged for other things. In the latter part is set forth the insufficiency of the whole world to be given, in case other things are to be exchanged for the soul.

20. xvii. 2—" And was transfigured before them: and His face did shine as the sun, and His raiment was white as the light."] This denoted who He was—viz., He that was spoken of in Dan. vii. 9, and Ps. civ. 2, 16–18.

21. xvii. 5—" While he yet spake, behold, a bright cloud overshadowed them: and behold a voice out of the cloud, which said, This is My beloved Son, in whom I am well pleased; hear ye Him."] This cloud was not bright merely as clouds are oftentimes very bright by the reflection of the light of the sun. But there was a more excellent and glorious brightness in it, which is a suitable symbol of the Divine presence, such as, perhaps, was in the Shekinah or cloud above the mercy-seat in the Tabernacle and Temple. Peter, speaking of the glory of this cloud, calls it " the excellent glory." (2 Pet. i. 17.) Luke says they feared as they entered into the cloud; it was of the appearance of Divine majesty and glory that was in the cloud.

22. xix. 17—" And He said unto him, Why callest thou Me good? there is none good but one, that is, God: but if thou wilt enter into life, keep the commandments."] Probably Christ, who knew what was in man, saw that this young man, though he had no notion of Christ's being a Divine person, and thought Him but a mere man, yet, thinking Him a prophet, came to Him, trusting in Him for eternal life in a manner that no mere man is to be trusted on, which is the reason why He says that to him, " Why callest thou Me good? there is none good but one, that is, God"—*i.e.*, there is none else who has a goodness that is to be depended upon but God. For Christ does not find fault simply with any man's being called 'good,' for He, using the same word, calls some men good, Himself, as Matt. xii. 25; so Luke xix. 17.

23. xxv. 12—" But He answered and said, Verily I say unto you, I know you not."] Rom. viii. 29—" For whom He did foreknow, He also did predestinate to be conformed to the image of His Son, that He might be the first-born among many brethren." To judge of the force of this expression, see Matt. xxv. 12; Deut. xxxiii. 9; Job ix. 21; Ps. xxxi. 7. In Exod. ii. 25—" God had respect unto them," in the original is, " God knew them." Thus the word in the Hebrew, is a kinsman or near friend, and also kindred and affinity, from the verb to know. See Job ix. 21, and Prov. xii. 10—" 'Regardeth' the life of his beast," in the original is, " 'Knoweth' the life of his beast."

24. xxv. 34—" Then shall the King say unto them on His right hand, Come, ye blessed of My Father, inherit the kingdom prepared for you from the foundation of the world."] That this has a special respect to the decree of election may be argued from Mark x. 40, and Matt. xx. 3. See Exod. xxiii. 20.

25. xxvi. 64—" Jesus saith unto him, Thou hast said: nevertheless, I say unto you, Hereafter shall ye see the Son of man sitting on the right hand of power, and coming in the clouds of heaven."] Christ's answer to the high priest is remarkable. The high priest asks whether He be the Son of God. He replies Yes; but says He, "Never-

theless, ye shall hereafter see the Son of man sitting," &c. He did not deny Himself to be the Son of man, though He preferred Himself to be the Son of God. He teaches the union of the human and Divine nature. It was wonderful, and what the high priest could not believe, that the Son of God should be arraigned as a criminal before His judgment-seat; and Christ tells him he should see another thing equally wonderful, and that is the Son of man sitting at the right hand of power, and coming in the clouds of heaven, sitting the Judge of the world, and be brought before His judgment-seat. Nevertheless though "I be the Son of *God*, yet ye shall see the Son of *man*, sitting on the right hand of power, and coming in the clouds of heaven."

26. xxvi. 65—"Then the high priest rent his clothes, saying, He hath spoken blasphemy; what further need have we of witnesses? behold, now ye have heard His blasphemy."] Contrary to that law, Lev. xxi. 10. This probably foreboded that the Levitical priesthood was soon to be abolished, their priestly garments to be rent, and they to be divested of the honours and prerogatives of their office.

27. xxviii. 9.] It may be pleasant and profitable to consider the various passions that these women felt in their hearts on this occasion. Christ was a person exceeding dear to them; and they lately had their hearts filled and overwhelmed with sorrow, upon the occasion of the cruel and ignominious death that they with their own eyes had seen Christ put to. (See chap. xxvii. 55, 56.) And they never expected to see Him alive any more; and they had with great art prepared precious ointment to anoint His body, and doubtless were much vexed that they could not have opportunity to do it, by the reason of the Sabbath coming on, till the third day after His death. And now they come very early,—the first day of the week,—greatly engaged in their minds to do it. But when they come there they find the sepulchre empty; they could not find the body of Jesus, as John informs us, and had the sorrow of the disappointment in their design of anointing His body, added to the sorrow for His death; while they stood here disappointed and sorrowful, not knowing what to do, two angels appeared to them and told them that Christ was risen and was alive. This filled them with surprise and joy. For it did not only take away their concern for their disappointment in not finding the body of Jesus in the sepulchre, but brought the unexpected and unspeakably joyful news that Christ, their dear Lord, was alive again. How suddenly did this turn them from the deepest sorrow to overflowing joy! It is said, in ver. 8. . . . How eager were they to impart the joyful news to their fellow-disciples, who were sharers in their sorrow for His death; and as they ran, Christ Himself met them, and in a friendly manner saluted them; and what a new surprise was this! Now they see with their own eyes the truth of what the angels had told them. How did it heighten their joy, now to see their dear Lord Himself, whom they had so lately seen put to so cruel a death, and never expected to see more, meet them alive, saluting them in a sweet and cheerful manner! and how do they express their joy and love to their risen Lord! They come and hold

Him by the feet and worship Him. They express their joy, and testify their respect to Him, in the most dear, humble, and adoring manner.

ST MARK.

28. vi. 8—"And commanded them that they should take nothing for their journey, save a staff only; no scrip, no bread, no money in their purse."] See Num. xxi. 18.

29. vi. 7—"And He called unto Him the twelve, and began to send them forth two by two; and gave them power over unclean spirits."] It was best, on many accounts, that two should go together; but this was probably one end—that their testimony might be valid, for the testimony of two witnesses is true.

30. x. 24–26—"And the disciples were astonished at His words. But Jesus answereth again, and saith unto them, Children, how hard is it for them that trust in riches to enter into the kingdom of God! It is easier for a camel to go through the eye of a needle, than for a rich man to enter into the kingdom of God. And they were astonished out of measure, saying among themselves, Who then can be saved?"] The reasons why they were astonished seem to be twofold: (1.) This was contrary to the notions they had of the Messiah's kingdom, as a kingdom of great temporal wealth and glory. They wondered, therefore, how it should come to pass that riches should exclude men out of it; and (2.) It was very contrary to the notion they had been brought up in among the Jews, who had a high esteem of rich men. They were their scribes and others that were their great men, that were rich, were in highest esteem among them, and supposed to be highest in favour with God. As to the poorer, meaner sort of people, they were low in esteem. In comparison of these they thought none so likely to be advanced as those, and therefore when they hear that those are like to be excluded, they say, "Who then can be saved?" Wherefore Christ greatly contradicted the notions of the Jews in the parable of the rich man and Lazarus, in representing a rich man and child of Abraham as going to hell, and not to Abraham's bosom, but seeing there, afar off, Lazarus, a poor stranger.

ST LUKE.

31. vii. 37—"And, behold, a woman in the city, which was a sinner, when she knew that Jesus sat at meat in the Pharisee's house, brought an alabaster-box of ointment."] This woman seems to have been before a common whore, and that precious ointment was what she kept to anoint herself with, to render herself agreeable to her

gallants, and particularly used to anoint her hair with, which was accounted the special ornament of women, and that she now makes use of as a towel to wipe Christ's feet; and having, now [that] she is brought to repentance, no further use for the costly box in that way, nor the precious ointment that is in it, she breaks the box and pours the ointment on Christ.

32. vii. 41, 42—"There was a certain creditor which had two debtors; the one owed five hundred pence, and the other fifty. And when they had nothing to pay, he frankly forgave them both. Tell me therefore, which of them will love him most?"] Christ plainly intimates that He is the creditor, or that He is the Being against whom sin is committed; for He is the person that forgives the debtor: verses 48, 49—"And He said unto her, Thy sins are forgiven. And they that sat at meat with Him began to say within themselves, Who is this that forgiveth sins also?" And He is the person the debtor loves for forgiveness of the debt: verses 44–47—"And He turned to the woman, and said unto Simon, Seest thou this woman? I entered into thine house, thou gavest Me no water for My feet: but she hath washed My feet with tears, and wiped them with the hairs of her head. Thou gavest Me no kiss: but this woman, since the time I came in, hath not ceased to kiss My feet. My head with oil thou didst not anoint: but this woman hath anointed My feet with ointment. Wherefore, I say unto thee, Her sins, which are many, are forgiven; for she loved much: but to whom little is forgiven, the same loveth little." And if Christ be the creditor, He is God.

33. viii. 1–3—"And it came to pass afterward, that He went throughout every city and village, preaching and shewing the glad tidings of the kingdom of God; and the twelve were with Him, and certain women, which had been healed of evil spirits and infirmities, Mary called Magdalene, out of whom went seven devils, and Joanna the wife of Chuza, Herod's steward, and Susanna, and many others, which ministered unto Him of their substance."] This company of women that followed Christ from city to city, ministering to Him of their substance, is a little image and resemblance of that blessed company of virgins that follow the Lamb whithersoever He goeth, spoken of in Rev. xiv. 4—"These are they which were not defiled with women; for they are virgins. These are they which follow the Lamb whithersoever He goeth. These were redeemed from among men, being the first-fruits unto God and to the Lamb."

34. xi. 24–26—"When the unclean spirit is gone out of a man, he walketh through dry places, seeking rest; and finding none, he saith, I will return unto my house whence I came out. And when he cometh, he findeth it swept and garnished. Then goeth he, and taketh to him seven other spirits more wicked than himself; and they enter in, and dwell there: and the last state of that man is worse than the first."] By comparing these verses with what goes before, it is confirmed that apostasy is one great ingredient or constituent of the unpardonable sin. For it is manifest Christ says this

of those same Pharisees spoken of before, that said He cast out devils by Beelzebub, the prince of the devils. It is more manifest still by comparing what is said in this place with Matt. xii. 22–25. There, speaking of the unclean spirit being gone out of a man, and returning again, &c., He adds, "Even so shall it be also unto this wicked generation." It seems there was a time when these Pharisees had much of the common influences of the Spirit of God, and the unclean spirit for a season seemed to be gone out of them; and this, probably, was a consequence of the awakening they were the subjects of by John the Baptist's preaching; but, after the illuminations they then had, it seems that their religion greatly degenerated, (though they were still very religious in their way.) They were exceedingly lifted up with spiritual pride, and fell into the condemnation of the devil, and at last into the unpardonable sin. Hence it is manifest that we nowhere in Scripture have any description of the unpardonable sin, but that apostasy is one thing that constitutes it.

35. xiv. 26—"If any man come to Me, and hate not his father, and mother, and wife, and children, and brethren, and sisters, yea, and his own life also, he cannot be My disciple."] We must 'hate' these, considered as an exchange for Christ, or as offered to us as inducements to forsake Christ. In the same manner as a just judge is said to hate gifts: Prov. xv. 27—"He that is greedy of gain troubleth his own house: but he that hateth gifts shall live." Are we to 'hate' father, &c.? It is not meant that the judge should hate gold, or silver, or goods, simply considered, but considered as offered as a purchase and bias of his judgment. And in the same manner as it is said in Cant. viii. 7—"Many waters cannot quench love, neither can the floods drown it: if a man would give all the substance of his house for love, it would utterly be contemned," not that it would be contemned simply and absolutely, but as offered as an exchange for those things which love seeks and desires.

36. xvi. 8—"And the Lord commended the unjust steward, because he had done wisely: for the children of this world are in their generation wiser than the children of light."] The meaning is, that the children of this world are wiser in their generation than the children of light are in theirs—*i.e.*, the children of this world are wiser in the management of their secular affairs to promote their worldly interest, and in contriving and disposing things that appertain to their generation,—that is, to the children of this world,—than the children of light are in the management of special affairs for their special interest. That this is the meaning, and not that the children of this world are wiser in temporal matters than the children of light are in the same matter, is evident by the following, where Christ advises us to be as wise for ourselves in special affairs as the children of this world are in temporal affairs.

37. xvi. 9—"And I say unto you, Make to yourselves friends of the mammon of unrighteousness; that, when ye fail, they may receive you into everlasting habitations."] *i.e.*, Make to yourselves friends in heaven of your earthly provision and substance; make God the

Father, and Christ, and the other inhabitants of the heavenly world, your friends, by bestowing the earthly goods that ye are stewards of upon them, as the unjust steward made himself friends by bestowing the goods that he was steward of upon them. Bestow your earthly goods upon them, by bestowing them on the poor, who are God's receivers: if it be bestowed on one of the least of Christ's brethren, it is bestowed on Christ. Then we shall make God and Christ and heavenly angels our friends, which friends will receive us when we fail. It is called the mammon of unrighteousness, because it is that which in time past we have, as it were, stolen and embezzled, and not improved them as God's stewards, but used them as if they were our own, as the unjust steward embezzled his lord's goods. It is for the sake of these worldly goods that we have been unjust, as the steward was unjust for the sake of his master's goods, that he might have them for his own and use them for his own private ends. Sin consists radically in the love of this world, and it is because this world is that which sin or the corruption of nature hath for its object, that it is called the mammon of unrighteousness. It is by our thus using the world that we come to be turned out of it, and to be separated from those worldly engagements by death, as the steward was turned out of his stewardship and was deprived of his lord's goods for his embezzling them. The sin by which man fell at first, and for which our first parents were turned out of the earthly paradise that God had committed to their care as stewards, to dress it and to keep it, was using it as unjust stewards, putting the goods committed to their care to a use contrary to the owner's command, and to serve their own private end. This will, therefore, be a wise improvement of the mammon by which we have lost our possession and enjoyment of all things here below, to make ourselves friends of it, "that they may receive us" when we are turned out of our stewardship and taken out of the world. Note, that expression, "that, when ye fail, they may receive you into everlasting habitations," thus explained, is a clear proof of the separate state of souls.

38. xvi. 12—"And if ye have not been faithful in that which is another man's, who shall give you that which is your own?"] By that which is another man's is represented this world's goods. The same with the "unrighteous mammon," as it is called in the foregoing verse; and by that which is "our own," is represented the blessings and enjoyments of heaven, the same that is called the "true riches" in the preceding verse. This world's goods are not our own; they are but lent to us for a little while, and are to be taken from us again presently. We are but stewards of them, according to the foregoing parable that gave occasion to these reflections. So the possessions of the children of Israel in the earthly Canaan are represented as not their own, but only what they improve as God's tenants and as sojourners with Him, who is their landlord: Lev. xxv. 23—"The land shall not be sold for ever: for the land is Mine; for ye are strangers and sojourners with Me." So here what we have in this world is represented as not our own, but God's, and we only as stewards.

But heavenly blessings are given to us as our proper inheritance, and that wherein our happiness consists. They are not lent to us, but given to us, never to be taken from us, but to be ours for ever. We are but sojourners with God on earth; but heaven is our proper home. Hence we may see the force of the argument. If ye have not been faithful in that which is another man's, who will give you that which is your own? If you be not fit to have something only committed to your care for a little while, that is quickly to be taken from you again, how much less are you fit to be trusted with things for ever; not only to have them lent to you or committed into your hands for a little while, but to have them given finally into your everlasting possession? If you cannot be trusted with something for only a few days, how much less can you be trusted with the eternal possession of a thing?

39. xvi. 16—"The law and the prophets were until John: since that time the kingdom of God is preached, and every man presseth into it."] Here I would observe, that when universal terms are used about redemption, they do not prove universal redemption, any more than the universal term here used proves that every man, in a strict and proper sense, did press into the kingdom of heaven since the preaching of John the Baptist. ("Every man presseth into it.") Christ is not so much speaking of what had already actually come to pass since John's time, as giving a description of that new dispensation that John began, and shewing wherein it differed from the old dispensation under the Law and the Prophets, as to the much greater numbers that are saved, and the multitudes that, under this dispensation that John's preaching was the dawning of, flock and press into the kingdom of God. The pouring out of the Spirit in John the Baptist's time, was the beginning of a glorious harvest of souls, that continued from that time to the end of that age, wherein multitudes of all sorts pressed into the kingdom of God.

40. xvii. 37—"And they answered and said unto Him, Where, Lord? And He said unto them, Wheresoever the body is, thither will the eagles be gathered together."] This is an enigmatical answer to their question; but yet by giving diligent heed to this answer, with due care to understand it, together with a diligent observation of events to be determined by it, when and where, Christ's answer is that these things that He speaks of shall be when and where they shall see the eagles gathered about the dead carcase. Now, the Roman armies bearing an eagle on their ensign, this might naturally lead them to think that the Romans were the eagles Christ spoke of. But what should lead them to think that Jerusalem was meant by the dead body? I answer, Because, when Jerusalem was besieged by the Roman armies, the city was filled with dead carcases. What innumerable multitudes were there that died in Jerusalem during the siege, by famine and by killing one another! When the Roman armies were gathered together about Jerusalem, then was it fulfilled that the eagles were gathered together about the dead carcases: or rather, by the carcase He means His own dead body that was killed at

K

Jerusalem. And after this the Jewish nation were like Christ's dead carcase, and not His living body as the true Church is; for His Spirit thenceforward left that Church and the Temple and typical ordinances of their worship; thenceforward it became as Christ's dead body. The Church, with its ordinances of worship, is the body of Christ. The Church, with the presence and Spirit of Christ, is His living body; but when deprived of it, His dead body. The Jews, therefore, killing Christ's body, killed then their own Church: by this means became a dead carcase and a fit prey for eagles. From the time the Jews killed Christ the Jewish Church was dead and putrified till they became a stinking carcase, before the time of their destruction, and their stink called the eagles together upon them.

41. xix. 12—"He said therefore, A certain nobleman went into a far country to receive for himself a kingdom, and to return."] Such a representation in this parable was the more familiar to the Jews because this had actually been the case with their late princes, Herod, Archelaus, &c. They, in order to receive their kingdom, left Judea for a season, and went into a far country—to Rome—to be invested with the kingdom by the Roman emperors, and then returned invested and in the exercise of their royal authority. So Christ went into a far country, and a greater city than Rome, to be invested with the kingdom over the Jews and over mankind in this world, His own country, by One infinitely greater than the Roman emperors.

42. ver. 14—"But his citizens hated him, and sent a message after him, saying, We will not have this man to reign over us."] They sent this message to that superior Potentate that was to invest Him.

43. ver. 17—"And he said unto him, Well, thou good servant; because thou hast been faithful in a very little, have thou authority over ten cities."] For now the nobleman was returned with kingly authority over the whole country, and had power to dispose of the government of cities.

44. xxi. 31—"And in the day-time He was teaching in the temple; and at night He went out, and abode in the mount that is called the mount of Olives."] By this it is evident that Christ was commonly wont to lodge in the open field—He had not where to lay His head in Jerusalem: He had no friend there to invite Him in, and He had not money to purchase entertainment at an inn, and therefore it was His constant manner to go and lodge at a certain place in the mount of Olives, which was the place where He and His disciples were found when Judas betrayed Him; and therefore it is said in next chapter, ver. 39, that that night "He came out, and went, as He was wont, to the mount of Olives; and His disciples also followed Him." And hence also John xviii. 1, 2. (See also John viii. with vii. 33.) Hence we may learn that what is spoken of Christ figuratively in Cant. v. 2, "I sleep, but my heart waketh: it is the voice of my beloved, saying, Open unto me, my sister, my love, my dove, my undefiled: for my head is filled with dew, and my locks with the drops of the night," was often literally fulfilled while He dwelt here on earth, and

that He often suffered greatly in being obliged to lodge abroad in the cold and rain.

ST JOHN.

45. i. 9—"That was the true Light, which lighteth every man that cometh into the world."] There is not now, ever was, nor will be, any man in the world enlightened but by Jesus Christ. Every man that cometh into the world, that ever is enlightened, is enlightened by Him; or hereby is meant that this Light is not only to enlighten the Jews, but that it enlightens indifferently every man, let him be of what nation soever. It was fit that the true Light, when He came, should be a general light. Moses enlightened only the nation of the Jews, because he was not the true light. See a very parallel expression, Col. i. 23—"If ye continue in the faith grounded and settled, and be not moved away from the hope of the gospel, which ye have heard, and which was preached to every creature which is under heaven; whereof I Paul am made a minister."

46. i. 18—"No man hath seen God at any time; the only-begotten Son, which is in the bosom of the Father, he hath declared him."] God under the Old Testament gave the images of things the substance and reality of which He gave in the New; and one instance of this was, that Christ so often under the Old Testament appears in human shape. This was an image and an earnest of His incarnation; and it is still God's manner to give the image and earnest of the glorious things that are to be brought to pass for His Church, and in the spiritual world, before He actually accomplishes them; and it was pleasing to Him to appear in human shape, whose 'delights were with the sons of men,' who delighted in the human nature, and in the thought of taking the human nature and a human body; He delighted in a human shape, and in the resemblance of His future incarnation.

47. ii. 4—"Jesus saith unto her, Woman, what have I to do with thee? Mine hour is not yet come."] This expression, as it was used in those times, carried nothing of disrespect by what was then understood by the expression and the force that words then bore; they were not looked upon as unsuitable to be used towards one most superior. This is evident, because the devil, when through the greatness of his fear he feigned himself a humble and earnest supplicant to Jesus Christ, used this expression: Luke viii. 28—"What have I to do with thee, Jesus, thou Son of God Most High? I beseech thee, torment me not."

48. iv. 36, 37—"And he that reapeth receiveth wages, and gathereth fruit unto life eternal: that both he that soweth and he that reapeth may rejoice together. And herein is that saying true, One soweth, and another reapeth."] He that soweth is Christ, the

ministers of the gospel they do but reap the fruit of Christ's labours. It is He that has, as it were, ploughed the field and fitted the ground, and sowed the seed, and He waters the seed sown. The Word, Ordinances, and Spirit, are of His purchasing and bestowing, hence ministers are represented as labourers that are sent into the harvest only to gather in the harvest—to gather in souls, the foundation of whose salvation is all already laid by Christ. He that sows is the Owner of the field and Lord of the harvest. Ministers are only labourers and servants sent forth to gather in His harvest that grows in the field, and springs from seed that He has sowed. He that sows and he that reaps shall rejoice together, as Christ and the seventy did when they returned and told Him of their success: Luke x. 17, 18, 21. (Ver. 37.) This was remarkably verified with respect to Christ and these His disciples, for Christ, when He dwelt on earth, sowed, laid all the foundation of His future Church, but the Apostles and other ministers gathered in the harvest after His ascension.

49. xiii. 10—"Jesus saith to him, He that is washed needeth not, save to wash his feet, but is clean every whit: and ye are clean, but not all."] Probably Christ may have some respect to the legal washings of the priests, who, at their consecration, even washed all over: Exod. xxix. 4—"And Aaron and his sons thou shalt bring unto the door of the tabernacle of the congregation, and shalt wash them with water;" but afterwards were required only to wash their hands and their feet at the laver. (Chap. xxx. 19-21.)

50. xiv. 13—"And whatsoever ye shall ask in myname, that will I do, that the Father may be glorified in the Son."] Christ speaks especially of those works or miracles spoken of in the foregoing verse, and therefore it is said 'that will I do,' and not 'that will I give.'

51. xvii. 24—"Also."]—Query—What doth this particle 'also' refer to? Ans. Christ had before prayed for His own glory. This He began with in ver. 1. This He repeats in ver. 5. And this He speaks of in the verses immediately preceding, 22, 23, He speaks of the glory which God had given. Here He prays that God would not only glorify Him, but the disciples also with Him and in His glory. He here explains His request that God would glorify Him, signifying that He meant not Himself singly, but with His disciples.

ACTS.

52. vii.] Rehearsal of Stephen—to shew how the Jews had of old resisted the Holy Ghost in the revelation and promises made. (1.) Revealed. (2.) The operation of the Holy Spirit to accomplish them within them. Resisted it by Moses and others raised up. Particularly insists on the promises made to Abraham that He would give to his seed Canaan for a possession, and therefore began with account of the promise and the circumstances attending it,—how God called

Abraham from his own country in order to making the covenant with him, and the bestowing of the blessing on him, and the circumstance that rendered the promise wonderful [and] demanded Abraham's faith in resting in it—viz., that for the present God gave him none inheritance in the land, &c., and when he had yet no child—how God confirmed the promise by the seal of circumcision. Next the step God took to the accomplishment of this promise. (1.) Joseph into Egypt to keep them alive in famine, lest Abraham's posterity should be extinct and so the promise fail. (Gen. xxxvii. 4.) Joseph, the first instrument God worked by, whom they resisted. Next their fathers being buried in Canaan, earnest of fulfilment. Next their miserable state. Next Moses—type of Christ. Next brought in by Joshua—finished in David and Solomon. Never fully accomplished till then. Then God trieth them by settled abode. No longer moving about in a tabernacle. (2 Sam. xii.) And then Stephen observes that notwithstanding God don't dwell in temples made with hands, that Solomon's temple was not the true temple of God by the account of their own prophets, whereby he justifies himself in what they accused him of in ver. 14 of chap. vi.

53. vii. 37, 38—"This is that Moses which said unto the children of Israel, A Prophet shall the Lord your God raise up unto you of your brethren like unto me; him shall ye hear. This is he that was in the church in the wilderness with the angel which spake to him in the mount Sinai, and with our fathers: who received the lively oracles to give unto us."] The things which Stephen observes of Moses in these verses serve the more to shew the comparison that he makes of the Jews' treatment of Christ with their fathers' treatment of Moses to be apt and pertinent, and to render the application he makes ver. 51—"Ye stiffnecked and uncircumcised in heart and ears, ye do always resist the Holy Ghost: as your fathers did, so do ye"—the more convincing; for here he observes that Moses himself compares the Messiah to him, and says that He shall be a Prophet like to him; and besides, their fathers in rejecting Moses rejected Christ, for Moses spake and acted in the name of Christ, and as His messenger and instrument, and Christ was with him in what he did and said, as Stephen observes, (ver. 38,) that Moses was with the angel (*i. e.*, Christ) in Mount Sinai, and spake to Him, and with our fathers, who received the lively oracles to give unto us; so that Moses spake His words, and [so] as that in rejecting Moses they rejected Christ's own words, and their murmurings against him and opposition to him was really opposition to Christ.

54. viii. 20–22—"But Peter said unto him, Thy money perish with thee, because thou hast thought that the gift of God may be purchased with money. Thou hast neither part nor lot in this matter: for thy heart is not right in the sight of God. Repent therefore of this thy wickedness, and pray God, if perhaps the thought of thine heart may be forgiven thee."] By what is here said it is evident that a man may contract fearful guilt, and may undo himself to all eternity by that which he has no great sense of the badness of in the time of

it, when he commits it does not seem heinous to him ; for Simon, he never seems to have had any great sense of any hurt in his proposal of buying the gift or power of conferring the Holy Ghost with money. He was very bold in his proposal, and in all likelihood it was very unexpected to him to meet with such a rebuke.

55. xiii. 39—"And by Him all that believe are justified from all things, from which ye could not be justified by the law of Moses."] This is true in two senses. (1.) The Law of Moses made no provision for the expiation of presumptuous sins: there were no sacrifices appointed for such sins: Num. xv. 30—"But the soul that doeth ought presumptuously, (whether he be born in the land or a stranger,) the same reproacheth the Lord ; and that soul shall be cut off from among his people." It was so ordered on purpose that man being kept in doubt, and their consciences not fully satisfied about their presumptuous sins, that when Christ came, and the gospel which declared the forgiveness of all sin through Him, ought to be the more joyful tidings. The forgiveness of sin was never fully revealed till Christ came. It is probable that the forgiveness of presumptuous sin had been a matter of great question and controversy amongst their doctors, and therefore Paul tells them that it is by Christ they are justified from those sins. And (2.) the sacrifices of the Law of Moses could not fully take away the guilt of any sin.

56. xvii. 27, 28—"That they should seek the Lord, if haply they might feel after Him, and find Him, though He be not far from every one of us: for in Him we live, and move, and have our being ; as certain also of your own poets have said, For we are also His offspring."] Alluding to the darkness in which the heathen world is represented.

ROMANS.

57. i. 32, ii. 1—"Who, knowing the judgment of God, that they which commit such things are worthy of death, not only do the same, but have pleasure in them that do them. Therefore thou art inexcusable, O man, whosoever thou art that judgest: for wherein thou judgest another, thou condemnest thyself; for thou that judgest doest the same things."] It seems to be a mistake of many that the Apostle in what he says of men's wickedness, in chap. i., has respect only to the Gentiles, and that in what he says in chap. ii. he has respect only to the Jews. It is true that in the first chapter he evidently has his eye chiefly on the wickedness that prevailed in the world, but that is not his professed design in it, only to describe the sin of the Pagan world, but the wickedness of the world of mankind. It is all unrighteousness and ungodliness, &c. And in the second chapter he has his eye chiefly on the Jews; but it is not his professed design to speak only of them, as appears by his beginning in

ver. 1.—The universal terms that he uses in it—"Therefore thou art inexcusable, O man," (not, O Jews!) "*whosoever* thou art" (of mankind, whether Jew or Gentile) "that judgest: for wherein thou judgest another, thou condemnest thyself; for thou that judgest doest the same things." In the last verse of the first chapter the Apostle speaks of the wickedness of mankind in general, and shews how *they hold the truth in unrighteousness*, as he had said before (ver. 18)—"For the wrath of God is revealed from heaven against all ungodliness and unrighteousness of men, who hold the truth in unrighteousness:" and the special design of that verse is to set forth how they are all alike and all agreed in wickedness, and in the same kind of wickedness, though they all have that light that is sufficient to teach them that those that commit such things deserve the condemnation and wrath of God, and so death and destruction; which they are very ready to acknowledge and declare in the case of others when they see their wickedness, their unrighteousness, covetousness, maliciousness, envy, murder, debate, deceit, malignity, &c. I say, though when they see others guilty of such things they can easily see that they are worthy of death, and are forward to express it; yet they do the very same things, and not only so, but they shew plainly that they have just such hearts; they shew a full practical consent to all the wickedness of others that they are forward to condemn and to declare worthy of death. Thus inexorable are they and inconsistent with themselves. Thus the beginning of the II. chapter comes in—"*Therefore thou art inexcusable, O man, whosoever thou art that judgest.*" Thou that art forward to condemn others as worthy of death—"*for wherein thou judgest another thou condemnest thyself*"—thou art very unreasonable and exceeding inconsistent with thyself,—"*for thou that judgest doest the same things,*" and shewest that thou hast pleasure in their practice. There is at the same time that you judge them a full practical consent to, and good liking of, the very same practices. So God of old condemned the Jews, for that in this practice they had justified Samaria and Sodom, and were a comfort to them, and yet had judged them. (Ezek. xvi. 51, 52, 54.)

58. ii. 21, 22—"Thou therefore which teachest another, teachest thou not thyself? thou that preachest a man should not steal, dost thou steal? thou that sayest a man should not commit adultery, dost thou commit adultery? thou that abhorrest idols, dost thou commit sacrilege?"] The Apostle, in these verses, seems to allude to these words, in Ps. l. 16-18—"But unto the wicked God saith, What hast thou to do to declare my statutes, or that thou shouldest take my covenant in thy mouth? Seeing thou hatest instruction, and casteth my words behind thee. When thou sawest a thief, then thou consentedest with him, and hast been partaker with adulterers."

59. iii. 10-18—"As it is written, There is none righteous, no, not one: there is none that understandeth, there is none that seeketh after God. They are all gone out of the way, they are together become unprofitable; there is none that doeth good, no, not one. Their throat is an open sepulchre: with their tongues they have used

deceit; the poison of asps is under their lips: whose mouth is full of cursing and bitterness: their feet are swift to shed blood: destruction and misery are in their ways: and the way of peace have they not known: there is no fear of God before their eyes."] The passages here quoted out of the Old Testament are to prove these things—(1.) That mankind are universally sinful—that every one is corrupt; that is what is aimed at in verses 10–12. (2.) That every one is not only corrupt, but every one totally corrupt in every part; that is aimed at in verses 13-15, where the several parts of the body are mentioned. (3.) That every one is not only in every part, but corrupt throughout in an exceeding degree, in verses 16-18.

60. iii. 23—"For all have sinned, and come short of the glory of God."] *I.e.*, The glory of the reward, as the phrase signifies, (chap. v. 2)—"By whom also we have access by faith into this grace wherein we stand, and rejoice in hope of the glory of God."

61. iii. 25, 26—"Whom God hath set forth to be a propitiation through faith in His blood, to declare His righteousness for the remission of sins that are past, through the forbearance of God; to declare, I say, at this time His righteousness; that He might be just, and the justifier of him which believeth in Jesus."] Sins that are past, *i.e.*, that were committed in past ages, before Christ died, as Heb. ix. 15—"For he saith to Moses, I will have mercy on whom I will have mercy, and I will have compassion on whom I will have compassion." And therefore it follows in ver. 26—"To declare, I say, at this time His righteousness; that He might be just, and the justifier of him which believeth in Jesus." Before, the Apostle was speaking of past ages; the righteousness of God in pardoning their sins then committed was not fully declared, then, in the time, but now it is at "*this time.*"

62. v. 13, 14—"For until the Law sin was in the world: but sin is not imputed when there is no law. Nevertheless death reigned from Adam to Moses, even over them that had not sinned after the similitude of Adam's transgression, who is the figure of Him that was to come."] There are two things the Apostle would prove in these words, one of which establishes the other. First, he would prove that all mankind were under the law God gave to Adam, that stated "death to be the wages of sin." This is evident, because that sin, as bringing death, was in the world before there was any other legislation or scheme, giving of law to mankind, besides what was to Adam, viz., in that space of time that was from Adam to Moses. There being sin, therefore, in the world, as bringing death in that space of time, before the giving of the Law by Moses, shews that there was a Law given of God before that time, threatening death that they were under; but this could be no other than the Law God gave to Adam. This proves that Adam was the legal head of mankind; that mankind were under the Law given to him, wherein God threatened death for transgression; and thus God, in this Law given to Adam, saying, "When thou sinnest thou shalt die," did not only speak to him, though He spoke in the singular number; but in him spoke to posterity also.

Hereby the Apostle prepares the way for the second thing he would prove in these words which he had asserted before, ver. 12—"Wherefore, as by one man sin entered into the world, and death by sin; and so death passed upon all men, for that all have sinned;" which he mainly aims at the proof, viz., that all mankind sinned and fell in Adam. This is evident by Adam's being the legal head of mankind, which is the first thing insinuated. For if God, when He spoke to Adam in the singular number, giving him a precept, spoke to him as representing posterity, so it will follow that He spoke to him as representing his posterity in the threatening; and this is further evident by this, that death did not only reign from Adam to Moses, but also reigned over them that had not violated Adam's law themselves by their actual personal transgression, as Adam had done.

63. vii. 13—"Was then that which is good made death unto me? God forbid. But sin, that it might appear sin, working death in me by that which is good; that sin by the commandment might become exceeding sinful."] This is to be connected with v. 11, with these words, *and by it,* (*i.e.,* by the Law,) *slew me,* and so with v. 10, *I found the Law to be unto death,* and that with v. 9, *when the commandment came, sin revived, and I died,* and that with the fifth verse, "For when we were in the flesh, the motions of sins, which were by the Law, did work in our members to bring forth fruit unto death."

64. vii. 14—"For we know that the Law is spiritual; but I am carnal, sold under sin."] Ahab sold himself to work evil, (1 Kings xxi. 20)—"And Ahab said to Elijah, Hast thou found me, O mine enemy? And he answered, I have found thee: because thou hast sold thyself to work evil in the sight of the Lord." He did it of choice, he was a willing slave to sin, voluntarily submitted and gave up himself to the dominion of this master. But the Apostle Paul was sold under sin as a poor captive against his will, as the context obliges us to understand.

65. vii. 15—"For that which I do I allow not: for what I would, that do I not; but what I hate, that do I."] In the original it is *ὀυ γινώσκω,* "I know not," which confirms that the Apostle here speaks in the name of a true saint, and not in the name of a wicked man. For surely a wicked man knows his sins in the common use of such an expression in Scripture for approve, own, as what is near to him and belongs to him; but the Apostle here speaks of his not knowing sin in that sense, he disowns and renounces it; he does not approve of it as that which he has any relation to, and accordingly it is not in the sight of God approved as what belongs to him. That this is the sense is confirmed by v. 17—"Now, then, it is no more I that do it, but sin that dwelleth in me," and v. 20—"Now if I do that I would not, it is no more I that do it, but sin that dwelleth in me."

66. viii. 23—"And not only they, but ourselves also, which have the first-fruits of the Spirit, even we ourselves groan within ourselves, waiting for the adoption, to wit, the redemption of our body."] The Apostle, in calling the redemption of saints the redemption of the

body, probably has in his eye that passage in Hos. xiii. 14—"I will ransom them from the power of the grave; I will redeem them from death: O death, I will be thy plagues; O grave, I will be thy destruction: repentance shall be hid from mine eyes."

67. viii. 29—"For whom He did foreknow, He also did predestinate to be conformed to the image of His Son, that He might be the first-born among many brethren."] This is the sum of what the elect are predestinated to—viz., to be conformed to the image of His Son, to be made like His Son, and to have communion with Him in His holiness and in His happiness. They are predestinated to be conformed to His Son in His death; in dying to sin and the world, and in His resurrection by being quickened from being dead in trespasses and sins: also in their bodies being raised. "Christ the first-fruits, and afterwards those that are Christ's at his coming." They are conformed to Christ in His justification. When Christ rose, He was justified, and believers in this justification do but partake with Him in His justification, in v. 34—"Who is he that condemneth? It is Christ that died, yea rather, that is risen again, who is even at the right hand of God, who also maketh intercession for us." They are conformed to Christ in His relation to the Father in His Sonship, and are made also the children of God, so that they are His children, only He is the first-born among them, as the Apostle here observes. They are conformed to Christ in the Father's love to Him, and are made partakers with Him in it as members. They are conformed to Christ in His being heir of the world, and they are joint-heirs. They are conformed to Christ in His exaltation and glorification, for He and they shall be glorified together. They are conformed to Him in ascension into heaven; they shall also ascend. They are conformed to Him in the glorification of His body, for their bodies shall be made like unto His glorious body. They are conformed to Him in His enjoyment of the Father in heaven: they by being members of Him partake with Him in His enjoyment of the Father's infinite love, and in His joy in the Father, His joy is fulfilled in them, and the glory which the Father has given Him, He has given them. They are conformed to Him in His reigning over the world. They sit with Him on His throne, and they have power over the nations, and they shall rule them with a rod of iron, and as the vessels of a potter shall they be broken to shivers, even as He received of His Father. They shall be conformed unto Him in His judging the world, for the saints shall judge the world, yea, they shall sit with Christ in judging angels. This glory, this excellency and happiness that consists in the saints being conformed to Christ, is the sum of the good that they are predestinated to, and the whole of their conformity to Christ is what the Apostle has respect to, and not only their being made like Him in conversion and sanctification.

68. ix. 3—"For I could wish that myself were accursed from Christ for my brethren, my kinsmen according to the flesh." In the original it is "that myself were 'anathema' from Christ."] The Apostle's meaning probably is, that he was willing that Christ

should so order it that he should in the world be cut off from the society and privileges of His visible people, as an excommunicated person, and also be cut off from the earth by an accursed death at last, dying under the hidings of God's face and dreadful fruits of His displeasure for a time, as Christ did; and thus to suffer from Christ for the Jews, as Christ, who was made a curse for us, suffered from God the Father, who was despised and rejected of men, cast out of the synagogue as an accursed person while He lived, and at last died an accursed death for us. As Christ loved us so the Apostle loved his brethren.

69. ix. 4—"Who are Israelites; to whom pertaineth the adoption, and the glory, and the covenants, and the giving of the Law, and the service of God, and the promises."] The same glory is doubtless here meant, whose departure was lamented when the ark was taken, when it was said by the true friends of Israel, The glory is departed from Israel, meaning the ark and the cloud of glory in which God appeared above upon it, or rather Jesus Christ, with respect to these tokens of His friendly presence.

70. ix. 22, 23—"What if God, willing to shew His wrath, and to make His power known, endured with much long-suffering the vessels of wrath fitted to destruction; and that He might make known the riches of His glory on the vessels of mercy, which He had afore prepared unto glory."] He does not say to shew His justice or righteousness, for that is as much observed in God's glorifying and making happy the saints, and much more in some respects. God's justice is more gloriously manifested in the sufferings of Christ for the elect, than the damnation of the wicked.

71. x. 3—"For they being ignorant of God's righteousness, and going about to establish their own righteousness, have not submitted themselves unto the righteousness of God."] The reason why the righteousness of Christ, from time to time, is called by the name of *God's righteousness*, may probably be this, that the grand difference between the righteousness of the two covenants is this, that one is a mere human righteousness, the other is a Divine righteousness, or the righteousness of a Divine Person; and not that one is our own personal righteousness, and the other the righteousness of Another that is our surety. For if Adam had stood, and we had been justified as in the way of the first covenant, we that are the posterity of Adam should not have been justified by our own personal righteousness, but should have been justified as much by the righteousness of another as now under the second covenant. God, in infinite wisdom, hath so ordered things to bring mankind to a greater dependence on God, that mankind should not be justified by their own righteousness, that is, by the righteousness of mankind, but by the righteousness of God, that they should have their happiness, their strength, their wisdom, and their righteousness, and their all in God, that God might not only be the sum of their objective good or good of enjoyment, (but) so (that) He should be the sum of their glory or good of excellency, recommending them to that objective good, and so that God should

be all in all: as there is a great disposition in man to seek his good in the creature, and to keep at a distance from God, and in opposition to that universal union and dependence on God which is the aim of the gospel, so there is a strong inclination in men to acquit themselves of guilt, and trust in a mere human righteousness and reject the righteousness of God. That this is the reason why Christ's righteousness is called *God's righteousness*—viz., to set it in a more clear opposition to the righteousness of men—is confirmed from the antithesis in Rom. i. 17, 18—"For therein is the righteousness of God revealed from faith to faith: as it is written, The just shall live by faith. For the wrath of God is revealed from heaven against all ungodliness and unrighteousness of men, who hold the truth in unrighteousness." Here the righteousness of God is set in opposition to the unrighteousness of men, and that is implied why the righteousness of One that is above men, the righteousness of God is necessary, because the righteousness of men or a mere human righteousness is insufficient, or because men have no righteousness or there is no human righteousness. This confirms that the righteousness we are justified by is called the righteousness of God—viz., to set it in the clearer opposition to the righteousness of the first covenant, which is the righteousness of mankind. The righteousness that Christ provided is properly called the righteousness of God, in opposition to the human righteousness of the first covenant, on the following accounts—(1.) That whereas the righteousness of the first covenant was a mere human righteousness, this is a righteousness of a Person infinitely above a mere human person, it is the righteousness of a Divine Person; (2.) It is from His divinity that it derives its value whereby it is sufficient to justify us, and so is fit to succeed in the room of that human righteousness which we have failed of; it is as it is the righteousness of God, that it is of any avail to our justification; (3.) As the righteousness of the first covenant was in man wrought out by man, we have this righteousness not by our works, but wholly and immediately of God, by His gift and imputation, when we have none wrought by us or inherent in us.

The Apostle by *God's righteousness* means the righteousness that a Divine Person hath or is the subject of, and is given to believers; and, by God's rest, the same Apostle means the rest which God or Christ hath, and is also given to believers. (Heb. iv. 5.)

72. xiv. 15—"But if thy brother be grieved with thy meat, now walkest thou not charitably. Destroy not him with thy meat for whom Christ died."] That is as much as to say, will [you not in] your meat put yourself as much out of the way as to restrain your appetite, though you thereby expose your brother to be destroyed, for whom Christ put Himself so much out of the way as to die to save him from being destroyed?

I. CORINTHIANS.

73. i. 27—"But God hath chosen the foolish things of the world to confound the wise; and God hath chosen the weak things to confound the things which are mighty."] God, by this method, shews Satan that His understanding and wisdom is of infinitely further reach than his. All Satan's strife and contrivances is to get the powers and honours and riches and wisdom of the world on his side, and to improve them in his interest. God shews that His wisdom stands in no need of such helps; but He knows how to order the meanest and most despicable means, so and so to contrive things with them as to baffle all the policy of Satan and confound all the strength that he has on his side; as a king would shew his superior policy if he should so contrive things as without the trouble of raising armies and fleets, and providing arms and ammunition, or taxing his country and the like, should successfully carry on a war against a powerful enemy with mighty forces, and should baffle and confound them from time to time, though they lay out themselves to the utmost, by some very inconsiderable means and with very little ado.

74. iv. 6—"And these things, brethren, I have in a figure transferred to myself and to Apollos for your sakes; that ye might learn in us not to think of men above that which is written, that no one of you be puffed up for one against another."] That is, above what I have just now written in the directions I have given in this Epistle, how ye should esteem ministers that plant and water, &c.

75. xii. 28—"And God hath set some in the church, first, apostles; secondarily, prophets; thirdly, teachers; after that miracles; then gifts of healing, helps, governments, diversities of tongues."] It being so that Christians, in those days, were so generally endued with extraordinary gifts of the Holy Ghost, it made the case of the Church then very different from what it is now. For, then, those that had these extraordinary gifts became pastors, in the exercise of those gifts, and so far as they were thereby qualified. Thus, any male member of the Church that had the gift of prophecy might do the part of a pastor, so far as the exercise of that gift extended, or in prophesying. So any one that had the word of wisdom or knowledge, or a spirit of revelation, or doctrine, or exhortation, or gift of tongue, might do the part of pastors in the exercise of these gifts. All that had these extraordinary gifts thereby became a kind of extraordinary officers in the exercise of those gifts, and so far as that extended; and, accordingly, used to officiate in the Church. This is evident by this and chap. xiv., and also chap. xii. to Romans. So far as any person had a miraculous gift by the immediate and extraordinary influence of the Spirit of Christ on their minds, so far were they (as Christ, who is the head and fountain of all Church-office power, and therefore when they were in the exercise of that gift) to be submitted to by the Church as if Jesus Christ himself spake and acted. For it was not they, indeed, that spake and acted, but Christ in them. Christ, by

giving to them such a miraculous gift, marked out the person for such work in the Church. But it cannot be argued from hence that there are so many distinct standing offices in the Church as there were extraordinary gifts. A spirit of government, or an extraordinary and miraculous qualification for the exercise of that part of the pastor's office which consists in judging, reproving, rebuking, admonishing, &c.: he that had this gift was authorised to do this part of a pastor's work, and the Church submitted to him herein that they had discerned had this gift. For they had a discerning of spirits—among other gifts of the Spirit—among them. But this no more argues that government was a distinct standing office than that exhorting was; for some that had a gift of exhorting were in the exercise of that gift to do the part of a pastor and no otherwise: Rom. xii. 8—"Or he that exhorteth, on exhortation: he that giveth, let him do it with simplicity; he that ruleth, with diligence; he that sheweth mercy, with cheerfulness."

One had an extraordinary gift of the Spirit in doctrine, another in counselling and exhorting, another in reproving, admonishing, and judging of offenders, but these are only so many parts of a pastor's office, and may indeed all be referred to preaching and declaring the word of God. All this is confirmed from Rom. xii. 6-8—"Having then gifts, differing according to the grace that is given to us, whether prophecy, let us prophesy according to the proportion of faith; or ministry, let us wait on our ministering; or he that teacheth, on teaching; or he that exhorteth, on exhortation: he that giveth, let him do it with simplicity; he that ruleth, with diligence; he that sheweth mercy, with cheerfulness." The Spirit in Christians, which they had in an extraordinary manner dwelling in them, sometimes directed in judging of offenders. Thus the Apostle, chap. v. 4—"In the name of our Lord Jesus Christ, when ye are gathered together, in my Spirit, with the power of our Lord Jesus Christ," directs the Corinthians to excommunicate the incestuous in the name of His Spirit.

76. xv. 21-23—"For since by man came death, by man came also the resurrection of the dead. For as in Adam all die, even so in Christ shall all be made alive. But every man in his own order: Christ the first-fruits; afterward they that are Christ's at his coming."] That is, all that are in Christ. The words import no more. For the Apostle speaks of no more being made alive in Christ than are in Him. The Apostle in these words has respect only to the resurrection of the saints, as is evident by the words that follow in the next verse—"But every man in his own order: Christ the first-fruits; afterward they that are Christ's at His coming." Indeed this resurrection only can well be called a being made alive, for this only is in Scripture called a resurrection to life. (John v. 29; Dan. xii. 2.) This resurrection to life is alone meant by the word resurrection elsewhere, as Luke xx. 35; Phil. iii. 11. And it is this resurrection to life the Apostle evidently has a special respect to in the foregoing verses;

GALATIANS.

80. iii. 16—" Now to Abraham and his seed were the promises made. He saith not, And to seeds, as of many; but as of one, And to thy seed, which is Christ."] The passage in Genesis here referred to, is doubtless that Gen. xxii. 17, 18—" That in blessing I will bless thee, and in multiplying I will multiply thy seed as the stars of the heaven, and as the sand which is upon the sea shore; and thy seed shall possess the gate of his enemies: and in thy seed shall all the nations of the earth be blessed; because thou hast obeyed my voice." For the promise made to Abraham that the Apostle is here speaking of, is, that all the families of the earth should be blessed, and this is expressly predicted of his seed, in anything that God says to Abraham, nowhere else but there; and the seed that is there spoken of, is spoken of in such a manner that it is most naturally understood not as a noun of multitude, or as containing a plurality, but only an individual, because the singular word *possess*, and the singular pronoun *his*, are used—" Thy seed shall possess the gate of his enemies," where the same seed is doubtless to be understood, as in the words immediately following—" And in thy seed shall all the nations of the earth be blessed." It is not usual in Scripture that a singular pronoun is thus annexed to the word " seed," when it is a noun of multitude. Christ, the seed of Abraham, in whom all the families of the earth should be blessed, is spoken of elsewhere in the Old Testament as a single pronoun, as in Ps. lxxii. 17—" His name shall endure for ever: His name shall be continued as long as the sun; and men shall be blessed in Him: all nations shall call Him blessed;" and the word seed, as used in the Old Testament, is sometimes understood of a particular person. Thus Eve says, on the occasion of the birth of Seth, (Gen. iv. 25,) " And Adam knew his wife again, and she bare a son, and called his name Seth: for God, said she, hath appointed me another seed instead of Abel, whom Cain slew." So Hannah says, (1 Sam. i. 11,) " And she vowed a vow, and said, O Lord of hosts, if thou wilt indeed look on the affliction of thine handmaid, and remember me, and not forget thine handmaid, but wilt give unto thine handmaid a man child, then I will give him unto the Lord all the days of his life, and there shall no razor come upon his head." " If thou wilt give thine handmaid seed of men," as it is in the original, meaning a man child.

81. iii. 14—" That the blessing of Abraham might come on the Gentiles through Jesus Christ; that we might receive the promise of the Spirit through faith."] The Spirit from time to time was promised of old by the prophets, as the great privilege of the happy gospel days which they foretold; but the promise was made to the seed or children of Israel and Abraham. See Isa. xliv. 2, 3—" Thus saith the Lord that made thee, and formed thee from the womb, which will help thee; Fear not, O Jacob, my servant; and thou, Jesurun, whom I have chosen. For I will pour water upon him

that is thirsty, and floods upon the dry ground: I will pour my Spirit upon thy seed, and my blessing upon thine offspring." Now the prophet puts the Spirit and the blessing together, as the Apostle does, in this verse. Again, in that great promise of the Spirit, Joel ii. 28; Isa. lix. 20, 21. So, from time to time, the great promises of the Spirit, in other places in the prophets, are to God's people Israel or Israel's and Abraham's posterity. Hence, a being endowed by the Spirit is, by the Apostle, spoken of as evidently being of the sons of God. Rom. viii. 14—"For as many as are led by the Spirit of God, they are the sons of God;" and of Abraham, in this chapter.

82. iv. 21–23—"Tell me, ye that desire to be under the law, do ye not hear the law? For it is written, that Abraham had two sons; the one by a bond maid, the other by a free woman. But he who was of the bond woman was born after the flesh; but he of the free woman was by promise."] These verses might be paraphrased thus, by which the Apostle's reasoning in them will be understood—"Is God's giving of the Law to the children, therefore, any way contrary to or inconsistent with the constitution He had before established with Abraham, that was by a free promise? No; by no means. Indeed if the Law that had been given at Mount Sinai could have given life, so that justifying the children of Israel could have been the real design of it, the children of Abraham would have been justified that way, and it would have been inconsistent with the preceding constitution of Abraham. But this is not the case, for the design of the Law was not to justify the children of Israel, but, on the contrary, to conclude them under, to prepare them by faith to receive, the promise made to Abraham, &c., and it was not a constitution inconsistent with the preceding gracious constitution with Abraham, but subordinate to it."

83. v. 17—"For the flesh lusteth against the Spirit, and the Spirit against the flesh: and these are contrary the one to the other; so that ye cannot do the things that ye would."] By this, with the context, it seems that grace in the heart is no other than the Spirit of God dwelling in the heart, and becoming a principle of life and action there, acting and exalting its nature in the exercise of men's faculties. (1.) By the Spirit here spoken of, that lusteth against the flesh, seems plainly to be meant grace in the heart, or the gracious nature in man or man's regenerated and renewed part, which is opposite to the flesh or to the corrupt part. For that by the flesh is meant the corrupt nature, is most evident by verses 19–21, and Romans vii. 5–18. By the Spirit, therefore, is doubtless meant the spiritual or gracious nature that is begun in man in his regeneration. Doubtless by the flesh and Spirit, that the Apostle says lust one against another, he means the same as by the "law of the members and law of the mind," that he says war one against another, in the VIIth of his Epistle to the Romans, at the 23d verse—"But I see another law in my members warring against the law of my mind, and bringing me into captivity to the law of sin which is in my members;" which is further evident in that the Apostle there, in the continuation of the discourse

of the same things, he uses the very terms of "flesh and Spirit" so much after the same manner as in this context, as may be seen by comparison, that it is most evident that he means the very same thing. (2.) That the Spirit spoken of here, and in other parallel texts, as signifying the gracious or holy nature in the regenerate, is the Spirit of God, seems plain by the context. For no doubt but the same is meant by the Spirit here, as in verses 16, 18–25; but is more clearly evident by the VIIIth chapter of Romans, where the Apostle is speaking of "flesh and Spirit" in like manner as here, and as we have shewn already by "flesh and Spirit" he there intends the corrupt and the gracious nature. And it is evident that the Spirit there spoken of is the Spirit of God or Christ, by the 9th, 10th, 11th verses, and by the 13th and 14th verses. Those extraordinary principles of operation that Christians in those days were endued with, were called the spirit of the persons that had them, because they were nothing but the Spirit of God dwelling in them, and becoming a principle in them of such a sort of operation. (See Note on 1 Cor. xiv. 32.) So the principle of grace or gracious nature that all Christians have, is called the Spirit, because it is nothing but the Spirit of God dwelling in them, and becoming in them a principle of gracious and holy exercises. For the better understanding why the corrupt nature and the gracious or regenerate nature are called "flesh and Spirit," it is to be considered that man, as he was first created, was endued with two kinds of principles, natural and spiritual. By natural principles, I mean the principles of human nature, as human nature is in this world—that is, in its animal state, or that belonging to the nature of man as man, or that belonging to his humanity,or that naturally and necessarily flow from the inner human nature. Such is a man's love to his own honour, love of his own pleasure, the natural appetites that he has by means of the body, &c. His spiritual principles were his love to God, and his relish of Divine beauties and enjoyments, &c. These may be called supernatural, because they are no part of human nature. They do not belong to the nature of man as man, nor do they naturally and necessarily flow from the faculties and properties of that nature. Man can be man without them; they did not flow from anything in the human nature, but from the Spirit of God dwelling in man, and exerting itself by man's faculties as a principle of action. So that man's entire nature, in his primitive state, was constituted of "flesh and spirit," that part of his entire nature that consists in the principles of the mere human nature, or that is the human nature in its perfect animal state, simply and absolutely considered, is flesh. The human nature or humanity, in that animal state in which it is in this world, is often called flesh in Scripture—Gen. vi. 12; Ps. lxv. 2; Isa. xl. 5, 6, and xlix. 26, and lxvi. 16; Matt. xxiv. 22; John i. 14. The human nature, as it is after the resurrection, is not called flesh, being then no longer in its animal state: 1 Cor. xv. 50—"Now this I say, brethren, that flesh and blood cannot inherit the kingdom of God; neither doth corruption inherit incorruption." That spiritual nature which he had, consisting in those holy principles that he had, was quite a distinct thing, and it was only the Spirit of God dwelling in man, and exerting its nature by man's faculties. Man's natural principles, or those principles of humanity that man had, were in his primitive state very good; because that man's spiritual principles that he had were to that degree as the Spirit dwelt and acted in him to that degree, that the natural principles were entirely subordinate to them. Then the flesh did not lust against the Spirit. These two natures, or two sorts of principles, were, by an entire, an absolute subordination of one to the other, united, so as to be, as it were, one nature. The spiritual principles bare absolute rule, and therefore man was then wholly spiritual, because he lived in the Spirit, and walked wholly in the Spirit, and the flesh was only a servant to the Spirit. But when man fell, then the Spirit of God left him, and so all his spiritual nature or spiritual principles; and then only the flesh was left, or merely the principle of human nature in its animal state. They were now left alone, without spiritual principles to govern and direct them, so that man became wholly carnal, and so wholly corrupt. For the principles of human nature, when alone and left to themselves, are principles of corruption, and there are no other principles of corruption in man but these. Corrupt nature is nothing else but the principle of human nature in its animal state, or the flesh (as it is called in Scripture) left to itself, or not subordinated to spiritual principles; and so far as it is unsubordinate, so far is it corrupt. When a man is regenerate, then again the Spirit is restored to him, and spiritual principles in a degree; so then again there is "flesh and spirit." But so little of the Spirit is given, that the flesh, or principles of human nature, are not absolutely and perfectly subject and subordinate, so that the flesh, or the principles of human nature, lust against the Spirit. And this is the reason that these two natures in the saints, the corrupt nature, and the gracious or regenerate nature, are called "flesh and Spirit,"—viz., because the corrupt nature is only the principles of the human nature, (which is often in Scripture called flesh,) yet in great measure not subordinated to spiritual principles. And the regenerate, or gracious nature, is only the Spirit of God dwelling in the heart, and acting and exerting His own nature by man's faculties. There are two things that do confirm that, by the "flesh" in this text and parallel places, is meant human nature left in a measure to itself. The first is, that the natural man and the carnal man are evidently synonymous in Scripture. (1 Cor. ii. 14, 15.) There we find natural and spiritual opposed one to another. "The natural man *receiveth not* the things of the Spirit of God." "But he that is spiritual judgeth all things;" and then in the next verse but one—viz., in the first verse of the third chapter—we find carnal and spiritual in like manner opposed, and as signifying the same—"And I, brethren, could not speak unto you as unto spiritual, but as unto carnal, even as unto babes in Christ;" where it is most evident that, by carnal and spiritual, he means the same as he did before by natural and spiritual. I would argue thus from it, that if natural and carnal are synonymous, then nature and flesh are synonymous. A natural man is one that has only the principles of human nature; the word ψυχικος in the original seems to hold forth thus much, and this is the carnal man. And then, secondly, which strengthens this, and is strengthened by it, is that the Apostle in the same context explains what he means by carnal—viz., walking as men, or, as it is in the original, according to man. (Chap. iii. 3,) "Are ye not carnal, and walk according to man?" or according to the humanity, or the principles of the human nature in its animal state as the governing principles. To the same purpose is that in 1 Pet. iv. 2—"That he no longer should live the rest of his time in the flesh to the lusts of men, but to the will of God." (See note in the place.) Corruption of heart is called "flesh" in Scripture, not chiefly because the corruption of man's nature in great part consists in the inordinancy of bodily appetites, as appears, because the Apostle in Col. ii. 18 does call the mind fleshly, particularly on account of its being corrupted with the other sort of lusts—viz., the lusts of the mind intruding into those things that he hath not seen, vainly puffed up by his fleshly mind. It is therefore not so much on this account that corruption is called flesh, as because it is from human nature left to itself. The Scripture does expressly explain itself as to the meaning of the word natural—that it is being destitute of the Spirit of God, and so having nothing above human nature, (Jude 19)—"sensual, having not the Spirit." The word in the original is the same that is translated natural in other places. That, by flesh or fleshly, as the words are used in the New Testament, as opposite to Spirit and spiritual, respect is not only had to those lusts or appetites that are appetites of the body or desires of the objects of the external senses, is evident, because these terms are applied to pride, the most special of all lusts. Col. ii. 18—"Vainly puffed up by his fleshly mind." So 1 Cor. iii. 3, 4—"For ye are yet carnal: for whereas there is among you envying, and strife, and divisions, are ye not carnal, and walk as men? For while one saith, I am of Paul; and another, I am of Apollos; are ye not carnal?"—Coroll. 1. Hence we may learn Christ's meaning in what He says to Nicodemus, John iii. 6—"That which is born of the flesh is flesh; and that which is born of the Spirit is spirit." There are then two natures in man—the flesh, or the mere human nature, and the spiritual nature. The aim of Christ is to inform which nature is of the first generation, and which of the second. By "flesh" Christ does not mean only the body, for there is more born by the first generation than that.—Coroll. 2. Hence we may learn what is the meaning of the word spiritual as it is often used in the New Testament. It is not intended in contradistinction from corporeal; but things are said to be spiritual as relating to the Spirit of God, especially as dwelling in the hearts of the saints. Thus the godly man is called spiritual because he has the Spirit of God dwelling in him, and acting by his faculties, as is evident by 1 Cor. xv. compared with the context, beginning with the tenth verse. (See "Mastricht Theologia de Regeneratione," p. 661, *a.*)—

Coroll. 3. Hence we may learn in what sense the body at the resurrection is said to be a spiritual body. 1 Cor. xv. 44—"It is sown a natural body; it is raised a spiritual body. There is a natural body, and there is a spiritual body;" not spiritual in opposition to material or corporeal—for a spiritual body in that sense would be a contradiction—but spiritual in this sense that has been mentioned in coroll. 2—not in opposition to corporeal, but to natural or animal. "It is sown a natural body; it is raised a spiritual body." It is sown with animal faculties and appetites suited to the needs and purposes of the animal, frail, corruptible nature. But when it shall be raised again, it shall be raised without these faculties and appetites; but all the faculties and properties that it shall be endowed with shall be directly suited and subservient to the purposes of the Spirit, of His gracious principle, or of that Divine and holy nature which God hath imparted to His saints. It is evident that the body in its present state is called a natural body, and in its future a spiritual body, with relation to that animal nature that we derive from the first Adam, and that quickening Spirit, or holy and spiritual nature, that we derive from the second Adam, by the following verse:—"But if ye be led of the Spirit, ye are not under the law."

EPHESIANS.

84. ii. 6—"And hath raised us up together, and made us sit together in heavenly places in Christ Jesus."] The meaning is not, hath made us sit together with one another, but together with Christ; as it is said in the foregoing verse, "He hath quickened us *together with Christ*," as the Apostle goes on in this verse, "He hath raised us up *together with Him*, and hath made us sit *together with Him* in heavenly places." This is more plain by looking at these two verses as in the original, συνεζωοποίησε τῷ χριστῷ—και. . . 'Iησοῦ. It is here evident that the συν with which each verb is compounded has respect to the same thing, and that each one denotes the communion the saints have with Christ, in being quickened and also raised up and set in heavenly places. The import of the original would perhaps have been more naturally suggested to us if the translation had been thus, "He hath jointly quickened with Christ, and jointly raised us up, and jointly set us in heavenly places in Christ;" and when, as in the last cause, there is added "in Christ Jesus," it is to denote that the saints ascend into heaven, and reign in glory there with Him, and in Him, which more fully expresses the manner in which the saints have communion with Christ in His ascension to heaven, and that dignity and glory that He possesses there, as sitting with Him on His throne.

85. ii. 12—"That at that time ye were without Christ, being aliens from the commonwealth of Israel, and strangers from the covenants

of promise, having no hope, and without God in the world."] The first of these things here mentioned is the foundation of all the rest that follow. A being without Christ is the foundation of being aliens from the commonwealth of Israel, and strangers from the covenant of promise, having no hope. And the last thing here mentioned is the sum of all the rest. A being without God in the world is the sum of all evil. A being without Christ, and aliens from the commonwealth of Israel, and strangers from the covenant of promise, and without hope, are all summed up in being without God in the world.

86. v. 18—"And be not drunk with wine, wherein is excess; but be filled with the Spirit."] The Apostle here seems to have reference to that in Cant. v. 1—"I am come into my garden, my sister, my spouse: I have gathered my myrrh with my spice; I have eaten my honeycomb with my honey; I have drunk my wine with my milk; eat, O friends; drink, yea, drink abundantly, O beloved." He was afraid that they would misunderstand that as a liberty to Christ's beloved ones to be drunk with wine; but he explains the meaning of it to them.—Coroll. Hence we may learn the authority of that book of Canticles.

PHILIPPIANS.

87. iv. 8—"Finally, brethren, whatsoever things are true, whatsoever things are honest, whatsoever things are just, whatsoever things are pure, whatsoever things are lovely, whatsoever things are of good report; if there be any virtue, and if there be any praise, think on these things."] The Apostle in the immediately preceding verses had told them what they should not exercise their thoughts about—viz., outward things, things pertaining to their worldly interests: ver. 6—"Be careful for nothing; but in every thing by prayer and supplication, with thanksgiving, let your requests be made known unto God." Now he tells them what they should think about—what should be the objects of the greatest exercise of their thoughtfulness and care.

COLOSSIANS.

88. ii. 16—"Let no man therefore judge you in meat, or in drink, or in respect of an holyday, or of the new moon, or of the sabbath days."] This does not preclude the Sabbath. The word is ἑορτή "a feast."

89. ii. 20—"Wherefore, if ye be dead with Christ from the rudiments of the world, why, as though living in the world, are ye subject to ordinances?"] This world is not the contrary of the Church.

Christ, after He rose from the dead, was no longer a proper inhabitant of this world, and therefore was no longer subject to the ceremonial Law. So is the Church which is mystical and dead, and risen with Christ. Christ is the representative of the Church, and therefore the Church has communion with Him in this alteration of His state.

90. iii. 9—"Lie not one to another, seeing that ye have put off the old man with his deeds."] The stops seem here to be wrong made, which make it more difficult to understand the sense. The stop that is made at end of the preceding verse ought rather to have been at the end of these words, "lie not one to another." For this is one of those disuniting sins mentioned, of which the words in this and the two next verses are mentioned as a common reason why we should avoid them—viz., because in the new man the disuniting distinctions by which the carnal world is divided are abolished, and Christ is all in all.

91. iii. 17—"And whatsoever ye do in word or deed, do all in the name of the Lord Jesus, giving thanks to God and the Father by Him." Question, Why must we do whatsoever we do in the name of Christ? Answer, Because nothing can be acceptable to God as from us, but in and through Christ, as Heb. xiii. 21, and 1 Peter ii. 5. Therefore when we come to God to do anything Godward we must always bring Christ with us, that what we do may be accepted—that is, we must have a sense of our unworthiness of acceptance in ourselves, and must hope for acceptance on His account. Question, But why can't what we do be accepted but by Christ? Answer, (1.) We are infinitely ill-deserving creatures, and all our good is nothing when put in the scales with our unworthiness; and then (2.) we are condemned creatures, and it is against the Law that anything should be accepted from us as we are in ourselves. (3.) The third reason why nothing that we do can be accepted but by Christ is, because there is nothing that we do but what is in a sense corrupt, even the holy actions and gracious exercises of the godly are so. They are not merely attended with the exercises of corruption that precede and follow them and are nursed with them, but they are themselves corrupt. Take them as they are in their dimensions and manner of exerting them, even the exercises of grace in a godly man are manifestations and expressions of corruption; the act most simply and absolutely considered is good, but consider it in its measure and the manner of exertion, and it is an expression of corruption. All the godly man's acts of love are defectively corrupt or sinfully defective. There is that defect in them that may be called the corruption of them. That defect is properly sin, an expression of corruption, and what tends to provoke the just anger of God; not because the exercise of love is not proportionable or equal to God's loveliness or to His kindness, but because it is so very disproportionate to the occasion that is given for the exercise of love, considering God's loveliness and the manifestation that is made of it, or the manifestation and exercise of His kindness and man's capacity, and the

advantages to be sensible of it, and the like, together. A negative expression of corruption may be as truly sin, and as truly odious, and as just cause of provocation, as a positive. Thus, if a man, a worthy and excellent person, should, from mere generosity and goodness, exceedingly lay out himself, and should with great expense and suffering save another's life or redeem him from some extreme calamity, and when he had done all, that other persons should never thank him for it or express the least gratitude any way, this would be a negative expression of his ingratitude and baseness; but it is equivalent to an act of ingratitude or a base unworthy spirit, and is as truly an expression of it, and brings as much blame, as if he by some positive act had much injured another person, and as it would have been in a lesser degree if gratitude was but very small, bearing no proportion to the benefit and obligation, or if for so great and extraordinary a kindness he had expressed no more gratitude than would have been becoming towards a person that had only given him a sixpence, or had done him some such small kindness. If he had come to his benefactors to express his gratitude, and had done after this manner, he might truly be said to have acted basely, unworthily, and odiously; he would have shewn a most ungrateful spirit, and his doing after such a manner would be justly abhorred by all; and yet the gratitude in that little that there was of it, and, so far as it went, was good, and so it is with respect to our exercises of love and gratitude to God. They are defectively corrupt and sinful, and might justly be odious and provoking to Him, taken as they are, upon the like account, and would be so, were it not that the sin and corruption of them is hid by Christ. God, as it were, don't see the odiousness and iniquity of them, and so accepts them for Christ's sake, which out of Him would be worthy of His detestation.—Coroll. Hence the saints may be said to be rewarded for their good works for Christ's sake, and not for the excellency of their works in themselves considered. For, as we have shewn, as they are in themselves, they are odious, and might be just cause of provocation. They are not rewardable, therefore, as they are in themselves; they are accepted through Christ, and it is therefore for Christ's sake that they are rewarded. For God's rewarding them is a testimony of His acceptance. They are rewarded for Christ's sake in this sense —viz., that it is for His sake that God looks upon them as fit to be accepted and rewarded.

I. THESSALONIANS.

92. iii. 13—"To the end he may stablish your hearts unblameable in holiness before God, even our Father, at the coming of our

Lord Jesus Christ with all his saints."] This and these other parallel texts—ver. 14 of chap. iv., and Jude 14—do plainly shew that the saints are in heaven with Christ before the resurrection.

I. TIMOTHY.

93. i. 9—"Knowing this, that the law is not made for a righteous man, but for the lawless and disobedient, for the ungodly and for sinners, for unholy and profane, for murderers of fathers and murderers of mothers, for manslayers."] This may be given as a reason why the precepts of the moral Law were not expressed by God to our [first] parents as well as that positive precept of not eating the forbidden fruit. There is not that need of God expressly and particularly forbidding these and other immoralities to one that is perfectly righteous in his nature, either for the making known his obligation, or for the enforcing it, as to one that is of corrupt nature.

God, in His infinite wisdom, never would have seen cause expressly to reveal the moral Law had it not been for transgressions, or man's disposition to sin.

94. i. 19—"Holding faith, and a good conscience; which some having put away, concerning faith have made shipwreck."] It seems that it should rather have been rendered the Faith—that is, concerning the doctrine of the Gospel; for in the original it is *περὶ τὴν πίστιν*, and this last agrees with the metaphor of making shipwreck. For herein the gospel, or doctrine of faith, is represented as a treasure committed to their care as a treasure is committed into a ship, and so to the care of the master, to be carried safe to such a port. But they, through their unskilfulness and carelessness, have made shipwreck of it and lost it: or if by faith is meant an inward qualification, doubtless they made shipwreck of it, as Simon Magus did, of whom we are told that he believed when others believed, but never had a true faith; for it is plain by what the Apostle Peter says, he then remained in the gall of bitterness and bond of iniquity; and it must be such a faith as the stony-ground hearers had, who, at the same time that they believed, had no root in themselves, and so were not true saints; and such a faith as those had of whom we are told that they believed on Christ, but Christ did not commit Himself to them, for He knew what was in man; He knew that what was in them was not true, was not to be depended upon.

95. v. 11—"But the younger widows refuse: for when they have begun to wax wanton against Christ, they will marry."] It appears probable from ver. 15, "For some are already turned aside after Satan," that the Apostle here has in his eye some particular instance of a strange behaviour of some young widows that had been taken into the number; a regard to which instances very much governs his language, as much as to say, If you take in young widows, no wonder

if they, through a wanton disposition, behave themselves as those which you have received of the sort. No wonder if they gad about from house to house, grow idle, trifling busybodies, and are wanton in their behaviour, and marry in a dishonourable manner such as they have first been wanton with. It is probable that in the instances which the Apostle had respect to, or one of them at least, a young widow that had been taken into the number, through her wantonness, had yielded to the enticements of a heathen man, and finally married him, which occasions such a manner of expression as "waxing wanton against Christ," and cast off their *first faith.* When the Apostle says, "For when they have begun," &c., the expression imparts no more than this :—There will be danger of such things happening in young widows.

96. v. 17—"Let the elders that rule well, be counted worthy of double honour, especially they who labour in the word and doctrine."] What the Apostle probably had in view when he used the expression of "double honour" to the elder, was the law that gave a double portion to the elder brother.

97. vi. 19—"Laying up in store for themselves a good foundation against the time to come, that they may lay hold on eternal life."] A most beautiful expression for the purpose that the Apostle intended it, naturally intimating that they that were rich had much to beat them back and to oppose and hinder their coming at so glorious a prize. The Apostle therefore would have them use those means he here directs to, as an earnest to obtain it, notwithstanding the peculiar difficulties that were in the way of rich men's obtaining it, if by any means they might violently press through the opposition and reach forward and lay hold of it. The Apostle probably had in his eye what Christ said concerning the difficulty of rich men's obtaining eternal life, and might possibly have some reference to what he himself had said just before. (Verses 9, 10,) "But they that will be rich fall into temptation, and a snare, and into many foolish and hurtful lusts, which drown men in destruction and perdition. For the love of money is the root of all evil; which while some coveted after, they have erred from the faith, and pierced themselves through with many sorrows." The original word seems to have very much the same force as our English word "lay hold," naturally intimating opposition to the obtaining a thing, or danger of missing it. So in Matt. xiv. 30, 31, where we read that when Peter was sinking in the tempestuous sea, Jesus stretched forth His hand and *caught him.* The word in the original is the same. See also how he uses the same word, (ver. 12,) where the Apostle speaks of fighting the way through to reach this prize, and seems to allude to those that strove for the prize in the Olympic Games.

HEBREWS.

98. i. 6—"And again, when he bringeth in the first-begotten into the world, he saith, And let all the angels of God worship him."] The Apostle has probably here some reference to the XCVII[th] Psalm, where we have a prophecy of the Messiah's coming into the world, on which occasion it is said, ver. 7, "Worship Him all ye gods." But the fact, the event (in which that prophecy was fulfilled) was what was at Christ's birth, that we have some intimation of in the II[d] chap. of Luke, where we are told that on that occasion there appeared a multitude of the heavenly hosts singing—"Glory to God in the highest, and on earth peace, goodwill toward men." At that time when the Son of God appeared a poor little infant in a stable and manger, when God said, "Let all the angels of God worship Him," and then the angels had a great trial of their obedience, greater than ever they had before.

99. ii. 5—"For unto the angels hath He not put in subjection the world to come, whereof we speak."] The renewed state of things brought to pass by Christ, called the new heavens and the new earth, is here called the world to come, although already come in its beginnings. Even as the blessings of Christ's kingdom and of this new creation are called good "things to come," *ἀγαθα μέλλόντα*, (Heb. ix. 11, and chap. x. 1.) Though they were already come in their beginnings, note that the time when Christ came, and offered up Himself, and ascended into heaven, is called the end of the world, (Heb. ix. 26,) *συντελείᾳ τῶν ἁιώνων*, the end of ages, the perishing as it were of the old world. So the kingdom of heaven, the new state of things that followed, is called the world to come, the new world, the future or succeeding ages.

100. iii. 1—"Wherefore, holy brethren, partakers of the heavenly calling, consider the Apostle and High Priest of our profession, Christ Jesus."] Not only the Apostle's brethren, but Christ's brethren, as in verses 11, 17, of chap. ii.—"Partakers of the heavenly calling." Not only partakers with the Apostle and partakers one with another, but partakers with Christ in His heavenly calling as an High Priest. "For no man taketh this honour to himself but he that is called of God as was Aaron." Christians are spoken of in chap. ii. 17 as the brethren of Him who is a merciful and faithful High Priest; and they are not only so, but they are also partakers of His heavenly calling as High Priest. For they also are priests unto God through Him, and as united with Him. (1 Pet. ii. 4, 5, and v. 9; so Rev. i. 6, and v. 10; and Exod. xix. 5, 6; Isa. lxi. 6.) They are priests with Christ as they are partakers of His heavenly calling and His holy vocation, 1 John ii. 20—"But ye have an unction from the Holy One, and ye know all things." Believers are followers with Christ in His anointing, as in chap. i. of this epistle, ver. 9—"Thou hast loved righteousness, and hated iniquity; therefore God, even thy God, hath

anointed thee with the oil of gladness above thy fellows." They are partakers with Him in His unction, as the precious ointment that was poured on Aaron's head ran down to the skirts of his garment. (Ps. cxxxiii. 2.)

101. iv. 4–6—" For he spake in a certain place of the seventh day on this wise, And God did rest the seventh day from all his works. And in this place again, If they shall enter into my rest. Seeing therefore it remaineth that some must enter therein, and they to whom it was first preached entered not in because of unbelief."] That when the Apostle speaks of them who have tasted of the heavenly gift, and were made partakers of the Holy Ghost, he has a special respect to them that had received the extraordinary gifts of the Holy Ghost, is evident from this, that the Apostle here has respect to the same persons that he speaks of in ver. 2; but there he is speaking of them that had been the subjects of the laying on of hands, which was a rite used in conferring the Holy Ghost in His extraordinary gifts.

102. vi. 8—" But that which beareth thorns and briers is rejected, and is nigh unto cursing; whose end is to be burned."] The malice of those apostates and persecutors who committed the unpardonable sin, is with special fitness compared to briers and thorns. (See Cant. ii. 2; Ezek. xxviii. 24; Mic. viii. 4; Ez. ii. 6; Isa. x. 17; 2 Sam. xxiii. 6, 7.)

104. vi. 11—" And we desire that every one of you do shew the same diligence to the full assurance of hope unto the end."] Here the words "to the end" are not to be joined with the immediately preceding words, "the full assurance of hope," but with those going before, "shew the same diligence." The Apostle, in the preceding verse, had observed the labour and diligence which had appeared in them. He here exhorts that this be continued unto the end, in order to the full assurance of hope. The Apostle is still pursuing the advice he began the chapter with, to avoid apostasy and to go on to perfection.

105. ix. 14—" How much more shall the blood of Christ, who through the eternal Spirit offered himself without spot to God, purge your conscience from dead works, to serve the living God."] The Apostle is probably led, when speaking of sins in this place, to make use of the application "dead" works, from allusion to pollutions by dead bodies, to the cleansing from which the ashes of the heifer spoken of in the preceding verse were appropriated. (See Num. xiv.)

106. ix. 26—" For then must He often have suffered since the foundation of the world: but now once, in the end of the world, hath He appeared to put away sin by the sacrifice of Himself."] At the end of the world—at the conclusion of the ages. So *συντελεία τῶν αἰώνων* is most exactly rendered, meaning the last of the dispensations God ever intended to give mankind.

107. x. 1–3—" For the law having a shadow of good things to come, and not the very image of the things, can never with those sacrifices, which they offered year by year continually, make the comers thereunto perfect; for then would they not have ceased to be

offered? because that the worshippers once purged should have had no more conscience of sins. But in those sacrifices there is a remembrance again made of sins every year."] Concerning the argument for the insufficiency of the ancient sacrifices from their being often offered. The wise man argues the vanity of all earthly enjoyments, and that temporal food is not man's true good from that, that the occasions for eating still return. If a man eats, yet the need of eating returns, satisfaction is not obtained; his need and his appetite remains, the demands of nature are not answered so but that still it continues demanding, so that after a man has repeated his eating from day to day many years, yet he needs and his nature craves as much as when he first came into the world, (Eccles. vi. 7, and also i. 3–9)—"All the labour of man is for his mouth, yet the appetite or (as it is in the original) the soul is not filled," with the context. The argument is of the same sort with that which the Apostle here makes use of, to shew the vanity of the ancient sacrifices, and their insufficiency to answer the end of a true atonement, that they did not satisfy, because the demand of justice still remained, and its appetite returned, as in the other case the demands of nature. They were never able to make the comers thereto perfect: the occasion of offering them returned autumnally; and therefore if Solomon's argument be good, the Apostle's is certainly good also.

108. xi. 37—"They were stoned, they were sawn asunder, were tempted, were slain with the sword: they wandered about in sheepskins and goatskins; being destitute, afflicted, tormented."] "They were tempted," that is, in the midst of their torments their cruel persecutors added earnest solicitations, persuasions, fair-tempting promises, and the like, if they would desert the cause they suffered for, which was verified in Antiochus Epiphanes.

ST JAMES.

109. ii. 8—"If ye fulfil the royal law according to the scripture, Thou shalt love thy neighbour as thyself, ye do well."] Probably so called because the law of love was by way of specialty the law of Christ the King of the Church. (See Gal. vi. 2; John xiii. 34, and xv. 12; 1 John iv. 21.)

110. iv. 14—"Whereas ye know not what shall be on the morrow: for what is your life? It is even a vapour, that appeareth for a little time, and then vanisheth away."] Here seems to be an allusion to that vapour in the breath, (that is as it were man's life,) sometimes while the breath is warm; but as soon as it is cool, vanishes away as it were in a moment. (See Job vii. 7, and Ps. lxxviii. 39.)

I. PETER.

111. i. 4—"To an inheritance incorruptible, and undefiled, and that fadeth not away, reserved in heaven for you."] This is probably here mentioned because those that the Apostle wrote this epistle to were strangers scattered abroad, ver. 1, out of their own land—the land of Canaan, not possessing that earthly inheritance of old promised to Israel, and cast out by their brethren according to the flesh for being Christians. (See Dr Goodwin's Works, vol. i., p. 44.)

II. PETER.

112. i. 28—"Knowing this first, that no prophecy of the scripture is of any private interpretation."] That is, it is not men's speaking their own sense of things or interpreting their own minds, but the mind of God. That which is their sense is not always the sense or interpretaion of Scripture. But that which was the sense of the Holy Ghost, the prophets did not always perceive the meaning of in their prophecies.

I. JOHN.

113. iii. 3—"And every man that hath this hope in Him purifieth himself, even as He is pure."] That is, in God or in Christ, the Person spoken of in the foregoing words ἐπ' αὐτῷ. The preposition ἐπὶ expresses, not the relation of hope to the subject of it, but to its object, as in many places of the New Testament. It signifies the relation of faith, trust, and hope to this object, as Matt. xxvii. 43—"He trusted in God;" Luke xi. 22—"Wherein he trusted;" xviii. 9—"Trusted in themselves;" Luke xxiv. 25—"To believe all the prophets," &c.; Acts ix. 42—"Many believed in the Lord;" xi. 17—"Who believed in the Lord;" Acts xvi. 31—"Believe in the Lord Jesus;" Rom. iv. 24—"Believe in Him;" Rom. ix. 33—"Believeth in Him;" x. 11—"Believeth in Him;" 13—"In Him shall the Gentiles hope;" 2 Cor. i. 9—"Should not trust in ourselves, but in God;" ii. 3—"Confidence in you all;" 1 Tim. i. 16—"Believe on Him;" iv. 16—"Hoped in the living God;" v. 5—"Hoped in God;" vi. 17—"Hope in uncertain riches;" Heb. ii. 13—"Trusting in Him;" vi. 1—"Of faith in God;" 1 Peter ii. 6—"He that believeth in Him;" iii. 5—"Hoped in God."

114. iii. 6—"Whosoever abideth in Him sinneth not: whosoever sinneth hath not seen Him neither known Him."] See 2 Sam. xii.

13—"For thou didst it secretly: but I will do this thing before all Israel, and before the sun." By this it appears that though David was so holy a man, a man after God's own heart, yet his deed was properly called sin; yea, it was mortal sin—sin that deserved death, as is implied. See also the terms used Ps. li. 1–5, 10, 16. So Job was a man that God gloried in,—that was a perfect and an upright man, one that feared God and *eschewed evil;* or which is the same thing, one that sinned not. He held fast his integrity to the end and eschewed evil, and made good God's boast of (his) eschewing evil under his temptations. And yet Elihu, who spoke by inspiration, was in God's stead, and the forerunner of God, and did not answer as his three friends did, but spoke that which was right, and was not reproved by God, charges him with sinning, Job xxxiv. 37—"For he addeth rebellion unto his sin; he clappeth his hands among us, and multiplieth his words against God." See also note on 2 Chron. xxxii. 31. It won't do to go about to solve the argument from these instances with the doctrine of falling from grace. This verse that we are now upon will not allow of that, (see note on latter part of the verse,) and if any should imagine that the kind of operation on the hearts of the saints in the New Testament which the Apostle John calls a "being born again," is something peculiar to them, and what God's people, under the Old Testament, were not the subjects of, and that regeneration is a thing peculiar to New Testament times, (though that may easily be disproved — (for) the Old Testament saints were circumcised in heart, and had right spirits renewed in them, &c., and therefore were born again,) yet we have a remarkable instance in one that was said to have followed Christ in the regeneration.—(See Matt. xix. 27, 28)—viz., Peter, who denied his Lord with oaths and curses. He was one that had been born again, and therefore was one of them that Christ called little children, and one that He spoke of: Matt. xviii. 6—"But whoso shall offend one of these little ones which believe in me, it were better for him that a millstone were hanged about his neck, and that he were drowned in the depth of the sea;" whom He called so on the account of their new birth, as it is manifest by the foregoing words, particularly the third verse of the chapter:—"Verily I say unto you, Except ye be converted, and become as little children, ye shall not enter into the kingdom of heaven," which is parallel with what Christ says to Nicodemus: "Verily, I say unto you, Except a man be born of water and of the Spirit, he cannot enter into the kingdom of God." The Apostle John says, in the latter part of this verse, "Whosoever hath not seen Him, nor known Him," but Peter had seen and known his Lord, and therefore Christ says to him, "Blessed art thou, Simon Barjona, for flesh and blood hath not revealed it unto thee, but my Father which is in heaven;" and Christ in His prayer in the XVIIth of John speaks of him with others of His disciples expressly as having seen and known Him: ver. 3—"And this is life eternal, that they might know Thee the only true God, and Jesus Christ, whom Thou hast sent," and then says in the 6th to 8th verses, "I have manifested Thy name unto the men which Thou gavest Me out of the world: Thine they were, and Thou gavest them Me; and they have kept Thy word. Now they have known that all things, whatsoever Thou hast given Me are of Thee: for I have given unto them the words which Thou gavest Me; and they have received them, and have known surely that I came out from Thee, and they have believed that Thou didst send Me." These last words then, by what the Apostle John himself says in this epistle, [shew] that Peter was born of God: chap. v. 1—"Whosoever believeth that Jesus is the Christ is born of God: and every one that loveth Him that begat, loveth him also that is begotten of him." So Eccles. vii. 28; 1 Kings viii. 46. So 2 Chron. vi. 36; Prov. xx. 9; John ix. 30, 31, and ver. 20, and ver. 2, 3; Ps. xix. 12, and cxxx. 3. There is sin in the New Testament saints as well as the Old. The wise virgins slumbered and slept; Rom. vii.—"The thing that I hate that I do;" Heb. xii.—"Let us lay aside every weight, and the sin which doth so easily beset us." James iii. 2. And this Apostle John himself in this very epistle several times speaks of those that are born again as liable to sin. It is by the new birth that they become as little children; the Apostle says, chap. ii. 1—"My little children, these things write I unto you, that ye sin not. And if any man sin, we have an advocate with the Father, Jesus Christ the righteous." And this is a confirmation that the Apostle has not only respect to sins that were committed before regeneration. In the words immediately foregoing, "If we say that we have not sinned, we make Him a liar, and his word is not in us." Again, it is by the new birth by which Christians are born of God, this epistle speaks of the brethren as liable to sin: 1 John v. 16—"If any man see his brother sin a sin which is not unto death, he shall ask, and he shall give him life for them that sin not unto death." And yet in the next verse but one, respects that saying that we are upon: "We know that whosoever is born of God sinneth not: but he that is begotten of God keepeth himself, and that wicked one toucheth him not," which confirms that the Apostle means, when he says, "He sinneth not," is not that he never is guilty of any sinful act. Such expressions in Scripture as this in the text, "sinneth" and "sinneth not," are not always to be taken for committing a particular act of sin, as that in Job, the draught and heat, &c. By them that have sinned, is not intended them that are guilty of a particular act of sin. That in Eph. ii. 3—"Fulfilling the desires of the flesh and of the mind," in the original ποιοῦντες, doing the desires of the flesh—that is making a trade of this. 1 Peter iii. 10—"If thou wouldst see good days, refrain thy tongue from evil, and thy lips that they speak no guile." It is not meant that to do one good action is the way to be happy, but a man's setting himself in such a course, making a practice and business of doing good. How often is the wickedness of the king of Israel and Judah expressed by that, "That they did evil in the sight of the Lord."

115. iii. 6—"Whosoever abideth in him sinneth not: whosoever sinneth hath not seen him, neither known him."] The words of the

next verse are a full confutation of them that from hence would argue sinless perfection. "He that doeth righteousness is righteous, even as He is righteous." There is no more reason to understand the Apostle of committing only one act of sin by the expression "sinneth," or "committeth," or "doeth sin," than to understand of one single act of righteousness, when by the expression, "doth righteousness," and so to understand the next verse thus:—"He that doeth any righteousness at any time is righteous even as God is righteous," whereas by doing righteousness the Apostle plainly means practising righteousness, or making that his practice in the course of his life. So there is equal reason when he speaks here of committing sin to understand him of practising sin, or making wickedness his trade or practice. See "doing righteousness," &c.

116. iv. 17—"Herein is our love made perfect, that we may have boldness in the day of judgment: because as He is, so are we in this world."] The sense seems to be this—our love is made perfect to give us boldness before Him (that is, before Christ) in another world, even by our being in this world as He is. Like Him in love, then is our love made perfect, when we love one another as He hath loved us. For it is that love that the apostle is speaking of in the preceding verse—"We have known and believed the love that God hath to us," and what that love is that God hath to us. The Apostle said in the preceding verses (9, 10)—viz., God's sending His Son into the world to die for us—and then says, ver. 11—"Beloved, if God so loved us, we ought also to love one another;" that is, we ought to love one another as God hath loved us, and as Christ hath loved us, and so we shall be as He was, and hereby we shall have assurance, as it follows, ver. 13—"Hereby know we that we dwell in Him, and He in us, because He hath given us of His Spirit"—made us to be of the same temper with Himself; and then the Apostle, in verses 14 and 16, further insists on the love of God to us in giving His Son; and in the 17th verse, repeatedly mentions our conformity to Him in this love as what will give assurance, and observes particularly by this it will give boldness at the day of judgment, when we appear before Christ, that in this world we have been like Him, and behaved ourselves as He behaved Himself in the world.

ST JUDE.

117. 14, 15—"And Enoch also, the seventh from Adam, prophesied of these, saying, Behold, the Lord cometh with ten thousand of his saints, to execute judgment upon all, and to convince all that are ungodly among them of all their ungodly deeds which they have ungodly committed, and of all their hard speeches which ungodly sinners have spoken against Him."] Inspired writers of the Old

Testament, sometimes, when speaking [of things] recorded in Scripture history many ages after their histories were written, do mention particulars not recorded in these histories; as particularly, Asaph mentions thunder and lightning that there was in the time when Israel passed through the Red Sea, as Ps. lxxvii. 15, and following verses. So David mentions a great shower of rain that there was when God appeared on Mount Sinai. Ps. lxviii. 8—"The earth shook, the heavens also dropped at the presence of God: even Sinai itself was moved at the presence of God, the God of Israel." So the prophet Habakkuk mentions thunder that arose at the conclusion of the twelve hours that the sun and moon stood still. See notes on Hab. iii. 11, and we must allow the same to the inspired writers of the New Testament. This prophecy of Enoch is probably the rather mentioned as applicable to those heretics and apostates he speaks of, because they strenuously derided and contemptuously ridiculed [Christ's servants].

118. 19—"These be they who separate themselves, sensual, having not the Spirit."] The Apostle uses this form of expression because he has reference to some spoken of in the Old Testament, that are spoken of as separating themselves. Either Ezek. xiv. 7 or Hosea iv. 14, or ix. 10.

DIRECTIONS

FOR

JUDGING OF PERSONS' EXPERIENCES.

NOTE.

See Introduction iii., p. 13, *ante*.—G.

DIRECTIONS FOR JUDGING OF PERSONS' EXPERIENCES.

See to it

That the operation be much upon the Will or Heart, not on the Imagination, nor on the speculative understanding or motions of the mind, though they draw great affections after 'em as the consequence.

That the trouble of mind be reasonable, that the mind be troubled about those things that it has reason to be troubled about; and that the trouble seems mainly to operate in such a manner, with such a kind of trouble and exercise as is reasonable: founded on reasonable, solid consideration; a solid sense and conviction of truth, as of things as they are indeed.

That it be because their state appears terrible on the account of those things, wherein its dreadfulness indeed consists; and that their concern be solid, not operating very much by pangs and sudden passions, freaks and frights, and a capriciousness of mind.

That under their seeming convictions it be sin indeed; that they are convinced of their guilt, in offending and affronting so great a God: One that so hates sin, and is so set against it, to punish it, &c.

That they be convinced both of sins of heart and life: that their pretences of sense of sin of heart ben't without reflection on their wicked practice; and also that they are not only convinced of sin of practice, but sin of heart. And in both, that what troubles 'em be those things wherein their wretchedness has really chiefly consisted.

That they are convinced of their spiritual sins, consisting in their sinful defects, living without love to God, without accepting Christ, gratitude to Him, &c.

That the convictions they have of the insufficiency and vanity of their own doings, ben't only from some sense of wanderings of mind, and other sinful behaviour mixed; but from a conviction of the sinful defects of their duties, their not being done from a right principle; and so as having no goodness at all mixed with the bad, but altogether corrupt.

That it is truly conviction of sin that convinces them of the

Justice of God in their damnation, in rejecting their prayers, disregarding their sorrowful case, and all desires and endeavours after deliverance, &c., and not merely any imagination or pang, and melting of affection through some real or supposed instance of Divine Goodness.

That they be so convinced of sin as not in the inward thought and habit of their minds to excuse themselves, and impliedly quarrel with God, because of their impotency: for instance, that they don't excuse their slight of Christ, and want of love to Him, because they can't esteem and love Him.

That they don't evidently themselves look on their convictions [as] great, and ben't taken with their own humiliation.

That which should be chiefly looked at should be *evangelical.* If this be sound, we have no warrant to insist upon it, that there be manifest a remarkable work, purely legal, wherein was nothing of grace. So with regard to Convictions and Humiliation; only seeing to it that the mind is indeed convinced of these things, and sees 'em [sees] that [which] many Divines insisted should be seen, under a purely legal work. And also seeing to it that the convictions there are, seem to be deep and fixed, and to have a powerful governing influence on the temper of the mind, and a very direct respect to practice.

See to it

That they have not only pretended convictions of sin; but a proper mourning for sin. And also, that sin is burdensome to them, and that their hearts are tender and sensible with respect to it . . . the object of their care and dread.

That God and Divine things are admirable on account of the beauty of their moral perfection.

That there is to be discerned in their sense of the sufficiency of Christ, a sense of that Divine, supreme, and spiritual excellency of Christ, wherein this sufficiency fundamentally consists; and that the sight of this excellency is really the foundation of their satisfaction as to His sufficiency.

That their conviction of the truth of Divine things be discerned to be truly some way or other primarily built on a sense of their Divine excellency.

That their discoveries and illuminations and experiences in general, are not superficial pangs, flashes, imagination, freaks, but solid, substantial, deep, inwrought into the frame and temper of their minds, and discovered to have respect to practice.

That they long after HOLINESS, and that all their experiences increase their longing.

Let 'em be inquired of concerning their disposition and willingness to bear the Cross, sell all for Christ, choosing their portion in heaven, &c.

Whether their experience have a respect to PRACTICE in these ways. That their behaviour at present seems to be agreeable to such experiences.

Whether it inclines 'em much to think of Practice, and more and more for past ill practice.

Makes a disposition to ill practices dreadful.

Makes 'em long after perfect freedom from sin, and after those things wherein *Holiness* consists; and by fixed and strong resolutions, attended with fear and jealousy of their own hearts.

Whether, when they tell of their experiences, it is not with such an air that you as it were feel that they expect to be admired and applauded, and [whether they] won't be disappointed if they fail of discerning in you something of that nature; and shocked and displeased if they discover the contrary.

Enquire whether their joy be truly and properly joy in God and in Christ; joy in Divine Good; or whether it ben't wholly joy in themselves, joy in their own excellencies or privileges, in their experiences; what God has done for them, or what He has promised He will do for them; and whether they ben't affected with their own discoveries and affections.

SERMONS.

NOTE.

See Introduction iv., pages 13, 14.—G.

SERMONS.

I.

Matt. vii. 14—"Few there be that find it."

Doc[trine.] 'Tis a hard thing to find the right way to Heaven.

I. There is a way to Heaven.
God has opened a door.

II. There is but one right way.

III. 'Tis a hard thing to find this one right way.
Appears: In that there are so few that find the way.
Tho[ugh] all have so much need to find.
Tho[ugh] so many desire to find and seek after it.
Tho[ugh] so many think they have found.
. . . . . . so many are mistaken.
That many of those that do find it, first take a great deal of pains.
Some for a long time.
Many prayers.
Many difficulties.
Reason: Negatively, not that [God] han't [has not] called us.
" " very plain in itself.
Reasons:
Many wrong ways.
Like travelling through a great wilderness.
Full of difficulties . . . dangers . . . .
But one right way.
[A] narrow way.
Many wrong ways.
Mention some of the wrong ways.
Do right in some things only.
Outward Religion only.
Affections that go away.
Religious out of regard to men.

Religious only out of fear of hell.
. . . . from self-love.
Don't love God for Himself.
Trust in their own righteousness.
Depend on the good opinion of others.
Apt to think themselves convicted when they are not.
High pride : apt to think well of themselves.
A little good looks great.
Don't see what is bad.
How many things men often think are CONVERSION.
2. Men's own lust blind[s] 'em.
The way is good and plain.
Right way is what men don't like.
Up-hill.
Contrary to all their lusts.
. . . . . to their pride.
. . . . . to their worldliness.
. . . . sensuality.
. . . . slothfulness.
Enmity against God.
Wrong ways are
Easy.
Broad.
Down-hill.
3. Devils.
Blind them and deceive them.
4. Things of this world blind 'em.
5. Wicked men implead (?) 'em.

APPLICA[TION.]
What a great mercy to have the Word of God.
Mercy that God has appointed ministers.
Great need of Prayer ——
Never without God's help.
Don't trust . . . v. 22 . . .
What need of God's power and striving.

DIRECTIONS.
Pray earnestly.
Not trust . . . . . [As above, v. 22.]
Take advice.
Begin soon.
Hold on and hold out.
Don't take hope *too soon.*
In every thing follow the Word of God.
You need to be much concerned.*

* It will be observed from the *facsimile* that the above Sketch of a Sermon is written on the leaf of a letter. Very many of Edwards's MSS. are thus written on all manner of kinds and scraps of paper.—G.

II.

2 Tim. iii. 16—"All scripture is given by inspiration of God."*
Doctrine: The Scripture is the Word of God.

I. There must be some Word of God.

'Tis unreasonable to think that God would always keep silence and never say anything to mankind.

God has made mankind and given him Reason and Understanding.

Has made him the chief of all the creatures.

Given him reason that he might know God and serve Him.

Did not give the other creatures reason: He did make 'em to serve Him.

Other creatures are made for man.

Man was made for God: to serve God, or else he was made for nothing.

But we may be sure He did not make such a creature as man for nothing.

But how unreasonable is it to think that God would make us for Himself and never say anything to us.

God is the King that rules over all nations.

But how unreasonable is it to suppose that He should be a King and never say anything to His subjects. . . . be a King and never tell them what His will or what His commands are, that His subjects may obey Him.

Is as a Father: all His Family.

But will a father be always dumb and silent, &c.?

God has given mankind speech: so that they are able to speak and make known their minds to one another.

And therefore 'tis unreasonable to think that God never would speak to men and make known His mind to them.

We need to have God teach us as much as a child needs to be taught by his father.

And since God has given mankind understanding He doubtless will teach him and instruct him.

How can we know Him to worship God if we have no Word of God to tell us?

We should not know what way of worship would please Him . . . . whether to pray to Him or to sing or to keep the Sabbath, or be baptized, or come to sacrament, or what else we shall do.

'Tis certain God has made us for another world. . . . Men but a little while here.

And how shall we know how God will do with us in another world?

How shall we know how He will punish such as do wickedly in another [world]?

* In the left-hand corner is written, "St:, Ind. Novem. '53." See Introduction iv., p. 14.—G.

What He will do for good men in another [world]?

Whether He will forgive us after we have sinned?

How shall we know what He expects we should do that we may be forgiven?

In what He will save . . . . Whether He will forgive great sins.

What will men do when they come to die if there be no Word of God to tell 'em?

How should we ever know how the world was made?

How should we know how God made man at first?

We see men in this world are very wicked: the world is full of wickedness everywhere.

Certainly God did not make man so.

How shall we know how mankind came to be so wicked?

We see how the world is full of death: full of war and all manner of misery.

How shall we know how misery and death came, &c.?

And how shall we know what way of salvation there is?

Where shall we find one to be our Saviour that will stand for us . . . if the Word of God don't tell us?

How shall we know what God will do with the world at last? how the world will come to an end?

We see that God is kind to mankind: takes care of 'em.

Therefore He can't leave 'em in darkness and take no care to teach 'em.

We see what necessity mankind stand in, of a Word of God to teach 'em when we consider how it is in those countries where they have no Word of God.

They are all in darkness and blindness about God and Divine things.

They think there is a God.

Yet don't know what He is.

Many think there is [are] a great many gods.

Worship "graven images" and stones.

Worship the devil.

Don't know how to serve God.

Know nothing how the world was made . . . . how man was made.

Know nothing what God will do with men in another world.

Don't know how men shall obtain forgiveness of their sin.

Some think [by] offering their own children. . . .

Thus we see there must certainly be some Word of God.

But where is any Word of God if it ben't [be not] in the Bible?

The Heathen han't [have not] no Word of God amongst them.

The Bible therefore is the Word of God, must be.

The Bible gives right notions concerning God.

Tells how God made the world . . . . made men . . . . how men became wicked . . . .

What God will do with men in another world.

What way we may have the forgiveness of sin.

What is the way of salvation?

What God's mind, and [what His] will, is.

All the Rules and Commandments in the Bible are holy.

Here told what man's duty is in many things.

All sin is forbidden.

How God will be served.

The great things God has done for His people through all ages.

What the Saviour did and suffered: how He ascended into Heaven.

How the world will come to an end.

How God will judge the world.

Another thing that shews that the Scriptures are the Word of God is this:—

That when God told the wise and holy men to write the Bible He gave 'em power to work great MIRACLES, to convince men that it was His work.

Moses was a man that wrote all the first part of the Bible.

And God, to shew that the Word he wrote was His word . . . .

And so the other Prophets that wrote other parts.

Jesus Christ gave us the Scriptures of the New Testament. He spoke the Word of God.

He, to shew that His Word was the Word of God, wrought great miracles.

He told His Disciples to write down what He said . . . . enabled them to do great miracles.

The Apostle Paul.

That there was such a man as Christ . . . . that great miracles [were wrought] even His enemies own: none deny it.

Another thing that shews the Scriptures to be the Word of God is that the Scripture FORETELLS a great many things.

The OLD TESTAMENT that was given to the Jews a great while before Christ was born foretold Christ's coming.

And a great many things concerning Him. All which are FULFILLED.

The Scriptures of the NEW TESTAMENT foretell a great many things . . . . all came to pass.

The Jews should become a *distinct* nation . . . . that the Pope shall arise . . . . many turn Papists . . . . just as it is.

The Scriptures we here read is the same Word that was given of old.

The same Word has been kept all along: it has not been changed.

Here it still is the same language in which it was written at first.

It must be the same that the Jews had, and that God's People had in Christ's and the Apostle's time.

It could not be altered since, because it was scattered about a great many nations all over the world . . . . which have had it ever since.

Therefore the world could not be cheated.

The Jews, to whom the Old Testament was given: they remain a distinct People still, and have had the Old Testament amongst 'em, written in their own language.

They are all over the world and can't alter it.

The Scripture has all along been among people that have been against one another in their OPINIONS . . . . could not agree to alter it . . . . if one altered the other would find it out.

Another thing that shews that the Scripture is the Word of God is this :—

That the Scripture has been the means of enlightening so many nations.

Many nations formerly in great darkness : but now . . .

All the greatest nations of the world . . .

No people in the world can come to have right notions of God and of another world any other way than by this Word.

Another thing that shews [it, is]

. . . Great opposition : the Devil and wicked men make against it.

Another thing that shews [that it is] the Word of God is this : it has PREVAILED against such great opposition.

When it first came abroad in the world all the wicked set themselves against it . . . kings . . . armies . . . [Christians] put to cruel deaths . . . yet it PREVAILED . . . overcame all the greatest and strongest nations.

Then there is this thing : those [who] first preached were poor men.

So many nations never could have been made to believe it if men had made it.

Not only foolish men, little men, but great men and wise men.

Another thing : no other Word ever was used as the means of bringing men to know the true God but the Scriptures.

Where the Scriptures have come there has been light : all the rest of the world has remained in darkness. So 'tis now all over the world.

Another thing that shews [it] is this : no man could make such a Book as the Bible. . . .

It must be made by wicked men or good men. . . . Wicked men would not make it. Good men could not.

Another thing : no Book reaches the hearts of men so much. No word so AWAKENS the conscience. No word is so powerful to change the heart. Great many have been made 'new men :' very wicked men.

No word so powerful to comfort the hearts of men . . . in death . . . cruel deaths . . .

Another : good men all love the Bible. Better they are the more they love it . . . the more they are convinced that it is the Word of God. The more wicked men [are] the more they are AGAINST it.

APPLICATION :

1. How thankful we should be to God. . . .

2. Hence we may learn that all the Scripture says to us is certainly true.

God knows . . . God cannot lie . . . God is very angry for sin.

About another world. There is another world. Good men die.

About Hell. The Scripture says there is a furnace of fire.

God will not hear. No rest.

Many are ready to think that it may be there is none.

About Heaven. About the Day of Judgment: rise again.

About the sorrowful, miserable condition man is in.

About the way of salvation.

Christ is the Son of God. No other Saviour. HE WILL SAVE ALL THAT COME TO HIM.

About the mystery of being 'born again.'

Some are ready to say in their hearts there is no such thing.

What we must be in order to go to Heaven—

Therefore let all men that are not 'born again' consider these things.

All these are not seeking their salvation.

3. Hence 'tis worth the while to take a great deal of pains to learn to read and understand the Scriptures.

I would have you all of you think of this.

When there is such a book that you may have, how can you be contented without being able to read it?

How does it make you feel when you think there is a Book that is God's own Word? That tells . . .

And you think with yourself that you are not able to read it. . . . See and think about it. All that you know is only what others tell you . . . see nothing with your own eyes.

Especially I would have you that are young people take notice of these things.

Parents should take care that their children learn . . .

This will be the way to be kept from the Devil . . . Devil can't bear [the Bible.] Kept from Hell. To be happy for ever.

But if you let the Word of God alone, and never use, and you can't expect the benefits of it. . . .

You must not only hear and read, &c., but you must have it sunk down into your heart. Believe. Be affected. Love the Word of God. Written in your heart.

Must not only read and hear, but DO the things. Otherwise no good; but will be the worse for it.

And you should endeavour to understand. To that end to learn the English tongue.

If you had the Bible in your own language, I should not say so much.

Endeavour to promote your children's learning English.

You that can read should often read . . . meditate . . . pray that God would enlighten you.

Consider how much it is worth the while to go often to your Bible to hear the great God Himself speak to you.

There you may hear Christ speak.

How much better must we think this is than the word of men. Better than the word of the wisest man of the world.

How much wiser is God than man.

Here all is true; nothing false.

Here all is wise; nothing foolish.

This is the GREAT LIGHT God has given to the world. To make use of this is the way to walk in the Light . . . to have our souls filled with Light. If we neglect this we shall walk in darkness.

We should value this more than the light of the sun. We see the light of the sun does a great deal of good . . . gives light . . . pleasant to see . . . 'tis comfortable . . . it gives life.

So Scripture gives light . . . gives life.

Should hear the Word: come to meeting. 'Tis the way to have God's mercy, to seek God in His Word. There we may expect to meet with God. God will respect His own Word for the good of men: what great good has been done.

God has often made it a means of great good. Conversion of many souls. Great joy of many. Many have been comforted in affliction . . . in death.

This will be the way to be wise with the most excellent wisdom.

III. and IV.

Rom. v. 1— . . . "we have peace with God." *

SUBJECT: Peace with God.

1. The nature of it.
2. How it is brought to pass.
3. The distinguishing marks of it.
4. The benefits of it.
5. The course that should be taken in order to it.

I. The nature of it.

Here I would observe that we ought to distinguish between that peace which is real and [which is] sensible.

The one consists in the state of the soul: the other in the sense of the soul. The one is the foundation of the other. That peace of God which is real or that consists in the state of the soul is the ground of that which consists in its sensation or apprehension. Both are called in Scripture by the name of PEACE; and are represented as the peculiar privileges of God's saints. And therefore I will something very briefly consider the nature of each.

1. That peace with God that is *real* is that state of a believer whereby he is in reconciliation and favour with his Creator. It consists in two things:—

   1. Something negative—viz., the removal of God's anger and displeasure . . . forgiveness of sin . . . total, (Isa. i. 18)—'White as snow,' . . . compared to the unrolling of a cloud, (Isa. xliv. 22, 23;) . . . as though they never had been, (Jer. l. 20;) 'sought for and shall not be found,' . . . 'depths of

* See division V. for commencement of the second sermon from this text.—G.

the sea,' (Micah vii. 18;) . . . everlasting, (Jer. xxxi. 34;) "make an end of sin." (Dan. ix. 24.)

2. Something positive—viz., as being received and treated as the objects of God's favour.

As the expression is used in Scripture [it is] something more than merely negative. . . . Title. Manifestation. Treatment.

Difference between love and favour, though sometimes called by the same names — Acceptance. Compliance . . . as entitled to a reward.

2. [That peace with God that is] *sensible* is that inward, holy calm and quietness of soul arising from a sense and apprehension of the soul's union with God.

A sense of this gives an inexpressibly sweet calm. This is usually intended by Christ. (John xiv. 27.)

This is twofold:—

1. Peace of conscience or a sweet calm from a sense of the pardon of sin and acceptance with God as righteous.

   Two things—

   A sense of sufficiency.

   An apprehension of the faithfulness of the promise.

   These things give a sweet rest.

2. That rest of soul that arises from the sense or feeling of a real conformity to and union with [Christ].

Peace of confidence consists in a sense of a relative union.

That is the rest that arises from hope: this from love.

II. How the children of God come to be made partakers of this benefit.

1. The first and highest source and spring of all is from God's eternal foreknowledge. . . . Choosing 'em, the particular persons by the Father.

Jer. xxxi. 3—"Everlasting love."

The love of the Father. Giving them to the Son.

The Son owing them . . . predestinating of them. (Ephes. i. 4.) Titus i. 2.

This is the first foundation.

2. The purchase of this blessing was made by the offering that Christ made to the Father.

Prince of Peace. (Isa. iv. 6.) Peace on earth. . . . Nigh by the Blood. (Ephes. ii. 14.) He is our Peace. In the text, peace with God through our Lord Jesus Christ.

The Way. Great High Priest. Offering is but one; but it is to be variously considered.

3. The way in which we come to have an interest in this.

Purchase: and so to be actually brought into peace with God is by being united to Christ.

Threefold union.

Most immediately by a legal union. . . . Real union foundation of legal.

Being in Christ, the believer, as it were, necessarily is a partaker.

4. The immediate efficient of this union is the Holy Spirit.

So Christ is in them, and they in Christ. (Rom. viii. 9, 10.)

The union is first by a communication from Christ ; and this is what is communicated.

The vine is united by deriving sap : the womb by deriving life.

Thus the Holy Spirit makes application. In this respect the peace with God is from the Holy Spirit.

5. The work by which the Spirit effects this union.

The qualification that the Holy Spirit works in the elect by which this union is effected is faith.

This is the uniting act. Therefore God looks on the sinner as one with Christ, because He has accepted of him ; and his soul has united [itself to Christ].

6. The end of this union, by which the soul has sensible peace with God, is sanctification of heart and life . . . including faith and all other graces.

And thus it is that the Spirit of God gives sensible peace.

This is the seal of the Spirit, (Ephes. i. 13 ;) earnest of the Spirit. (2 Cor. i. 22.) By this 'tis a spirit of adoption.

III. Distinguishing marks of it, whereby it may be distinguished from the false appearances of it.

1. In those that have a true peace with God their sensible peace has its foundation laid in conviction.

There is a false peace.

Preparation . . . legal conviction.

Immediate foundation : . . . spiritual conviction has its foundation in light, and not in darkness . . . encreased by conviction.

2. In those [that have peace] that quietness and rest of soul they have is not only their comfort but their virtue or nature. (?)

3. Christ is the foundation of all.

4. In those [that have peace there is] a sense of glory and suffering precedes a sense of propriety [= property, possession].

A more principal foundation.

5. . . . a rest of choice and love precedes a rest of hope.

The rest of the faculties of the soul in God is the Church's God . . . goes before a rest in Him as our God. . . . As a rest in His favour.

6. In those [that have peace] there is a union of heart with God and Christ, attended with a relinquishing all other things.

7. Attended with an irreconcilable war with God's enemies.*

* In a smaller character there is added here—

1. Conviction, . . . legal, . . . spiritual. . . . 2. Divided from that in which it sought peace. 3. Christ is the foundation. 4. Union of heart with God and Christ, attended with relinquishing [of all else.] 5. An irreconcilable war with sin, . . . an holy peace and rest. 6. A sight of excellency and suffering procures a sight of rest. 7. A rest of choice and love precedes a rest of hope. 8. A sweet, humble, peaceable frame of life. These are 'Notes' of a recapitulation of the Discourse thus far, preliminary to a second, which consisted of the remaining head V., amplified from the 'Notes.'—G.

IV. Benefits.

1. A being infinitely above the reach of everything that might make them men. . . .

I say infinitely above. . . . Infinitely strong defence . . . as impossible as to destroy God Himself . . . infinite wisdom . . . infinite strength engaged . . . infinite price . . . infinite truth. . . .

Dwell "on high" . . . infinitely high.

Foundation in that which is eternal: from eternity to eternity. . .

Oath of God. (Heb. vi. 17, 18.) . . .

2. A being at peace with all God's creatures. In different senses.

Angels. . . . Saints. . . . Sun, moon, stars. Beasts. Stones, (Job v. 23.)

Water and fire, (Isa. xliii. 2.) . . . Whole creation 'groans.'

Poisonous things, (Mark xvi. 18 ; Luke x. 19.) . . . Wicked men and devils — All things for them, (1 Cor. iii. 21, 22.)

3. Communion with God.

4. An holy and sweet walking and friendly conversing with God.

Amos iii. 3—"Two walk together." . . . "Called you friends."

5. More and more conformity and assimilation to God.

6. Communion with saints, (1 John i. 3-7.)

7. An irrefragable title to eternal glory.

8. Steadfastness under the changes of life. Anchor to the soul.

A steadfast calm in the midst of storms. A steadfast meekness in the midst of oppositions.

9. A strong and conquering support and comfort under the troubles of life. . . . Waiting our death.

10. Joy unspeakable.

V. Course to be taken in order to the obtaining this peace with God and enjoying the benefit of it.

1. A sense of the great breach. . . .

2. A sense of their misery by reason of the breach, and the absolute necessity of reconciliation. All false rest must be destroyed. The world. Own righteousness.

3. A conviction that God may justly refuse ever to be at peace with us.*

4. An eternal divorce of the heart from that which made and which maintains the breach.

5. The Prince of Peace must be resorted to and embraced.

6. An high war must be maintained with God's enemies.

7. A spirit of peace and love must rule in our hearts and lives.

This is the end of union between God and the soul. And this is the end of union between Christians, one with another. If we are much under the influences of a spirit contrary to this, we can't expect to have the sensible peace of God. But if you live in the lively exercise [of this] it will be the way to love.

The feeling of this gives sensible peace, as I observed before.

* Interlined here—"It is the foundation for spiritual light and knowledge."—G.

And it tends to give the other sort of sensible peace, that which consists in hope. "For perfect peace casts out fear."

V. and VI.

Acts xxiv. 25—"And as he reasoned of righteousness, temperance, and judgment to come, Felix trembled, and answered, Go thy way for this time; when I have a convenient season, I will call for thee."*

I. The subject of the Apostle's preaching.
II. How Felix was affected by it.
III. How he conducted himself in these circumstances.

SUBJECT: Sinners delaying in putting off the great concern of their souls till a supposed more convenient season.

1. How sinners oftentimes do delay.
2. The reasons or causes why sinners do thus.
3. The end of it.

I. I would briefly observe how sinners do frequently delay and put off the great concern of their souls till a supposed more convenient season.

(1.) They sometimes put off to certain times they set, when they intend. . . . Children sometimes. . . . Shall know more—Know better how to pray and perform other duties of Religion that grown-up persons perform.

'Tis a common thing for young people. Till settled in the world. "More convenient season:" a better inclination . . . . not so much inclined to mirth and youthful vanities . . . . fewer temptations . . . . out of the way of young company . . . . more in the way of those who are solid and serious persons.

They esteem the present season very inconvenient for religion . . . . being so very convenient for other purposes. . . . Now a very convenient time to take liberty in mirth and youthful delights.

Many that are past their youth put off to a supposed more convenient season . . . . when got through such and such particular affairs wherein they are now involved . . . . when they hope they shall be more at liberty . . . . or till in this and the other respect they are got into more convenient circumstances.

(2.) There are many that delay and put off without fixing any time in their mind . . . . hoping for a more convenient future time. . . .

The present time appears peculiarly inconvenient . . . . feel a great opposition . . . . have many temptations . . . . hope it will be

* In the left-hand corner is marked, "Novemb. 1749," and a little beyond, "St Ind. = Stockbridge Indians, Aug. 1752." See Application for the second sermon. —G.

better with them . . . . not feel such an aversion . . . . fewer temptations. . . .

Wait to have the Spirit of God strive with them.

Now a time of general deadness, and very inconvenient on that account . . . . all the talk is of other things . . . . put off till a time of the outpouring of the Spirit of God. . . .

Or, perhaps, they are hoping for some greater advantage in other respects, some better means than now they enjoy, or a better concurrence of circumstances to favour a design of seeking God and their salvation.

II. The cause of persons thus delaying.

1. Stupidity . . . . senselessness of their danger and necessity.

Insensible of the reality . . . . insensible of the greatness . . . . senseless of the heinousness of their sin . . . . a brutish stupidity. . . .

2. The importunity of lust. . . . Job xx. 12—"Wickedness is sweet in his mouth ; he hides it under his tongue ; he spares it, and forsakes it not, he keeps it still in his mouth."

3. Aversion to their duty.

4. Ignorance of themselves and self-confidence.

Trust in wisdom . . . . strength . . . . steadfastness. . . .

5. A spirit of self-blinding. . . . The blinding influence of a sinful self-love . . . . promise themselves future opportunity . . . . better opportunity . . . . that God will hear. . . .

6. The subtile temptations of the Devil. . . .

III. The evil of it.

1. 'Tis exceeding wicked.

Direct disobedience . . . . wilful, resolved, wickedness . . . . determine to continue in sin, and an allowance of it. . . .

'Tis not only designedly committing one act of wickedness, but deliberately determining on a course of it . . . . a course of manifested wickedness . . . . neglect of many commands . . . . gratification of many lusts . . . . horrible ingratitude, abusing the past "long suffering" . . . . horrible presumption on future mercy . . . . contempt of offered mercy. . . .

2. 'Tis exceeding foolish. . . . Hereby they reject and miss a good deal of present good . . . . wilfully continue in a miserable state . . . . bring a great deal of certain future misery upon them. . . .

They run a dreadful risk . . . . depend on innumerable uncertainties . . . . life continued . . . . means of grace continued . . . . use of reason . . . . disposed . . . . "more convenient season" . . . . given one . . . . if disposed whether succeed . . . . whether God won't give over to delusion and to hard-heartedness. . . .

Depend on many things that are not only uncertain, but very improbable . . . . disposition . . . . convenient season . . . . thought when they were children . . . . make their case more and more dangerous . . . . depending on greater conveniences they make inconveniences for themselves . . . . and by this means many thousands are actually undone. . . .

Application :*—

This may be of warning to sinners not to delay and put off. . . .

You have heard how common this is. . . . Men are exceeding prone to it. . . . Does your own experience confirm what has been said in this matter? And are there not some here who are now doing as has been represented? Have we not reason to think that there are many here present that say as Felix, "When . . . ." &c.?

Undoubted, by what is everywhere to be seen at such a time of general deadness and regardlessness of religion as this is: a good evidence of the exceeding proneness to put off. . . .

Let all take warning. . . .

You have heard something in general of wickedness and folly; but here consider more particularly—

1. What guilt you contract: what a horrible thing it is to live in known and wilful disobedience to God; . . . . what great light ye will sin against if you . . . .

2. What would you think of your delays if God should say to you, "Thou fool, this night . . . .?"

3. If the future time you are putting off to should never come, how far it will probably be from being a "more convenient season." . . .

In many respects, far more inconvenient . . . . God's anger increased . . . . your heart harder, more stupid . . . . every evil habit established . . . . sloth . . . . a carnal, worldly disposition . . . . an habitual making light of things affecting such awakenings. . . . Satan's great opportunity to establish his interest . . . . commonly an increase of inconvenience of outward circumstances . . . . increase of temptations . . . . commonly many inconveniences arise that never would be thought of . . . . less likely ever to set about the work . . . . Satan hath greater advantages if they do . . . . more likely to be unsteady . . . . more likely soon to be discouraged . . . . the work is greater and harder that they have to do . . . . less time to do it. . . .

4. Others have lamented their folly in delaying . . . . many when under concern . . . . I who have long been in the work of the ministry . . . . many on a death-bed.

5. How much otherwise you deal with God, and desire that God should deal with you.

6. If you continue still to delay after the warning you have this day, how aggravated your wickedness will be!

How have you been warned hereof before . . . . and how have you gone from the meeting-house and still . . . .

How can you excuse yourself to go home to-night and do nothing? or to do a little this evening, and then to-morrow, or in a few days? . . .

* The text is again placed above "Application," shewing that *it* formed a second sermon.—G.

Consider how unreasonable this is. . . .

And if now again, ... and there be a God, ... how may you reasonably suppose He will resent it?

7. If you still . . . . what danger that you will be utterly given up before the time comes. . . . Giving up a common thing. . . .

8. Enquire whether you yourself don't believe [that] there are many now in Hell through this very means?

Here some, perhaps, may say, to excuse themselves, and quiet their own consciences with respect to this, "I don't delay and put off the concern of my soul. I am in a way of seeking my salvation."

Here I would put two or three questions to such persons.

1. Whether you are in a way of minding this affair more than all others? "Seeking FIRST the kingdom of God,"—"*one* thing." . . .

2. Is your reformation universal? Sins of omission . . . . commission. . . .

3. [Do you feel] as much pains as ever you take will be needful? Forsaken all practices you think you would need to forsake? Complied with all duties? As earnestly? . . . . Do you intend to continue? How has secret, closet religion been with you? How have you kept the Sabbath? Attended the sermons? If not, . . . you are guilty of the forementioned wickedness, . . . wilful disobedience—guilty of folly. Therefore, if you have any regard to . . . . think on your mercies, and "turn your feet," . . . . and whatever "your hands find to do." . . .

VII. and VIII.

1 Pet. iii. 19, 20—"By which also he went and preached to the spirits in prison," &c. . . .*

Two things it is my present purpose to observe concerning the spirits or souls of those wicked men that Noah preached to. . . .

1. How long ago they lived.

2. How those souls are here spoken [of] as to their present state, "spirits in prison."

DOCTRINE.—Those wicked men who lived before the flood, and went to Hell in Noah's time, are there still.

1. I would give some reasons why they have remained in Hell so long.

2. Observe in some respects in what circumstances they remain there all this while.

I. Give some reasons.

Negatively.

1. 'Tis not because Hell has been tolerable to 'em.

2. 'Tis not because they ben't convinced of their former folly, . . .

* In left-hand corner, marked "June 1749." See 'Directions' for second sermon.—G.

that they have not yet been brought to their right mind or to their judgment of things.

3. 'Tis not because they are careless about their own welfare and ease, and not willing to be at any possible labours or cost in order to escape, if there were any hope of deliverance. Not because they don't wish and long . . . . not thoroughly overwhelmed . . . . not because they ben't in earnest . . . . that they ben't thoroughly engaged in their spirits . . . . not yet disposed to own that the courses that they went on going weren't good . . . . not disposed to attend to any offer of mercy . . . . because they begrudge . . . . would be unwilling to lay out themselves . . . . not because they are covetous . . . . not willing to be shewn. . . .

4. 'Tis not because they were weaker than the generality of men. Many of them were giants.

5. Not because there is not a great number of those who are disposed to unite their strength to burst prison.

Affirmatively.

1. Their souls are immortal . . . . made for eternity . . . . of a nature agreeable to this design. . . .

Though they desire it, they can't return to nothing. "Seek death and cannot find it." Extreme torment, but no tendency to annihilate the soul . . . . tendency to sink it, but not to reduce it to nothing. 'Tis not with the soul as 'tis with the body in its present mortal state . . . . extreme oppression tends to destroy it.

2. They are not in a state of probation.

3. Their debt is what they can't pay. . . . Great debt to Divine justice. Have not wherewith. . . . Nothing to pay. . . . Cast into prison till they should pay the last mite. . . .

4. THERE IS NO GOSPEL PREACHED IN HELL. Christ did not die for the damned. . . . Had no respect to that world . . . . to those in this state . . . . any more than to the devil. No means of grace. Means of grace not accommodated to that state. No manner of provision made in any respect for their relief. No aid. Preaching of the Word don't reach them. The prayers of saints, of godly friends, don't reach them.

5. The place and state they are in was never designed for the exercise of mercy.

God is infinitely merciful; but the exercises of mercy are not for ever. . . . Limited by Wisdom in various respects: has declared what the purposes of His wisdom are with respect to the exercises of His mercy. As to the kind of beings; fallen men and not angels. . . . His declarations are according to truth. . . . His purposes are not altered. . . .

Hence no mercy in Hell. . . . Though their pain is extreme . . . God don't pity 'em. Though their wishes for deliverance are great . . . . though their cries are loud . . . . though long continued . . . . though it be exceeding intolerable.

6. By being longer in Hell, they have not become any more fit for any other state . . . . don't make 'em better . . . . although indeed

their judgments are convinced, yet their hearts are the same. No change in their dispositions. There are no conversions in Hell. The wrath makes a great change indeed; but no saving change. The wicked in Noah's days were most of them very wicked on earth, yet, in some respects, they became worse when they went to Hell. Not fit for Heaven. Not fit to come and live in this world. Fit for no other place. That is the place provided and fitted for such.

7. The prison is strong that holds them. Delivered up into the hands of Satan . . . . against whom they have no strength. And his cruelty is as strong as his power. And what is much more than devils, God confines them . . . . irreversible sentence binds them. Omniscience opposes them. No escape by subtlety unobserved. Often here, in this world, persons break prison by stealth . . . . get away by night, when no one observes them. . . . And God's Almighty power holds 'em down. And God ever lives. He is unchangeable. He never will alter His purpose . . . . never will forget His own Son . . . . never will forget His righteous sentence. . . .

II. Observe, in several things, in what circumstances they have been in, all this so long a time.

1. They have not been in a state of insensibility. "The Rich man." Not less their sensibility by long-continued torment and misery . . . . hence not been deprived of the use of reason.

2. Have had no time of respite all this while. No rest. Rev. xiv. 11—"No rest day nor night." Both day and night are mentioned, because the night in this world is a time of rest. Have never been asleep . . . . never find any resting-place. Never find out any assuaging medicines . . . . any cool shadows . . . . cooling green . . . . never found a drop of water . . . . never found any expedient for mitigating their torment.

They have had much to goad 'em, in exercising their invention. Necessity is the mother of invention. But their inventions have not saved them . . . . have had nothing to divert them . . . . no amusement to take off their attention. . . .

3. Have not forgotten things that were so long ago, or when they were on earth. "Son, remember." . . . Will remember over all at the Day of Judgment. Have not forgotten pleasant circumstances they lived in . . . . swam in delights . . . . their lives were long . . . . the wickedness they committed . . . . the opportunities they had . . . . the warnings . . . . Noah's preaching . . . . their folly . . . . the thoughts they had concerning God and His testimony.

4. Their misery is not grown more tolerable by their being so long used to it.

5. The great additions that have been made to the numbers from their time has been no comfort to 'em.

6. They have had no hope all this while . . . . have none now . . . . though their torments have been so long continued.

This is verified concerning all that go down to the pit of Hell. (Isa. xxxviii. 19)—"They that go down to the pit cannot hope for Thy truth."

USE:

May be of warning: Let sinners in these days take warning. Those that now live in unbelief and impenitence are in danger of the same.

1. Let me call upon [you] seriously to consider how long a time those who have been spoken of have already worn out [themselves] in Hell: they have been there 4000 years. How many ages? How many and great changes, and successions, and transactions? How many generations have passed? How many successions of those who had come into being, gradually grown up, and grown old, and then died?

Not only have many generations gradually come upon the stage and have died; but many great and populous nations have come into being, and have flourished, and made a great figure in the world for many ages, and then by degrees have dwindled and wasted, swallowed up by other nations and come to nothing, and nothing of them now known but by history. And some of them very ancient and powerful, so that even the very history of them is almost come to nothing and vanished; and all since they have been suffering the flames of Hell, without any cessation or rest. The world has been peopled .... subdued .... many mighty princes have appeared and made a good bustle, and none .... whose memory is now almost forgotten. .... Very great and magnificent cities .... and now 'tis hardly to be known where they stood. Many kingdoms, yea, many great monarchies. .... Those four monarchies of the world. How many things have worn out! The strongest fortunes .... strongest empires .... most durable monuments .... pillars of brass .... monuments of marble stone. .... Languages used as the common speech of large countries. Such things have gradually perished, and length of time worn 'em out; but yet the torments of the "spirits in prison" yet remains .... not come to nothing .... are as fresh and lively and in as great vigour as the first moment.

The souls who are the subjects of these miseries were sinners, and their miseries immortal. Since they have been in Hell there has been a long series of wonderful dispensations of God towards His Church and the whole world. After the flood, the nations degenerated .... fell off to idolatry .... Abraham was 'called' .... children of Jacob became a great nation .... Christ was foretold of old, from time to time .... anciently prefigured .... and in the fulness of time Christ actually came into the world .... all these ancient prophecies and ancient types were fulfilled .... the Jews, God's ancient people, rejected .... Gentiles called .... prophecies were given .... a mighty change made in the Roman kingdom .... Antichrist arose .... reigned for long time .... but at length the Reformation came. .... During all those mighty changes on earth those souls spoken of in the doctrine, continued without ease day or night or one minute's respite, wrestling with the mighty torments of Hell; and so they continue still .... torment not abated. These great and mighty changes on earth have not affected them to cause any change there. There have been many good times on earth: days of great good; but . . . .

2. How we may suppose the things which they remember of their past lives now affects them . . . . their worldly enjoyments . . . . the length of the time of their past ease and pleasures . . . . they lived long lives . . . . their past opportunities . . . . their long warnings . . . . the preaching they had . . . . their folly and stupidity . . . . obstinacy . . . .

3. How many since have followed their steps and have gone to Hell in like manner. 'Tis not the manner of men to take warning by those that perish before them. . . . . Those that are gone before can see the folly of those that come after, whom it will do no good. The rich man in Hell. Those that went to Hell in Noah's day, see the folly of those that come to 'em from generation to generation. But those that follow after don't see the folly of those who went before, and so they follow them. . . . .

4. They that have worn out so many ages in Hell, are never the nearer any end of their misery. The time is very long that they have suffered . . . . many tedious days . . . . tedious years . . . . and tedious ages one after another. . . . . They must wear out another space of time as long as this in Hell flames, and another after that. . . . . Soon the time will come when they will actually have worn out a million such as . . . . yea, a million and millions. . . . . God foresees the time . . . . knows the particular passage of the day. Yea, as many such ages as there are particles of dust on the globe of the earth. . . . . And even then NO MERCY. It will be without end. FOR EVER, YEA, FOR EVER. Therefore take warning. If you neglect to take warning you will go to Hell . . . . and the time will come when you will have been as long as they now have been . . . . and you must also be there millions of millions . . . . and you will be no nearer . . . . yea, will be in absolute despair as they are . . . . your wishes, and cries, and strength, and entreaties will be in vain. You in like manner will reflect on and curse your folly.

5. The torment that those spoken of in the doctrine have endured for so long a time, is but an imprisonment in order to execution. "Spirits *in prison*." "Chains of darkness." There is another day. Their misery is great now. We learn by the parable of Dives and Lazarus. . . . . I know nothing by which it can be determined that the misery will not be a thousand times as great. . . . . They 'tremble.' The chains are strong. There is no hope . . . . no relief to them.

6. The means and opportunities they enjoyed were nothing to yours. Little revelation of a future state.

7. God has an appointed time to wait on you. 'The Spirit will not always strive.'

8. Consider the sudden, unexpected manner in which they were destroyed (Luke xvii. 26, 27.) . . . . You will probably be surprised as they were. They had as much reason to flatter themselves as you, (Job xxvii. 20)—"A tempest stealeth him away in the night."

DIRECTIONS : *

1. Avoid those things by which the men that went to Hell in Noah's time undid themselves . . . . particularly sensuality, (Gen. vi.; Luke xvii. 27.) . . . . So it was with Sodom. Violence. "Evil imaginations." They would not hearken. They grew hardened to long-continued calls and warnings . . . . habitually made light. Is there not reason to apprehend that this is the case with many here? You must reform your life . . . . thorough reformation. . . . .

2. You must in this respect be as Noah was in the generation of those souls that are "castaways;" particularly

1. You must avoid those liberties of young people that are customary.

2. Another thing that is apparently become customary, and doubtless is very provoking to God, is pride and extravagance in apparel. Not that I condemn all adorning the body. 'Tis evident by Scripture that some moderate degree of this is lawful. Oil that makes his face to shine, (Eccles. ix. 8; Matt. vi. 17; Prov. xxxi. 21, 22; Exod. iii. 22.) But yet 'tis apparent that there is a most sinful extravagance in this kind, (1 Tim. ii. 9; 1 Pet. iii. 3, 4; Isa. iii. 16, 18, &c.) Appears to be very provoking to God . . . . when persons go beyond their rank. One end of apparel seems to be to distinguish. (Prov. xxxi. 22, 23.) Common people to shew an affectation to be like those of high rank; country towns to affect to be like the metropolis. When they go beyond their estate, disable themselves from paying their debts; deprive themselves of other things more necessary and more profitable; disable themselves much from deeds of charity. An affectation to distinguish themselves in imitating the fashions of the more gay part of the world. Complying with the general customs of a country in clothing is not vulgar. On the contrary, 'tis not decent to be singular. But some fashions in themselves are ill . . . . extravagance . . . . very costly . . . . immodest. . . . .

All this care, and pains, and cost to adorn themselves shews persons to much affect outward ornament . . . . seem to shew that they make much of themselves . . . . all that which tends to encourage a general excess. Such things as these have been condemned by wise men of all nations.

'Tis a time when the nations here have got to a vast excess. The land is become exceeding extravagant. More so than in England in proportion to our ability and ranks. Prevents great good that might be done . . . . is continually running in debt. The main thing that brings our greatest national calamities . . . . particularly the present state the country is in with regard to a medium.† And is the main source of that general injustice that has been so long complained of . . . . keeps the country in constant distress . . . . maintains constant injustice . . . . threatens us with ruin. . . . . We in this

* Text and Doctrine placed here, shewing a second sermon commenced at this point.—G.

† That is, "the currency," coinage.—G.

town* are evidently got to a great excess. Boston is extravagant beyond London. And we, considering all things, I think beyond them . . . . how far below we fall short in rank . . . . state . . . . education and our situation in the world . . . . far beyond them.

I had occasion to observe the people at Portsmouth, in both the congregations in that place. That is a place very much famed for politeness, and is a city much like Boston in many respects. I judged the apparel of our congregation was fully as costly. Many things that might make it proper for them to go beyond us.

Such excess in gaiety and costliness of apparel is a manifestation of great vanity of mind. It seems to shew a great senselessness of our own vileness . . . . becomes us to go modestly . . . . modest apparel would better become such sinful creatures. Do not consider the end for which clothing was given . . . . to hide our shame . . . . that deformity that is the first of sin . . . . senselessness of what our bodies are coming to . . . . shews vanity of mind, as it shews the heart to be set on that which is exceeding vain and empty . . . . great want of a sense of the worth of those spiritual ornaments that are infinitely more valuable.

If persons had a proper concern for their soul, there surely would not appear very much affectation to . . . .

If religion should greatly revive it would undoubtedly make a great alteration.

This is one thing, among others, that tends to prevent its reviving.

God has of late awfully testified His displeasure for the extravagance of the country's manner of living.

3. You must not only seek, but strive. You must make it a business . . . . main business . . . . thorough . . . . How plain the necessity of it! How often in the Word of God! How plain by experience! On many accounts necessary . . . . How much you have had to convince you of the necessity! And are you, after all, in any sense awake? And how can you excuse this folly?

4. Be seasonable.

The sinners of the old world perished by the Flood because they were not seasonable. They doubtless, many of them, used means afterwards. Had need to make haste. . . . . So we are directed from time to time. "Haste" . . . . "escape for thy LIFE." On many accounts necessary. How many have we reason to think perish through delay!

5. Not only engage in but go through that great work that is necessary in order to your escaping eternal damnation.

Do in this respect as Noah did for the saving himself and his house from the Flood.

6. Don't waste time in halting between two opinions.

How there seem to be some things that give special encouragement. Isa. lv. 6, 7.

* Viz., Northampton, New England.—G.

BALLANTYNE AND COMPANY, PRINTERS, EDINBURGH.

Dear J.M.B

By

S.D Lawton-Betts

Searching for meaning
A quick session
Let me holla at you real quick.
Quick note from Dymil
Dear J.M.B
Trust
Dear J.M.B
Reassurance
Dear J.M.B
Communication
Dear J.M.B
Understanding
Dear J.M.B
Passion
Dear J.M.B
Clarity
Dear J.M.B
Vision
Dear J.M.B
Dear Love, I'll always be around.

The Allure of Love and Pain

If only there was a moment in time where love was not subjective. Where love was a shared reality and a concept that wasn't just a mere speck of the cosmos. Allure is the basic understanding that something is out of your reach, we as humans tend to perceive that love is not in our grasp but pain is. Pain has become the new love embodiment.

If you become hurt then you learn to hate. When you hurt others you then become the one hated. The everlasting allure of love and pain. We as humans shoulder guilt and because of this guilt we understand such pain. Our generosity to others just becomes second nature.

Our human nature tends to boast a selfish aura of wanting to preserve peace that initiates war. We tend to inflict hate to protect our love. The Allure that these nexuses causal relationships can be separated is a mere futile spec of hope.

What allure do you consider your reality? Are you in the allure that you build hate, resentment and other harboring feelings to call it love? Do you shatter the heartbreak and protect yourself from love and then call it pain. The underlying mystery here is that maybe, love and pain are synonymous. Maybe their nexuses relationship is the trajectory of hope. So again I ask, what is your Allure, Love or Pain?

Open your mind and allow perspective to flow. It isn't always that love isn't for you, sometimes we just are in our own way and speak it so much that the universe says fine…then you won't have it….

Thank you, If no one told you today then let me be the first,

You matter,
You are real,
You are seen,
You are beautiful,
You are magical,
You are a gift,
You are worth it,
YOU DESERVE IT.

Dear J.M.B,

With you I want you, the actual person of who you are and who you really are!

I think to be honest I never looked at it as settling. I looked at it for the first time in a long time as I felt whole. I felt like I found someone who saw me and wanted me for not what I had or what I did but wanted me. Someone who wanted to just love me. So honestly I felt like being with you was one of the biggest wins never a settle.

I'm sure because things with you are just easy (outside of the growing pains in relationships).

I'm sure because I feel connected to you. Even the first time we talked you just felt like home. You felt like we been married for 50 years and got reborn to just find each other again and pick up where we left off.

I'm sure because, as much of a tough front you put up or on, I know you love me and I know you feel safe here. You want to just be soft and let everything go with me but you are afraid of a lot .

I'm sure because when I look at you I see me and I see your heart . I'm sure because I found you in a space / time that I wasn't looking to find anything. I was only looking to grow closer to God and then I found you.

I'm sure because I think about you all the time. I want you around me all the time. I want to just be in your presence. I want to just see you, hear your dreams and goals. Hear you talk. Laugh. Cry. Be vulnerable. I like hearing your pain because it lets me know that you trust me and that I can be a safe space for you . I like seeing you smile when I love on you because I know that deep down it's healing some part of you and that makes me smile because I just want nothing but the best for you and you to love your best life smiling as you deserve.

I'm sure because I feel the weight come off of you when you are in my arms. I'm sure because you may fight the world but with me you can be soft, free and the version of you that you want to be but don't have the space to do so.

I'm sure because you are the first person I think of when I wake up. You are the person I want to run to when something is wrong. You are the person I want to tell when something is good. You are who I want to celebrate with. You are the one who I want to laugh and cry with. Fight and make up with. I know Because I can't sleep without you. I miss you when I don't talk to you or just don't hear from you.

You are different because you truly care about me. You run to me when something is wrong. You want to be connected to me. You want to learn me. You want to grow and build with me. You are different because you love me from a place of just being. You are different because you show up and you come to me. You always come "home". You are different because you want to learn me to love me, not to use me or anything. You are different because I feel like you really want to protect me and my heart from anyone or anything.

Idk maybe it could all just be me. I do know, I love you and I rather go out loving you and trying than not trying and not loving you at all.

So like I said I'm here and I'm in this for the long run. I want you not the idea of you and being with you is never settling it is always winning.

Trust: The ability to believe in the truth, ability, reliability of someone.

Even when we fall.
I'll always hit the ground first.
Keep your trust in me.
This will be ok.

I don’t Trust you,

But I didn’t hurt you.

Blindly we are…

It’s not that I don’t trust you.
It’s really, I just trust you so much to be
Exactly who you are.

Show me your heart so I can trust your intentions.
Show me your actions so I can trust your word.
Show me your patience as I give you this mended heart
Hoping you wont be another repeated
Cycle.

Trust is a vase
Once you break it
You can try to fix it
However, it will never
Be like it
Was.

Trust don’t work on borrowed money!
Meaning just because they didn’t pay
You back before me don’t mean I’m responsible
For their debt.

“Trust me” Screamed Love
“We can’t” Screamed our past.

Hi.

I am, love nice to meet you!

Nah, we don't trust you!

But why?

We have seen this movie before.

How? The opening scene just started.

Dear J.M.B

I know I told you I will love you forever.

However, I feel myself becoming so upset
because I feel like

Forever isn't long enough.

Reassurance: Removing doubt & Fears

I promise you it isn't on purpose.
Sometimes I don't feel worth it and

I just need to hear it.
Let me see you show it.

Removing your doubts and fears is something you should never feel bad for needing while seeking love.

I am an overthinker
So I need a lot of Reassurance and for that I'm not
Sorry!

You make me happy.
Even after it all
How I feel for you
And my love
Will never diminish!

Reassurance is never for you,
It is to calm those narratives made
In their minds.

It’s simple. They tell you what they need and you do it,
Or move the hell out the way!

She never will “ just “ know.
She needs elegant reassurance and where she stands.
Let her hear it!

Relax
We are just people on this earth.
It is like a breath of fresh air.
To feel and be needed / wanted.

Dear J.M.B

"Home to me is a sacred place. Everyone shouldn't have access to it. It's where you go when you need to be free, where you can hide when you don't want to be bothered, where you can cry, scream, laugh, be whatever or whoever you need to be. It's nice and warm at home. It holds you like a Hermes blanket. You never want to leave, and every time you have to leave, you get sad because you just want to be in your place of comfort. A place where you are most understood and most like you."

That is what you feel like, a place where I can be me and I'm safe. No one has to know where I am because I'm with you and it feels warm and peaceful…..

Communication: It is a long-life skill that should be learned at minimum and practiced every day at maximum.

I only want you to tell me the love I seek is real.

I don’t want to hear it only with words.
I wan’t to feel it with your actions.

Talk to me in actions.

Stop listening for what I’m saying
And
Hear everything I’m not saying.

Our relationship thrives on communication.
When it fades we begin the inevitable path
To the End.

She talks in emotion.
He talks in Logic.
They both Talking
Just hearing different languages.

Her: Talk to me.
Him: I tried, and you showed me, I’m not safe here!

Him: Tell me what's wrong.
Her: I did, and you did the same thing.
Him: I'll fix it.
Her:…………………
(You get tired of talking so you don't)

Dear J.M.B

Loyalty is hard to define.
Like you have it in you or you don't.
You know right from wrong.
Good from bad.
So don't do anything that will go against me and get you
.....yeah

Communication is a lifelong language.
You will always have
To learn and study.

Understanding: The ability to make sense of something.

It is always beautiful
To be with someone
Who just get's you.
You don't say anything

But you know they know.

You shouldn’t only understand because it happens to you!
You should just understand.

U- UNIQUE
N- NEVER DULL
D- DOING FROM LOVE
E- EMPATHY
R- RESELLIENCE
S- SUSTAIN
T- TRANQUILITY

A- ASCENSION
N- NEW VISION
D- DELIVERANCE

Sometimes we all have to stumble or fall
to truly see
where we once stood.

In love, stop trying to figure out why.
There is no reason,
Love is one hell of a drug and addiction.
It is meant to be felt and understood.

All of life's beauties are not meant to be understood.
Rather to be enjoyed.

Your anger blocks understanding.
But.
Your lack of acceptance
Blocks your ability to see.
Beyond.

No one will ever understand you
When you only want to be misunderstood.

Dear J.M.B

I can't breathe when you are around.

life without you won’t be good.

When I’m somewhere I always wish you were there.

Passion: A deep desire to indulge in intimacy

A sweet glaze coats her lips
It's so sweet it makes me indulge again and closely stay gripped to her hips.
The thing about it is, I know who I am
A strong passionate sex healthy Man
Who is deeply in love with quickly falling into your sand.
I don't mean no disrespect when I say I want to split you lips.
This moment I want to lose our morals and disregard our values.
Let me slide into your plate
Clean it and then use our bodies as the towels
See how I figure it is today I want to fu….
Not make love.
I want to forget our current age and act like we are 19.
Let's forget the rules because we breaking all the above.

Our love is romantic.
And
Passionate while being dirty and disrespectful.

I crave to choke you,
Spit in your mouth
And
Call you my good girl.

Sex isn’t only physical.
The energy is happening before.
The passion of the small touches.
The eye glances.
The intention of desire.
She should cum before you are even inside of her.

Every time, I taste you
I indulge in a treasure beyond this world.

The way our bodies connect is a true bliss.

I don't want to ever hurt you
But
In this passion I will leave some ass smack whelps.

Your Grace,
I clean my face….
Please have a seat on your Throne.

Clarity: Always be clear with me even in the storm I wanna know where we are going…

It’s not that I need it to be certain.
I need it to be clear!

When searching for your own light
You must first see your own darkness.

The drug I need is clarity
The fix you keep giving is confusion.

Things are only blurry because your glasses
Are not fitting your prescription.

I had to see clearer
I accept how you are
Not how I want you to be.
However, The person you are is dope for someone
Just
Not
For
Me……

I need you to be clear with me.
Tell me what it is.
Tell me what it isn't.
Just like GPS I need to know the directions
And
Destination we are going.
I rather not be led to the unknown just because you find
It
Hard to be straightforward.
I'll make it easy, we won't go forward
On this journey!

I’m an overthinker. So be clear with your instructions and directions.
Calm me with your reassurance.
I promise I’ll be ok!

Dear J.M.B

.....I love you

....With the whole world watching I only see you.

.... I am proud to love you for the rest of our lives.

...Thank you, for just being.

Vision: Your eyes are not the only way you are meant to SEE

If your eyes could talk
They would mostly lie.
Our vision at best is
Only meant to pry.
So see me without
The lines
See my heart as we travel through loves time!

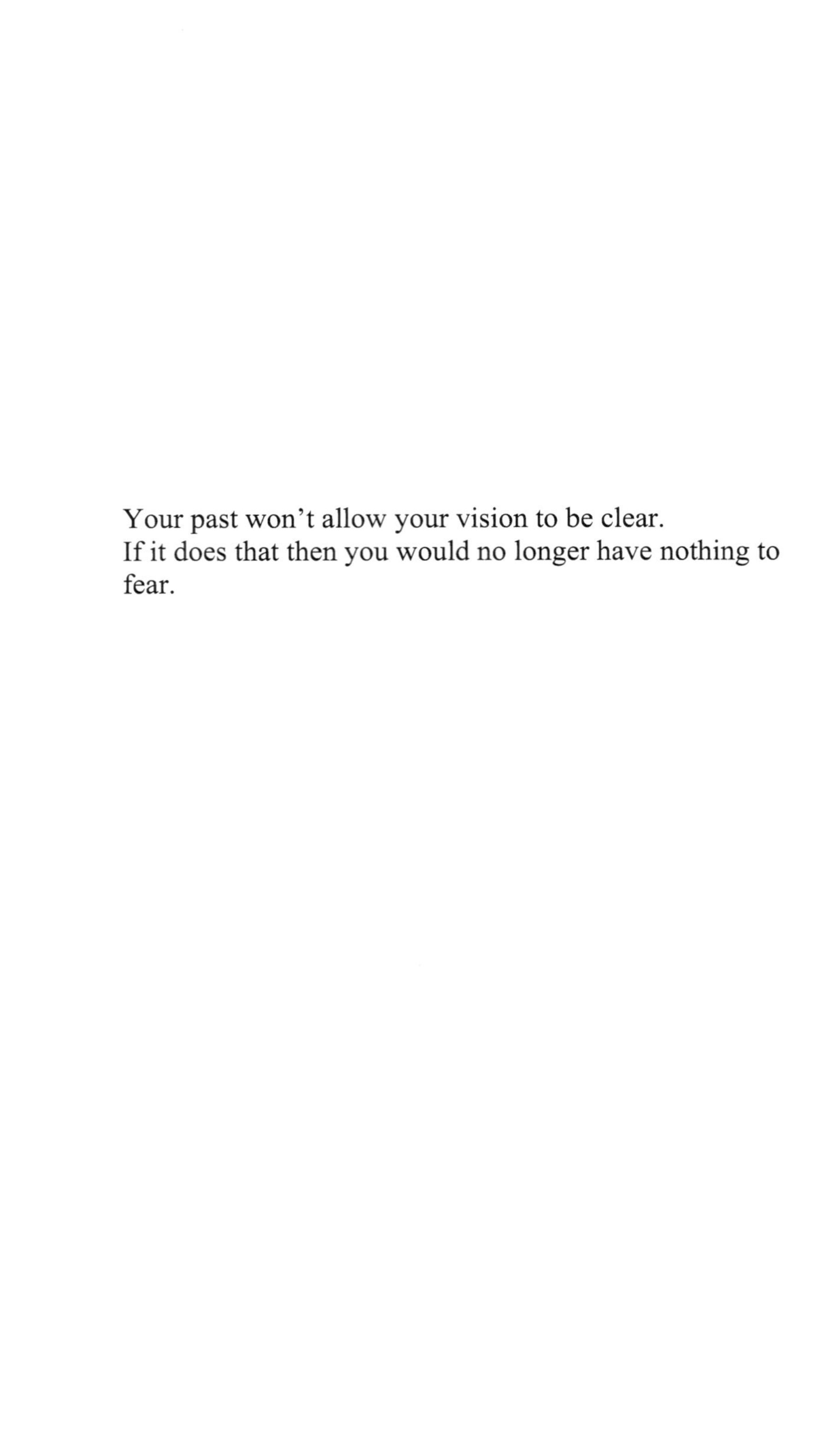

Your past won't allow your vision to be clear.
If it does that then you would no longer have nothing to fear.

Dear Love,
Why can’t you see me reaching for you?

Dear You,
Why can’t you see I’m already in you!

It’s not that I don’t want to accept their growth.
It just means I also have to accept everything I told
Myself to see about them was not true!

I don't want to trade places with you.
I want to trade spaces so you can get a
Glimpse of what you look like from my POV.

Let’s Trade eyes
So for just a moment
You can see you
In all the glory that I do.

I didn’t look pass your demons,
I saw them and still thought you were beautiful.

Pain has made you blind to what your heart wants you to see!

Dear love,

Dear love, I promise I'll always be around.

I promise to hold you close.
I promise to love you from a forgiving place.
I promise to do you no harm.
I promise to be patient with you.
I promise to only be nasty to you in a way that makes
your natural juices flow.

So love until we meet the final clock,
I will leave it at

Hey

J.M.B

In this world we only have the moments that we stand in.
Tomorrow is just a dream that we hope to wake up into.
Yesterday is a memory that we will forget.

The way to Agape is through selfless love.
Believe in you. Believe in love.
Believe that you DESERVE IT.

S.D Lawton- Betts

Lawton-Betts Publishing

IG- sdlawtonbetts
Tiktok- Locdinwithmilsz

Made in the USA
Columbia, SC
07 October 2024